SIAMO
FORESTI

For Randi & Alan

Best wishes

John

SIAMO FORESTI

A Venetian love story...

Written and illustrated by

JOHN G. RAWLINGS

ISBN: 1539183785
ISBN 13: 9781539183785

"...na scarpa e un zocolo..."

"...neither a shoe nor a clog..."

Grazie Matteo

CONTENTS...

For Souheir
Ti amo sempre

Chapter 1

FIRST OR LAST?...

I would like to begin with a confession...
The real motivation for writing this first chapter is to talk myself into writing the rest of the book!

I mean why write any book?

It's bound to be a great deal of work, and it's summer. I'm sitting, looking out of the windows of my home, at the Salish Mountains which sweep up from the other side of the valley, (which we have always called "our valley".) I'm definitely not in work mode, and there is little on the horizon that would seem to be capable of motivating me to be otherwise.

Why write a book on Venice when there are already so many great anthologies of historical and contemporary narratives that tell the story of this remarkable city? Some do it with wondrous story-telling skills, while others can't help themselves, and drone on in that sterile hum some historians seem incapable of avoiding. However, they are all stuffed full of facts and figures that I don't carry around in my head. Nothing I could write would, for a moment, challenge any of their historical storytelling.

Some contemporary 'in vogue' books are characterized by personal insights into the lives of Venice's high society...Its patricians. Gossipy, insider stories gently reveal the Achilles' heel and sometimes the soft underbelly of this ancient city. These stories resonate so well with the insatiable appetite and need of 'the masses' to know intimate details about the rich and famous, that they are considered required reading. They are "de rigueur" for visitors to Venice and can be found on their own separate shelves in the cute little bookstore on the corner of Calle Canonica and a canal of the same name which passes beneath the Bridge of Sighs.

I don't know any Patricians or famous Venetians; can't think of a single thing that I could tell you that would even remotely resemble an 'exposé' and, although it may sound conceited, I'm not much of a gossip.

So what is it that beckons me into this task? What compelling reasons move me even vaguely in this direction? If all the books on Venice have been written, what on earth do I think I could write that has not already been said? As an artist, I'm happy to describe myself, even explain myself by my processes and techniques. But I'm very aware of the fact that I would never, ever use the words 'writer' or 'author' to describe myself.

So I'm no author, no grand repository of historical facts, and know no one rich, famous, or scandalous that I can gossip about...

The prospects of a book are rapidly shrinking to an essay about the size of what might have been a first chapter! However I'm being slightly disingenuous here. I do have a somewhat different perspective than those expressed in the authoritative books that deal with Venice. My view is unique and insightful in a rather pedestrian way, but if one were to canvas the millions of visitors who annually visit 'La Serenissima', the largest portion of them would fall into this pedestrian category.

What about 'Joe Blow' (or is it Joe Shmow?) who walks off the vaporetto at San Zaccaria carrying a backpack containing a bottle of water, a sandwich, and a map, which once unfolded, requires a PhD in Origami to restore it to its original format?

He's going to spend a WHOLE DAY wandering the streets, discovering Venice. Of course he's not going to do more than scratch at its surface. Who could disagree with such a statement? However, whatever experiences he has during this day will become 'his' Venice. He will describe it and evaluate it, all the time speaking authoritatively, for he has been there IN PERSON, no matter how superficial his observations may be.

What about Mr. and Mrs. Junket who, like the lettuce in the insalata, have been shipped in from some foreign place to spend a few days, even a week in the Serene City?

The choreography of these groups is a military two-step with lots of 'swirls'. They are marched through the streets in tight little knots which by the end of the day, fatigue affecting both the group and the 'sheep-dog-like' tour guide, will take the form of what I call a 'straggle' of tourists. They are whirled through museums, churches, glass factories and trattorias at such a pace that I wonder what they actually see. Once again these experiences will create for them their own Venice that will find voice in the slideshows and power points they create back home in their native lands.

My point is that Venice is many more things than are described in historical texts and travel literature.

A fact not often embraced with enthusiasm by society at large, is that those of us employed in the plastic and graphic arts (artists), are trained in the art of observation, and as such are often able to 'see' details that do not even register on untrained eyes. Perhaps then, one thing that I can bring to these pages, through the eyes of an artist, is some careful observation.

One of the things that most attracted me to the Italians is their cuisine. Food is a feature of their everyday lives and it is not just the wonderful flavors and presentations that I find impressive, but rather the way that they build their lives around it. Their food responds to seasons, festivals, regions. It is written about with passionate enthusiasm in books, magazines, and daily newspapers. It is a major feature of Italian pride. As the horror of popular culture's eating habits slouches toward the neutral textures, colors, and flavors of mass produced 'fast food', the Italians cling fiercely to the richness of their own cooking and embrace 'slow food'.

I fancy myself as a bit of a cook…a minor chef. It's something that I love to do, and nothing pleases me more than to have a group of friends come to my home so that I can cook for them. I am an inveterate collector of recipes and one entire section of my library is given over to cookbooks…The greater proportion of them are books of Italian recipes. I took two of them to Venice in January of 2007.

One, from my favorite celebrity chef Jamie Oliver, "Jamie's Italy", published in 2006, is a wonderful collection of recipes, photographs, and stories from his trip through Italy in 2004. He embodies my own enthusiasm for their food and the culture that surrounds and supports it, and this book has become one of my favorites, (which means that many of the pages are dog-eared and stained with olive oil).

The other book that I carried with me is a gem that I found in a second-hand bookstore many years ago. It is called "Venetian Cooking" by H.F. Brunning Jr. and Cav. Umberto Bullo. Published in 1973, it is a wondrous collection of 200 recipes written with such enthusiasm and love that I have attempted to cook them all. Cav. Bullo adds a comment to each recipe, and these little addendums were often the reason that I decided upon that specific recipe.

Here's an example:

In the introduction to "RENGHE SALAE SOTO OGLIO" (Venetian for Salted Herring Fillets under Olive Oil),
    "This dish serves as an antipasto, but the result is so delicious one can eat them in abundance, especially if accompanied by polenta. In that case the stomach must be in good form, for salted herring brings on a great thirst for wine!"

Marvelous stuff!

So another feature of this book will be my descriptions of foods, with the occasional recipe. Once again there will be no attempt to compete with food/cookbooks that your local book store is awash in.

The final element that might be a feature in this book is entirely personal, even private, and I had to think long and hard before deciding to commit it to writing. However, it addresses a question that I was constantly asked by tourists who were attempting to 'find their way around' Venice.

Passing the age of 60 was not a particularly harrowing experience for me, and apart from the fact that I no longer look the way I did 30 years ago, there are only a few physical changes that have affected my life. I still run regularly, albeit a good deal slower than I used to, and my eyesight and hearing are not as sharp as they used to be. But the great discovery awaiting me beyond 60 was the fact that I had a prostate! Never knew it was there before! In the process of dealing with prostatitis I have become a male member of the human species that needs to pee regularly, and unfortunately, urgently. So the last element I will include will be: "Where to pee in Venice". I swear I was asked this by tourists who were perfect strangers, and can only surmise that I had that pinched look that fellow sufferers recognized.

Whatever. Knowing 'where to go' was very important information to me and ultimately played an important part in my sojourns around the city.

Perhaps I can compile a collection of observations and experiences that will resonate with a broad spectrum of folk where the common denominator is simply Venice. A book for the masses... "The proletariat in Venezia!"

I know...I know...The 'author' has slipped into an egocentric hole the size of the Bacino di San Marco. However, even such silliness has a grain of veracity to it. It is patently clear that the Venice of the Venetians is a very different place from the Venice of its visitors. It is a "them and us" situation that plays itself out in countless subtle ways, adding spice and color to the everyday life of this city.

So if I go ahead with this project, what format should it take? How do I want it to read?

First let's grind a few axes... (Oh yes, I should tell you I am not without prejudices!)

I intensely dislike books where the author uses words like 'insouciance' on the first page, thereby establishing the superiority of his/her intellect and vocabulary. I promise not to use such verbiage. I promise to write with as little 'flower' as possible...Nothing too insouciant! I hope it is becoming clear that I don't take myself too seriously. I'd tell you that I'm pretty good at self deprecation, but then there would be some pompous word on page 6.

Where was I? ...Oh yes, format.

I don't want to write a day by day diary of events, although there is, in truth, a sequence that proceeds over the period of time from January to May of 2007. Observation is always a process of synthesis, and what you learn today you take into tomorrow, growing it into more complex, hopefully more complete information. It took a long time and many repetitions before I started to see some of the things I will share with you, so there is, inherent in all of these stories, a sense of calendar, a moving forward in time.

I find that in the conversational retelling of my experiences, I tend to follow themes.

If I'm talking about a meal or a recipe, then the conversation continues on into other descriptions of food. It seems to be my natural way of organizing information, and in an attempt to sustain this 'natural' quality, each chapter will be at least nominally thematic.

And so we have reached the moment where I need to commit.

This is, of course, the place where I should introduce myself, for surely dear Reader, you have made a commitment to get this far, and deserve to know where this is coming from...And where it might go!

My name is John Rawlings. I am a sculptor/painter, and I taught Drawing and Art History at a small community college in northwest Montana. In 1985 and 86 while teaching at the University of Alaska, I spent a sabbatical year in Florence, Italy with my wife and daughter. Since that time my family has carried on what can only be called a love affair with Italy...And all things Italian.

We have made many visits since 1986, and over the past decade or so have organized and chaperoned student tour groups to Italy almost annually. Initially these trips were the typical 'junket' arrangement comprised of 10 days of intensive travel, sleeping in a different city most nights, eating communally at the cheapest trattorias that we could find. They were student tours. First consideration?...Cost. To be kept as low as possible.

I zealously attempted to give my students a glimpse into the Italy that I had come to know; Stood them in front of all the 'important Artworks'...Extolled the virtues of my favorites ...Introduced them to Italian friends. I wouldn't cast a completely dismal light on these tours, however, because I worked hard at making them as unlike group travel as possible. We ate local food. Drank the local wine. I organized plenty of unstructured time into each day, and encouraged students to wander off in small groups or even alone. The end product was always remarkable. In a traditional classroom setting, even an exceptional teacher can only hope to see a few 'light bulbs turn on' when he or she is lecturing. As my students stepped off the aircraft...All the lights went on! It's an amazing experience to be with a group of students who are so completely engaged.

However, each time I returned home, I was left with the empty feeling that I had not quite achieved what I had hoped to. I worked hard at improving these tours, and focused on my language skills, knowledge, 'street smarts', comfort level in new places, and as I did, I of course became more enamored of Italia. Dragging a group of young people halfway around the world, moving them through the cattle lots called airports, across multiple time zones, compressing them into a seat for a day where they inhale other people's exhales, creates an exhausted person... Tired, irritable, disoriented... Jet lagged. Landing a bus load of these individuals in Rome is a formula for disaster. Why? Because the city is huge, noisy, fast, impersonal. Tired students become the fodder of slick, streetwise Romans. I never really considered such an entry into Italy, and initially landed in Milan at Malpensa airport from which we bussed to Venice.

Venice turned out to be the perfect place to begin these tours as it was quiet, had no motor vehicles, was safe, and above all didn't seem to intimidate anyone. After the horrors of a transatlantic flight I can't even begin to describe the calming effect of a slow walk through the midnight streets of a sleeping Venice. I came to realize that I was more at home in Venice than in any other Italian city. I literally never worried about the students in my care, and they in turn seemed to affect an easy independence that they did not exhibit elsewhere.

My wife and I slowly changed our tactics and the tours became less micro managed and organized around us, and more focused on individual experiences. The tours eventually took on a more leisurely, open ended quality with our goal being group travel that somehow didn't feel that way. Individuals were encouraged to seek out their own personal 'places', which fostered research and reading before we departed.

This format was so successful that we eventually decided there was a good deal more merit in staying in Venice for 10 days with the chance of getting a better understanding of it, than hopping all over Italy, ending up exhausted and in "information overload".

Our tours do travel as a group, moving through the airport system collectively. I go into what my wife Souheir calls my 'sheep dog' mode, as I help them navigate their way. Once in Venice, they are housed in one of my favorite little hotels in the world, in double room occupancy.

Travel and accommodation is basically what the traveler pays for up front. Once they have arrived, however, I offer them complete flexibility. I meet the whole group each day at 9:30 am in the Campo Santa Maria Formosa. I usually sneak them back against the ochre walls of the old church and tell them what I have planned for the day. Where I'm going. What I'm going to visit. They choose to accompany me or not. They decide where and when to eat, and may do so singularly or in small groups. In this way they take control and ownership of their travel experience and the breadth of their understanding of Venice is increased immeasurably. This format has proved so successful that we have continued to use it over the past few years.

In 2006 I became eligible for another sabbatical leave, and applied for it accordingly. It was approved, and I elected to spend the spring semester of 2007 in Venice where I hoped to accomplish two things. The first was to attend a one month long intensive Italian Language course, and the second was to do a preliminary study that would explore the feasibility of organizing a 'semester abroad' program for the school where I taught.

The following pages contain thoughts, observations, and stories from the months that my family and I spent in Venice from January to May of 2007. I wrote a continuous journal of sorts, following a format that seemed to make sense at the time. Initially they were quite detailed entries, but I realized that this was actually taking up a good deal of my time. This was time that I should have been spending outside in Venice.

I changed to pages of fairly cryptic notes, thinking that I would connect all of these thoughts in a narrative at a later time. In reading some of these notes, however, I have decided to leave them as diary entries because they have an immediacy that I can't seem to achieve from my desk in northwest Montana.

Chapter 2

LA SERENISSIMA

In 1853, just north of Amsterdam, a major land reclamation project was undertaken. A large, fairly shallow lake was drained with skill and attention to detail that only the Dutch can do. First an earthen wall, a dyke, was thrown up around the complete shoreline of the lake. Then a canal which was engineered to have a positive downhill flow toward the nearest river was dug into the top of this dyke. A string of windmills was then constructed on top of this dyke and through the use of the ancient water screw the water was pumped into the canal and the lake slowly drained away. The lake had for years been plied by small boats and as the water level slowly dropped a number of wrecks were found on a sandbar which occupied its center. The Dutch sailors knew of this place and avoided it at all costs. They named it for the boats that it had claimed. Schiphol in Dutch translates to ship's grave ... And on this shallow sandbar, which is now an outcropping of land, the main traffic control tower of one of Europe's busiest airline hubs stands, and the airport takes its name from this place. Schiphol is one of my favorite airports, which as a statement is somewhat inaccurate, because in fact I am not enamored of any airports. Stated more accurately; I should tell you that it is the best of a bad lot.

It's interesting that a short train ride away from Amsterdam - the city that makes Las Vegas look like Disneyland; the city whose calm canals are black and putrid, and whose streets are only slightly more clean, the Dutch have built one of the most pristine, clean, and efficient airports in the world. It is sensibly laid out with wonderful signage and easily understood public announcements. It has long moving walkways that whisk you along concourses to the jetway of your choice. At the end of each of these moving walkways a charming female voice reminds you to "mind your step". Another marvel of this airport is that this is the interchange where a Northwest Airlines jet that we have been imprisoned in for nine hours over the Atlantic, hands its passengers over to Royal Dutch Airlines. KLM. The transition is amazing. We move from plastic cutlery and cups to real metal and porcelain, from uniforms that are downright dowdy, to tailored suits of a gorgeous mid-blue color. Sadly, we also move from an attitude that clearly states "I don't have to be civil to you when I serve you", to one that takes pride in its ability and genuine friendliness. The Dutch speak English in a beautifully neutral accent that always makes me feel that I am hearing my own language for the first time. It is spoken in crisp clear, absolutely understandable words, only serving to increase your level of incomprehension when they repeat their announcements in Dutch--which is singularly the most impenetrable language that I know.

We have escaped the transatlantic monster, breathed deeply of the scrubbed Dutch air, had some food and excellent strong coffee, and are now back on a 737 that is slowly descending over the glorious snow-covered landscape of the Alps into northern Italy. It's early January of 2007 and I am sitting next to a young man who has been plugged into his iPod or the plasma movie screen attached to the rear of the seat in front of him for almost the entire duration of the 11 hours of flight. Needless to say he has not been an outstanding source of conversational exchange. He is my son Tarik. The aircraft is slowly descending out of the cold, turbulent air over the Dolomites, and we can begin to see the green patchwork created by the agriculture of the plain below us. It is the Veneto. The coastline of the Adriatic is rushing towards us and the aircraft is making a long sweeping left-hand turn to begin its commitment to the runway of Marco Polo airport when Tarik pops the headphones from his ears.

"Oh my God, Dad! Look. Look! It's Venice!"

And there she was.

It was a cool, blustery day with scattered white clouds and not quite warm sunshine. But sunshine nonetheless....no fog. A cluster of buildings that seem to float in the middle of the grey-green lagoon, vaguely white and coral even at this distance, has snapped him out of his trans-Atlantic torpor.

"Quite a sight huh?"

I smile a warm, gratifying flush that I always feel when people that I bring to this city respond with such awe.

Marco Polo is not a large airport; has recently been renovated; and is laid out in a fairly sensible fashion that allows passengers to pass through it quickly. Our family of four stands outside the arrival hall looking down the long, covered walkway toward the direction of the water's edge. We are not here for the weekend and consequently have two pieces of luggage each, and a guitar. It is one of those "so far, so good moments", and even though my body clock is set for a time zone considerably west of here, and is nagging at me to take a nap, I am filled with the anticipation that starting an adventure of this sort can generate.

I run through a mental list of my "next to do moves". We have previously rented an apartment through that amazing--and to me still arcane thing--called "the Web". I made euros in Amsterdam, have all of our luggage... and it's only midmorning. We can actually get lost for quite a long time before night falls. I need to walk us down to the lagoon, negotiate a price with the water taxi driver, give him the telephone number of the landlord who will tell him where to drop us off, and schlep stuff to the apartment.

Halfway there! The water taxi driver rolled his eyes at the luggage and asked how long we were staying. It was certainly a facetious question. I answered "Quattro Mesi", and he obviously appreciated both my attempt at Italian and the fact that we were not normal tourists. However when you turn up with so many bags there is an assumption that only wealthy people travel with that much 'stuff', and the price of the ride is adjusted correspondingly. The damage is done however, and I agree upon the hundred euros that he wants for the crossing. Truthfully, I really don't care and settle back in the soft seats of his boat as he whisks us across the lagoon. Of all the ways that you can enter Venice this, in my opinion, is the only way that you should do it. As you skim over the lagoon along the roadways marked by pilings driven into the mud of the lagoon, the city of Venice slowly comes into view. It seems to rise slowly and majestically out of the grey-green water which is now a million mirrors in the warm sunlight.

I look across at Souheir my wife, and my sons Tarik and Tamir, and they all have that look of rapture and wonder that I know is on my face.

I love this place.

You cannot be in Venice for more than a few moments before you start asking questions. Everywhere you look there is something that needs explanation. It is, of course, historically rich and complex, and this complexity continues into every aspect of the life, architecture, technology, art forms, and politics that are woven into the fabric of this amazing city. It's not enough to consult historical texts looking for answers, although this indeed is an extremely important part of the process. So many books purporting to be history books have been written, and so much rivalry occurs between these authors, that those of us who are the readers are confronted with the daunting task of deciding their veracity... Which is History with a capital "H", and which with a lowercase "h"? Can a "guide book" be trusted to pass along facts, or are they only compendiums of age-old fables? My answer is to attempt to read it all in the hope that I will begin to recognize common threads and relationships. At present I don't think that I can report a great deal of success in this venture... However, I have done a great deal of reading!

But it is not enough to just read. I have walked countless miles through the streets of Venice, consciously standing in places where important events transpired, looking so I could actually see and know of the space/form arrangements of streets, bridges and canals... perhaps hoping that in some weird homeopathic way that a few molecules of these people could still be accessed if only I looked earnestly enough. It is a little like trying to discern the vibrations of a person after they have left the room. Dangerous stuff indeed, because you inevitably begin to see what you want to see.

La Serenissima she is called... The most serene one.

If you consulted the book of the world's greatest and most powerful empires you will find her listed there. She has, at the same time, been the richest, most prosperous commercial center in the civilized world and its most powerful maritime force. This small city once controlled the entire Mediterranean Sea, extracting taxes and tariffs from as far away as Gibraltar. She was an independent republic for over 1000 years and served as the crossroads between the East and the West, the clearinghouse for goods from as far north as Sweden and as far east as China.

The Venetian lagoon is quite large... About 200 square miles in area. However, much of this water is seldom more than waist deep. It is a large expanse of turgid water that owes its opaque nature, its murkiness, to both the sandy, muddy bottom and the swirling currents that are the result of the outfall of three rivers and their interaction with the tides of the Adriatic Sea. Almost centered in the lagoon is a cluster of 117 small islands that collectively constitute only about 1800 acres of land surface. On these islands resides the city of Venice. The shallow waters of the lagoon are laced with treacherous currents and their opacity makes it impossible to see the navigable channels that meander through the lurking sandbars that, by their soft and muddy nature, will hold tight to any hapless vessel that should stray there. In current times as you ride the many kinds of boats that work the lagoon, you realize that the navigable waterways; the roads through the lagoon, are clearly marked with a system of pilings rising above the water. This is a system very similar to the roads that cross our Montana valley in the wintertime, where snow blankets both road and field alike, and one navigates by the reflective posts that are driven into both sides of the road. You don't really see the road...rather where it is. In the past, whenever Venice was threatened from outside, the pilings were quickly removed and any advancing enemy stood little chance of negotiating their way across the lagoon. This system proved to be so effective that almost no other defensible architecture was necessary and the buildings of Venezia took on a fineness and delicacy that few other ancient cities could afford. When compared to many of Italy's mainland cities that are girded about with walls, moats and other defensible elements. Venice presents a decidedly feminine beauty that the maleness of military defense precludes.

A great deal has been written about the architectural style that became the signature of Venice, but in truth the plural should be in use here, because the history of Venetian architecture parallels its civic and religious history and reflects the many changes and influences that were a part of her formative past. It has been written that Venice was born Greek and raised Italian, but it is clear that she owes a great deal also to her early Roman roots. It is the charming way that she admits and absorbs this broad variety of architecture that I find so captivating, and of course the fact that these buildings, which have stood for five or more centuries, present themselves as a living-history laboratory that makes them unique in the world.

If you ride the number one vaporetto from Piazzale Roma to San Marco, you will be treated to a slow, stop-by-stop, tour of the Grand Canal. This central waterway is encrusted with Palazzo after Palazzo on both sides, and it will take more than just one ride before you have actually looked at all of them. The richness of these buildings defies description and few people make the ride without openly wondering how it must have looked before the ravages of time removed much of the luster. Years ago I received a postcard from an old teacher of mine who was visiting Venice and I still clearly remember his descriptions,

"She is something of a dowdy old dowager now, but as you travel along the Grand Canal, you can't help but wonder at how beautiful a princess she must once have been."

Many of us are not aware of how inculcated into our very being are elements from our Greco-Roman ancestries, and are perhaps not even cognizant of the fact that we expect our architecture and town plans to be geometric and regular. The organic nature of the layout of Venetian streets and canals simply overwhelms most of us. Try to give even the most basic directions to a restaurant or bar and you'll know what I mean by this. Nothing is regular or regulated. Some streets that begin between walls 30 feet apart find themselves squeezed into a space only 4 feet apart. Streets seldom intersect each other at right angles and this maze of walkways is further complicated by the network of canals and bridges. Nobody can decide whether it's 409 or 412 but it's safe to say that there are more than 400 bridges in Venice.

A map is an essential tool for the first-time visitor but is by no means a guarantee against endless wandering. I can be pretty sure that any of my students who tell me that they didn't get lost on their first day in Venice probably didn't leave the vicinity of their hotel. To explore and discover Venice is to be lost in Venice! A favorite story tells of a visiting Englishman who was discovered, sitting most forlornly, by a friend of mine at the central Police Station or Questura. When my friend asked if he could be of assistance, the man told him that his wife and he had arrived from London that morning and once in the hotel, his wife decided to take a nap while he had a 'quick look around'. He left the hotel without a map, without the name of the hotel, and apparently without a sense of direction. After hours of wandering he finally ended up at the Questura, but could give the Police no information they could use. He simply had to sit there and wait for his wife to report him as a missing person!

The water taxi enters Venice and sliding under a low bridge close to the Fondamente Nuove vaporetto stop, begins to wind its way through the 'backstreets' of Venice. Nothing seems to respond to the orders of horizontal or perpendicular and the buildings list and lean as if answering the call of gravity was an act of choice. What's actually happening is that the ancient building techniques used by the founders of this city are still exerting their influence. Many of the 117 Realtine Islands that make up the center of Venice were very small and it was not too difficult to simply join their land masses by filling in the little rivers between them. These streets are still called by the name of Riva. The process of erecting buildings, however, was much more difficult. Below almost all of the city of Venice is the same ooze that constitutes the floor of the lagoon. Pilings up to 30 feet in length and approximately 6" x 6" were driven down into the mud in such a way as to leave no space between them. What was created was a raft of pilings spearing down into the mud in the hope that some firmer ground could be found. Because there are no wood-eating marine worms in the Adriatic, and as long as the pilings are driven to a depth that keeps them below low water mark and the oxygen that would rot them, they are still sound after all these years. A foundation of dark stone--which is water-repellent--is then laid on the wooden raft and above the water line, the foundations are completed with a white stone which usually came from Istria, across the Adriatic. The houses were then built from small terracotta bricks called altinelle.

All of this of course is heavy, and many of the foundations have subsided a little, which results in the obvious tilt and lean of many structures.

All of Venice then, floats on platforms of wooden pilings driven down into the mud. Santa Maria della Salute, the giant church designed by Longhena and built as an act of gratitude at the end of the 1777 plague, is said to be built on a raft of 1,156,627 pilings.

Apart from the churches and their attendant bell towers or campanile, most buildings are barely 5 stories high, although this is never very obvious because the narrowness of the streets and canals gives them a feeling of verticality that is really an illusion. The general feeling when walking in most of Venice is that you are down in it...If that makes sense.

A young, red-headed woman waves to us from a small wharf and the driver allows the taxi to slide smoothly alongside with not even a nudge. She introduces herself as Agnese, but the wonder of the Italian language turns this rather flat-sounding Anglo name into a small musical phrase...Ahn yay say...

The driver passes our mound of luggage to me and my sons and we stack it against the wall that is flaking paint and large chunks of stucco. I'm immediately fascinated by the textures in such proximity. Smooth, green glossy water, grey weathered wood, and this amazing wall. All of this slides beneath the exchange of names and the fistful of Euros that I pass to the water taxi driver. Agnese's English is almost textbook which doesn't mean she is immediately understood because she is speaking in an entirely formal way and still clings to the "adjective after the noun" organization of the Italian language. We all laugh at the process of understanding each other. All of our luggage has wheels which are a perfectly sensible thing when motoring through vinyl and carpet clad airports, but looking down the narrow alleyway in front of us and its organic flow of cobblestones, I'm pretty sure it's not going to work out quite the same here. So much for sneaking into town. Collectively we sound like some fair sized agriculture machine and our rumblings are amplified by the walls of the houses on both sides of this narrow alleyway. Venetians know the sound well, and we will quickly also realize that this sound foretells the approaching presence of tourists.

The small street that dead ends into the canal is San Moise and we pass a hotel of that name and then take a left-hand turn into Calle delle Veste; walk about 50 meters and stop in front of a five-story building that is a nondescript color close to that of an old Manila folder. A restaurant occupies the ground floor and sandwiched between its front window and the next building there is a door that Agnese slips a key into, opens, and with a smile, ushers us inside. Stairs. Lots of them. Four flights of them! Souheir goes ahead to open the apartment, the boys follow lugging one bag apiece. I follow, then make three more return journeys with the luggage everybody else seems to have forgotten. Finally I struggle into our new home with the last of the bags and attempt to catch up on the tour of the premises that has been going on for awhile. Agnese is from the rental agency which turns out to be one of our most important discoveries in Venice. They have filled the cupboards and the refrigerator and have even left a stocking full of candy and chocolates for the boys. I thought it was a belated Christmas gift but it turns out that tomorrow is St. somebody's day and Italian kids get a stocking from "Befana" (literally Grandma Witch!) The boys enter into the spirit of this festival immediately and the consumption of chocolate begins.

Agnese shows us how to operate the appliances and the heating system, opens the windows in the sitting room to reveal a clothes line that is attached to the side of the building, gives us all a welcome hug and closes the door behind her as she leaves. It is now very quiet in the small apartment and we just stand looking at each other in our jet lagged stupor.

"We are here" I say, stating the obvious to my family. "There's no longer any need to rush about, so I suggest that we all take a nap and try and catch up on some sleep".

Tamir is already sleepwalking toward his bed. Tarik is kicking off shoes and shrugging out of his sweatshirt. Souheir and I walk into our new bedroom, pull back the cover on the bed, strip to our underwear and snuggle down. She pulls the cover up beneath her chin and smiles at me over it's brocaded edge.

"Welcome to Venice" she says.

I feel an almost unnatural sense of accomplishment and smile back at her. "Thanks... Grazie".

Chapter 3

..."IT'S ALL IN ITALIAN!"...

I can't remember the first meal that we cooked at Calle delle Veste, because I can't remember much of anything of the first 24 hours in our new home. I've had varying degrees of jet lag before, but nothing like the mind numbing lethargy that I experienced then. Souheir and the boys seemed to join me in this grey stupor, and looking back it occurs to me that perhaps the reason that we so completely relaxed is because we could. When I arrive as a chaperone of a group of students, no matter how long or ghastly the journey has been, the one person in the group that cannot afford to be asleep is me. There are always a hundred things to do as you collect 20 people <u>and </u>hopefully their luggage from the airport, walk them to the lagoon, put them aboard a water taxi, motor them across to Venice, and book them into a hotel. In all of this, I am the one person in the group that has to be alert. Even when we visit without a group we are always aware of the fact that we only have a finite time available to us, and we make heroic efforts to "get onto Venice's clock" as soon as possible in an attempt to avoid wasting time. None of that mattered this time, however, we were here for months, and this luxury allowed us to sleep.

I awoke to shafts of light sneaking into the room between old wooden shutters, looked around this completely foreign bedroom once or twice, staggered to the tiny bathroom with a latch that was actually a cleverly disguised monkey puzzle, sometimes working and sometimes not. Looked in on the boys, lifeless lumps in foreign beds, and always collapsed back into what was now "my bed" where Souheir softly snored.

Eventually we all awoke. Not at any prescribed time, nor with any purpose other than the fact that our bodies had decided that they were ready to function again.

One of the keys on the small mirror table in the hallway was gone, replaced by a scrawled note:

"Gone for a walk...Tarik"

"Do you think he is OK?" asks Souheir.

"I think it's wonderful that he feels comfortable enough to go off exploring by himself" I reply.

We sit at the table drinking coffee and eating bread and cheese that we'd found in the small refrigerator. Tamir staggers into the kitchen looking like he's coming out of hibernation.

"Where's Tarik?"

"Gone for a walk"

"Can I go for one too?"

"Absolutely, just make sure you know the way home...and take a key".

He immediately brightens, drags on a jacket and some shoes and we hear him galumphing down the stairs as he makes his way to the street.

Souheir smiles at me over her coffee cup.

"Good morning"

"Is it?"

"I haven't got a clue"

We both laugh and decide to unpack suitcases and settle into our little apartment.

The boys return at different times with stories of discovery and acquisitions of sweet foodstuffs, and Souheir and I can't stop feeling proud of them.

In the late afternoon I step out of the door into a cool, grey mist that seems to be sitting on the rooftops, turn to my right and follow delle Veste down its shining flagstones to a very grand street lined with expensive clothing boutiques. Calle Larga 22 Marzo. Five minutes of wandering meanders brings me to a small salumeria tucked into a tiny campo with a bridge on both sides. I buy water, salami, mozzarella, a couple of tomatoes and bread and retrace my steps, entering the apartment as if I am Santa Claus with a bag of gifts.

So I suppose our first meal was sandwiches…panini…with salami, tomatoes and mozzarella. What I remember clearly is the beginning of a conversation that stretched over the entire period of our time in Venice. It was always a dialogue about how good all of their food tasted. Perhaps we were enchanted from the start, bewitched by geography and our own expectations, or perhaps these people are so connected to good food and all its subtleties that they simply won't buy anything else.

We have a weekend to settle in, find our bearings, and to prepare for the intensive language course that begins at 9:00 on Monday morning. Agnese has left us with a map bearing the pencil marks and labels of her suggestions for everything from supermarkets to wine stores, and we spend the next day buying brooms and cleaning materials and 'other stuff' that a household requires. In the food stores we are a little timid at first and seem to arrive home with many small parcels.

We were truly kids in a candy store, and the most amazing thing of all was that the shopkeepers didn't mind that we bought small amounts of differing foods. In fact after watching the local Venetians, we realized that buying small amounts of food was what everyone did. Diversity of flavors and the foods are always fresh. Shopping for this day's food is a natural part of this day…Every day. We acquired 4 different kinds of olives, 5 different varieties of cheese, and I learn my new favorite words.

"Duecento cinquanta gramme!"

Two hundred and fifty grams…About a half of a pound.

Our first organized meal was simple fare that would never be remarkable in the US

In a pan I warm olive oil and then brown a couple of chopped onions and a crushed garlic clove. Introduce 250G of ground beef and continue to brown. Add one box of Pomi tomato sauce, a handful of dried basil and a good splash of red wine. Cook it slowly for 45 minutes and serve over pasta with good crusty bread.

We followed this with an insalata mista dressed with balsamic vinegar and olive oil and washed it all down with a bottle of Valpolicella..

The kitchen is small, and by the time the food is prepared we are all crammed into it tasting the sauce and sipping wine. Tarik begins what will become a small culinary ritual that will become something of an addiction during his stay in Venice.

He cuts the bread into chunks and dips them into a bowl full of Olive oil and Balsamico.

He will consume gallons of this stuff before we depart.

Sitting in the front room, which contains a couch, the television, and a dining table we toast our first complete day in Venice, and laugh our way through the meal.

It is delicious. This recipe has never tasted better, and we are off again about how wonderful the food is. The washing of dishes after the meal is cause for further laughter as we attempt to crowd around the small kitchen sink, washing the dishes in a plastic bowl and rinsing them in another, jostling each other as we reach into the small sink alcove to dry the dishes.

We return to the front room with glasses of wine and the boys turn on the television, surfing through the 20 or so available channels. They finally settle on a newscaster who is covering a story about the lack of snow in the Dolomites. Tamir looks across the room at Souheir and me, and theatrically gestures toward the television,

"Hey, it's all in Italian!"

We don't know why it's so funny, but none of us can stop laughing. I'm choking on my wine. We are ready for this adventure!

Chapter 4

"IN ITALIANO PER FAVORE"

I have no rational explanation for the phenomena that affects people from all over the world, creating an irrational desire to speak the Italian language. However, the fact that it resists explanation and definition in no way diminishes this universal attraction, and I'm amazed at the breadth and variety of folk who are afflicted. I'm one of those sufferers, but must quickly insert a disclaimer here, lest you, dear Reader, jump to any conclusions about my ability with this beloved 'lingua'.

In the inimitable words of my son Tarik,

"…Dad, you suck at this…"

I'm amazed that I can actually speak English. It would come as no surprise if my mother told me that I did not speak until I was seven years old! I love this Italian language, but speak it abominably. Before you write me off completely though, be informed of the fact that I consider myself a work in progress, and have every intention of affecting great improvement…May be even fluent one day. That day, dear Reader, is not today.

So what is the attraction for this language? It certainly is not main stream to commerce, banking, specific scientific disciplines or computer applications. There are no great stretches of Geography that will resist your entrance without this Italian language.

Outside of this Mediterranean peninsula and its immediate neighbors there are literally no places where you will be required to speak it. The Albanian language is close to it, and I am always amazed at how quickly the French learn it. (Apparently the rules of grammar are exactly the same). It is, of course, the closest language to the precursor of all romance languages...Latin.

I have absolutely no problem with pursuing an explanation that is not based on linguistic insight or expertise. For me it is simply the music of the language that I find so attractive. I'm not sure that I would've been so instantly besotted by this language if it had been offered up to me as a study of an abstract topic at a 'book' level. It was simply the sound that captivated me. Italian was introduced to me in the mayhem of the railway station in Florence in the early morning of a day in June of 1982. It then 'swirled' around me for the next couple of weeks as my newly minted bride and I honeymooned around Northern Italy. The language became welded to sounds and tastes. The smell of the morning cappuccino; the expectation of the coming meal...Primo piatto. The warmth and friendliness of the people who spoke it and who then so patiently encouraged those first words from us:

"Il conto, per favore"

"Why Italian?"

It's 1985...

I'm part of a group of students being led on an orientation tour of Florence. The person asking the question (that I'm hoping desperately is rhetoric), is a pretty young woman who is a language instructor at Florida State's Study Center in Florence. We are standing on a street corner at the rear of the giant Santa Maria dell' Fiore Cathedral, and the blaring noises of the city fills in the pregnant pause. She gestures upward to the great tiled dome soaring above us,

"This building in English can be called…elegant…In Italian it is elegante… It sounds like ey..ley..ghan…tey"

The English just disappears into the street sounds. The Italian hangs like a clear musical note. I love to listen to the way it trembles and rolls, the way it stretches the speaker's mouth open wide. Big open sounds that seem always to be accompanied by the conducting hands of the speaker.

I have way too many excuses when it comes to questioning the shortcomings of my efforts with the Italian language, but some of them surely are valid. Prior to the classes that I have taken at the Istituto Venezia, I have never studied any language other than English. I briefly acquired a number of Spanish words while in Mexico in 1975, but never examined structure or syntax nor received any formal classroom instruction in Spanish.

In truth the few words that did 'stay' with me simply confused my early efforts with Italian. It took a great deal of effort for me to replace the Spanish word for two (dos) with the Italian (due), and I have no idea why. What I do know is that the entire process is quite intimidating to me, and once again I am left with nothing but questions as to why this is so.

I never questioned the profound Anglo prejudice of my education which was standard fare for Australia in the 1950's. In the fourth grade my teacher read us an 'important book'. She sat us down and began to read Don Quixote…
I don't mean Don Key..ho..tay
I mean Don Quicks..oat!
I had very nearly graduated from high school before I was aware of the Spanish pronunciation! (I have never quite consoled the contradiction that surfaces around the English word "quixotic", however.)

We Anglos emerge from the education process without really understanding the basic qualities of our own language. We are seldom told that some languages are finite (Italian) and some are not (English). However both of these languages grow in different ways. The Italian language grows by adding words from other languages. It is not uncommon on a Friday afternoon to be wished "buon weekend" by Italian friends. This cross fertilization creates quite a fuss among the French language purists who see it as an attack on their tongue. It is the aggressive quality of an ever-growing language that is often the reason for this attack. The English language grows itself at an astounding 1000 words per year, and this dynamism is one of the main reasons that makes English so difficult to learn. It also accounts for confusion among its own native speakers who are trying to understand its inner workings.

Rather than rules, it is a language of exceptions to rules

"I before E…EXCEPT after C"

When I ask my students about formal or informal language, they mostly decide that we are having a discussion about courtesy.

Yes please

No thank you

Excuse me

Pardon me …

In fact these courteous phrases come with the understanding of what in some places are called manners. We are being courteous. When we use these manners, our demeanor changes, but our language doesn't. I suspect that deciding that the youth of today is not as courteous as the previous generation is an age old complaint, and the fact that this resonates with me is probably just a comment on my age. However, it seems to me that colloquial language appears to be aimed at the destruction of this formality and courtesy.

Younger students infrequently use courteous phrases when talking with each other, and many of them have stopped using them at all. The language of 'the street' is apparently trimmed of these things…A sort of egalitarian leveling process. We largely live in a "Hey you" world, and most Anglos confronted with the concept of a formal language, that is even more so in its written form, are lacking a basic concept that places them at a distinct disadvantage.

And then of course, there is the subject of gender to deal with.

"Is the Moon masculine or feminine?"

This question is almost non sensible in English. In Italian, however, not only is it a sensible question, but everyone knows the correct answer! The English language carefully names both genders of almost all of the animal kingdom, but leaves most inanimate objects without gender definition. It's not something that we English speakers have to contend with.

All of the preceding verbiage may be informative, but be aware, dear Reader, that it is primarily offered up to justify my very mediocre Italian language skills.

Campo Santa Margherita is an irregular shaped open space ringed about with three and four story secular buildings, each with its own architectural character, quality and texture, while somehow presenting itself as a continuous perimeter; like trees that were planted close together and intertwined their branches as they grew to become almost one giant tree. Buildings lean on each other, often slouching in the same direction. The campo has chestnut trees planted down its length and beneath them, benches. Sitting on one of these you can look down to the old Scuola dei Varotari (tanners and furriers) which now serves as a municipal office, and beyond it to the square campanile of the Chiesa dei Carmine that looms over the rooftops.

It's in the university district of Dorsoduro and the flow of the foot traffic through this campo is brisk and constant, as it is also a thoroughfare for the bus station in Piazzale Roma.

It has a bookstore, a pizzeria that sells it by the slice, a wonderful bakery that is always sold out by 2:00pm, a wine store where you can fill your own container, and an array of stalls that sell fruit, vegetables and flowers that somehow miraculously are folded up and whisked away at the end of the day. On Tuesday through Saturday there are also three fishmonger stalls (there are only a select few in Venice that are outside of the central fish market). These are the Pescivendoli, and the sound of their voices calling out prices mingles with the cries of the ever opportunistic seagulls that seem always to be in attendance.

The most numerous stores in the Campo are bars and trattorias, and they seem to serve a continuous clientele day or night. As the weather warms, each of these establishments will increase their presence by creeping slowly out into the campo with their tables and chairs. This space in front of their premises is called the plateatico, and they must pay the city a tax for using it. It is not uncommon to see policemen with measuring tapes checking to see that only the space allocated is being used, but it is also clear that on warm days when the tourists are present, the tables and chairs seem to multiply. It's a little like walking through a crowded restaurant, rather than crossing a square.

It is a place where university students can buy single glasses of wine from the Enoteca, standing in animated groups arguing and laughing, a place where lovers exchange passionate kisses, where people walk dogs of almost unbelievable variety and size… Grandfathers dodder after tottering 2 year olds. It is obviously so much more than just a public place and is an extension of each of these private lives. It's the front yard of these folk…and the back yard.

If you cross the Rio di San Barnaba on the Ponte Puglia (where it is said that sailors and fishermen settled their differences in public fist fights) you will enter a street that leads you into Campo Santa Margherita. On your right, just as you enter the campo, you come upon an old metal gateway sandwiched between a coffee bar and a hardware store. Behind this gate a flight of well worn stairs leads up to the piano nobile (first floor). It's an old palazzo that shares the marks of its age with the surrounding buildings, and from the street there is nothing that would mark it as extraordinary. It is the Istituto Venezia, the language school that we have come to attend.

It's cold and wet. Moisture clings to all surfaces and the little group of people that is my family carefully ascends the slippery steps and opens the tall, narrow doors that are the entrance to the Istituto. It's our first day of school. I want to use the word 'intimidated', but if I'm at all honest the word needs to be 'terrified'. I really don't want to do this.

The reception at the Istituto is warm, professional, even inviting, and I have no idea why I'm so overwhelmed by the prospect of attending classes. We are shown to a room and given a very basic written and oral examination so that we can be placed in classes that match our competence. I'm mentally heading for the entry level class before even completing the test. Souheir, who has had some previous formal Italian language classes, and who clearly masters new languages better than the rest of us, is directed to the intermediate class, while the boys and I head for level one.

The grand conundrum for me was somewhat resolved. Was it better to be in a class with your wife or your children? I'm a pedagogue, so I know that the perfect world would find us each in our own class. No spousal or sibling rivalry would be great, but that was not among the possibilities. Souheir was raised by Egyptian parents in a bilingual home, and while I may just once again be grasping at straws to justify my shortcomings, I'm sure that folk who are raised with multiple languages, exhibit a much higher level of linguistic competence than those of us who weren't.

She is the best friend that I have in the world and in our everyday life we are always 'there for each other', helping in hundreds of ways. I really didn't want that to affect this learning situation we were entering. I had to do this on my own. The complication, of course, was that I was now in a class with my two sons, and my initial concern was with their response to that situation. Let me just jumble all of the emotional and familial elements into one pile so that you can get some idea of what was going through my mind as I walked down the polished marble hallway to the "elementary" room.

I'm a college professor. It's a long time since my degree-gathering days. I'm good at what I do, but old enough and smart enough to only do the things that I do well. I'm competitive, and while I have learned to be magnanimous in defeat, I don't like it. Did I possess the required humility to enter into this course of study and be able to deal with the fact that no matter how many degrees I have, and how successful I've been in my work, there was a very good chance that I was not going to "shine" here. All of this in front of my own children? This scenario did not simply manifest itself at the moment, and perhaps part of my dread was steeped in the fact that I had been considering these elements for some time. I was fairly sure that my ego was strong enough to take the coming 'dents'; and was driven by a genuine desire to gather as much of this language as possible.

The three of us stood in front of the tall paneled door like small children on their first day of school. The door handle was a bronze casting of a lion's head, perhaps one of the most ubiquitous images in Venice, however, the symbology of Saint Mark was completely lost on me, and I knew we were entering this animal's den.

I turned to Tarik and Tamir, placed a hand on each of their shoulders and said,

"Come on guys…we can do this".

And we did!

Nobody enjoys watching a good teacher at work better than another teacher.

We were treated to pedagogic skills that were well honed, competent, wonderfully patient, and above all, knowledgeable.

Two young teachers, Gregorio and Rosanna, marshaled us into the classroom and began a discussion that outlined what would transpire in the next four weeks. Our class consisted of a young Dutch woman who spoke excellent English, and was a student in hospitality management, a young German man who was a Lufthansa pilot, a Parisian girl who looked as if she was carrying a minor in 'Haute Couture' fashion, a well- preserved English woman who was currently living in Monaco, and three mature, retired dentists from Sweden. Toss the three of us with the Australian/Montanan elements and I think you have an excellent working definition of multicultural!

Each day was divided into two sections. One was from 9:00am to 11:00am followed by a half hour coffee break, and the other from 11:30am to 1:00pm. Gregorio taught the first section and Rosanna the second. Total immersion is an interesting terminology that took on an entirely new meaning for me. Classes were conducted entirely in Italian, and a remarkable skill that both teachers exhibited was their ability to sustain this. They both spoke excellent English (and other languages too!), and if the immersion became too much for you and you found yourself swimming upward to take a gulp of English, they would simply just look at you and with a smile, shake their heads and say,

"In Italiano per favore"

At break in the local coffee bar they could be induced to enter an English conversation but never in the classroom. Looking at almost any text on the basics of Italiano will give you an idea of what we covered in those weeks, because the class followed a careful and thorough structure aimed at conveying these elementary principles. The dynamics of the class, however, were a constant delight of discovery and invention as this small cluster of students went to work. I was constantly in awe of the speed with which the Dutch and French girls mastered certain aspects of our studies, and of course felt like an idiot when paired with one of them for a 'buddy conversation'.

The folk who really fascinated me were the Swedish contingent. Two women in their early sixties, and one man of the same age, who somehow looked older than they did.

They spoke wonderful English, but did so with a very strong accent. The class quickly divided itself by age, and of course I was constantly thrown in with the Swedish dental corps. The three of them had clearly attended some formal instruction in Italian because at an academic level they were streets in front of where I started. They could conjugate verbs, were expert at singular/

plural and gender. I kept asking the question "Why are they in this elementary class?"

Lui ...Is the Italian word for "He"...a pronoun in constant use.
    On the first day Gregorio pointed at me and said,
    "Lui E....
    In my head I wanted to point out to the young teacher that he had forgot-
ten my name.
    My name was not Louie!...It was John!...Even Giovanni!...My hand was
moving upward to correct this naming mistake when a small bell rang way
back in the dark recesses of my brain, and a voice said,
    "Don't do it, John".

I'm sharing this information to give you some idea of how limited my exposure to Italian was... And by comparison how superior to me this trio was.
However, the Dental Swedes were still in the elementary class, and each day it
became clearer why that was so. They simply seemed incapable of setting aside
their dictionary, which apparently ranks among the most heinous of linguistic
crimes. Rosanna and Gregorio were constantly asking them to not use their
dictionaries; but they never complied. Perhaps they didn't understand! And
this is the part of this chapter that I have been waiting for...

When I told you that I speak Italian poorly; (OK abominably)... I was talking
about the language as a whole. I'm actually quite good at some of its parts. It's
a constant source of surprise, but I somehow have the ability to carry around
in my head single Italian words...Hundreds and hundreds of them. I am
the dictionary! Together, Souheir and I can talk to anyone. She supplies the
grammar and structure, and I keep feeding her the words. Pretty strange stuff,
yes? It turns out that my comprehension is quite high even though my speaking skills come nowhere near that mark.

The Dental Swedes were clearly sophisticated, intellectual beings, but it
seemed to me that they had fallen into the trap that I was so determined

to stay away from. They considered that because they were the recipients of University degrees and had proved their intelligence, they would obviously do well at this new academic endeavor. They were horrified and shocked to find out that this was not the case. I can't begin to tell you how bothered they were by the fact that I could just blurt out a word while they were frantically thumbing through their dictionaries in search of it. They would fuss and fume over these dictionaries, and while they could easily work out the written exercises given them, the vocalization of the language was another task indeed.

Two of the trio were a married couple, and I watched with interest the reactions between them. I did not envy them this closeness and was acutely aware of the fact that I was glad that Souheir was two classrooms up the hallway away. Their shared exasperation spilled into the oral exercises, and the fact that I seldom understood their Italian sentences simply added fuel to the competitive fire that burned between them.

"Dove questo..." Became "Doovy kwistor", and only after they had repeated each sentence several times was I capable of translating it out of Dental Swede into Italian and finally English. It was excruciatingly painful, but very instructive, and I realized that I must sound pretty strange to the locals, with my Austro-American accent. I spent a great deal more time with my pronunciation after my sessions with the Swedish folk, and they had no idea how their efforts motivated and helped me.

Our month in the program moved slowly along its daily passage and was dotted with pinnacles and valleys of personal success and defeat. I never quite overcame the strange sinking feeling in my stomach when it came my turn to give an answer or to enter into a discussion, but it diminished greatly and my internal dictionary grew by hundreds of words. Above all I learned the courage to always make an attempt at conversation, and in doing so immediately won the admiration of the Venetians who are so encouraging when you attempt to use their language. Our linguistic growth was simply a part of the change in our overall comfort level that increased daily as we settled into our adopted home.

Through the Istituto we made many new friends and the boys slowly began to exert an independence that allowed Souheir and me to escape for quiet lunches and cups of coffee at newly discovered trattorias and bars. Perhaps being in class for 4 hours every day with their father drove them off into adventure. Perhaps like their mother and I they just needed some time by themselves. Whatever the reasons, they disappeared at 1:30 pm and we seldom saw them again before dinner time that evening. We were still working our way through our Italian cookbooks and most evenings were spent concocting meals, enjoying newly discovered wines, and then splashing through the carnival that was washing the dishes.

The evening of our last class was an auspicious occasion and we decided on a "graduation dinner" to celebrate. At the mid-morning break in class I went down into the campo to the fishmonger and bought 16 large scallops. They are called in Italian, "Capesante", and the "pescivendolo" carefully wraps them with the rounded half of their shell. He also leaves attached to the white meat of the crustacean its liver, which is a bright orange color…It is called the coral. They were not inexpensive, but as I paid for them I told myself we had earned such an extravagance.

CAPESANTE AL FORNO
Finely chop two or three large cloves of garlic

¼ cup of lemon juice
¼ cup finely chopped parsley
¼ cup olive oil
½ cup dry breadcrumbs
16 scallops with shell

Mix all of the ingredients in a bowl…Remove scallops with their "coral" from their shells…spread a small amount of mixture in each shell…Replace scallop and coral…Sprinkle rest of mixture over the scallops (do not heap it up)…Place the scallops on a baking tray and place them under the broiler…leave them there until the breadcrumb mixture is golden brown (probably only 5 minutes)…serve!

Dessert was a box of small sweet cakes from a famous pasticceria over by the Frari, and we washed them down with limoncello. Souheir, her eyes shining over the sunshine yellow of the drink in her hands, said quietly to me,

"So now that we are finished with the language school, what are you going to do with your time?"

I allowed a small swallow of the golden citrus to slide down my throat before answering.

"I'm going to walk down every street in this city."

Chapter 5

ALL ROADS LEAD TO ?...

Following Jamie Oliver's lead we had decided to explore the prospects of 'real Italian peasant food', and had decided to make our first ribollita. Ribollita is a Tuscan dish that Souheir and I often ate during our stay in Florence. We weren't sure how many of our neighbors ate such a dish, but felt they would at least appreciate our effort at "authenticity". It is basically a soup so hearty that it would be called stew almost anywhere else that has three main ingredients. Beans…Cabbage…and stale Bread!

Take about a pound of dried cannellini beans and soak them in water overnight

In a large pan of water combine the drained beans, a bay leaf, a small peeled and quartered potato, and a crushed tomato…Cook until the beans are tender…(this will take some time)…When they are soft, drain them and discard everything except the beans.

Finely chop 2 carrots, 2 red onions, 3 sticks of celery, and 3 cloves of garlic and gently cook them in a large pan with generous olive oil. When they are soft add a large can of plum tomatoes and then turn up the heat…then simmer it all for 5 minutes. Add cooked beans and a cup of water. Bring to boil. Stir in a pound of cavolo nero (a local black cabbage)...tear the leaves so that they are not too large, and finely chop any stalks. Add half a loaf of stale bread that has been cut into cubes. If the soup gets too dry just add a little water (a splash of white wine works well too!) Continue to cook for about 30 minutes... season with salt and pepper and when you serve it, drizzle generous amounts of olive oil over each bowl.

All of Jamie's suggestions and directions were (of course) perfect... What didn't appear in any of his directions were any precautionary statements about how olfactory the process might be! Don't get me wrong here, the smells are wonderful and tantalizing, but there was no way to confine them to our little appartamento on the fourth floor. Open a window and it's only 2 meters to the next building where an open window embraces the sumptuous aroma of our cooking cavolo nero.

We have been saving bread for a couple of days to give us the stale bread that is the base of its rich creaminess, and as we stir it down into the wonderful concoction of vegetables and oil, the aromas are absolutely overpowering. I remember that we are out of red wine and excuse myself for a quick dash downstairs and around the corner to the local enoteca. I love the proximity of everything in this city. A little out of breath, I'm back at the entrance to our building and slide my key into the old worn lock. As the door opens I am instantly assailed by the smell of cooking ribollita...four floors below the kitchen it is being cooked in! The aroma increases in intensity as I ascend the eight flights of stairs, and by the time that I step into the apartment, I am giggling almost uncontrollably.

Souheir and the boys of course want to know what is so funny, and I tell them of my discovery. Tarik and Tamir immediately disappear down the stairs, only to reappear several minutes later also overcome by mirth. It is a kind of embarrassed laughter, but we seem incapable of curbing it, and literally laugh through the entire meal, which by the way was delicious. Thanks Jamie.

Washing the dishes, we are all a part of a discussion that wonders if our neighbors think that the 'stranieri' on the fourth floor have suffered some culinary disaster, or if they are impressed by the fact that we have cooked something so classically Italian.

We, of course, never find out, but the smell of ribollita took a day or two to dissipate.

Souheir and I were sitting at the dining table savoring the last of the chianti which had been a wonderful accompaniment to our ribollita.

"So where are you going to go?"

"You're invited too, you know", I reply.

"I'll meet you for coffee afterwards. Where are you going?"

"Well, I'll walk to Piazza San Marco then down the Riva degli Schiavoni, up to the bridge by the Museo Navale, then up to the Arsenale, cut through Castello into Cannaregio, back across the bridge by the railway station, down through Santa Croce to the Frari, catch a traghetto to San Tomà, and then walk back here"

"And how long will that take?"

"Dunno…never done it before"

And so it was that the next morning I stepped out into Calle delle Veste, took a right down to XXII Marzo and began my exploration of Venezia…street by street.

Have you ever looked at the streets of your town and wondered what process was used to decide upon this organization of roads and structures? If you travel northwards into western Montana you will pass through some of the most remarkable mountain scenery in the world. Eventually, however, you will find yourself confronted with the final range of mountains that stand between you and Canada. At the base of these mountains nestled up to a lake that bears its name, is a town that I adopted 20 years ago, and that I have come to love. In some ways it is a rather typical western town with an "old side" and a "new side". It has a thriving "downtown" that is currently resisting the tentacles of the encroaching linear development called highway sprawl and its attendant box stores. It is at least making efforts to ensure both preservation and uniformity by enacting legislation that controls the process of development and rapacious building so often lumped under the title of progress.

It is a prosperous town and in the 20 years that we have lived here, we have watched an ongoing program of improvements. The new library, the performing arts center, the ice rink, the athletic club have all taken root and blossomed during our tenure.

All of these things are wonderful and obvious. Surrounding all of this is something that is infinitely less so, even though it is ubiquitous, and a part of everything...the road system.

It is absolutely organic, and each year is resurfaced, repainted, repaired and refined.

The roads actually get wider. I watch with interest the process of adding sidewalks and curbing to the edges of roads that have previously only been a strip of bitumen with gravel edges. The road never gets narrower... Always creeps outwards. It is clear that the automobile reigns supreme and that the sidewalks, added as an obvious afterthought, are achieved at the price of a wider road. But go beyond these observations: How did this road get here in the first place? In the center of town it is obvious that after the decision to begin a town was made (and who knows how that was achieved?), that designers used mechanical devices to draw straight streets that intersected each other at ninety degrees. What about the roads that snake up the mountainside, or wind along the river's edge? How do you explain that beautiful sweeping "S" of the road that cuts through the meadow near the golf course?

Does it follow high or rocky ground that would have enabled pioneer folk to drive their wagons through the pasture without becoming mired? Was there always a path through the meadow? Perhaps a game trail that habituated deer followed moving away from the Native Americans who were hunting them eons ago? All roads and streets have a story, and the longer the imprint of civilization, the more obscure that story becomes.

I took a slight detour from my planned route and passed under the sotto-portego that leads to the Campo San Zaccaria. Its little space, and its quiet emptiness belies its proximity to the tourist throngs that are close by. (Sotto is 'under'... portego is the central part of the first floor of a house or palazzo... These are literally passageways beneath houses, linking streets together. They are not clearly marked on most maps and create a particular problem for lost tourists). One of my favorite bars looks across this space to the magnificent structure that is the church of San Zaccaria; and believe me, even though it always tastes great, it's not the coffee that keeps me coming back. I'm not sure that there is anywhere else on the planet where you can sit with a coffee, and view such splendor.

If it's not already obvious, I will tell you that this is my favorite exterior of any religious building in the world. It has just been uncovered after a long period of hiding behind the scaffolding that was part of a major cleaning and restoration project. Its striking pearly-white exterior literally takes my breath away each time I pass it, and I remember clearly the tears that sprang to my eyes, the first time I saw her after she had been uncovered.

San Zaccaria is a sacred building...a church. It is filled with artworks that are the envy of every major museum in the world, and I visit this place regularly with my students. As you enter its rather gloomy interior you are almost immediately felled by the power of the Zaccaria Altarpiece by Giovanni Bellini that gleams jewel like from the left wall, and that is just the beginning. Every wall surface seems to be covered with painting, and for an extra 2 Euros you can enter the Sacristy to see early Gothic works by Antonio Vivarini and

Giovanni d'Alemagna. However, no matter how impressive the contents of this building may be, it is the exterior that I find so compelling. What kind of people would build a church to look like this? Perhaps it was this question that drew me there this morning. You see, I was sure that, given time, I could form my own opinion about contemporary Venetians. But who were the ancient Venetians? The people who were responsible for so much of the architecture that still exists today? There is a long and complicated story here, let me briefly sketch some of it for you.

The most successful thing the ancient Venetians did was to escape.

Third and fourth century Italy saw the final deterioration of the Roman Empire. Constantine moved its capital (and a good deal of its art and booty) to a safer place, and, consistent with the ego of a living God, called it Constantinople. What was left of the Western Empire consolidated itself for a short while in Ravenna, a city only 100 miles south of Venice, but this was a last gasping effort, and the last Roman Emperor, Romulus Augustus, was captured there by Odoacer in 476 AD. Odoacer and his warriors (there is conjecture as to whether he was a Hun or a Goth), were just one of the nomadic tribes that raided the Empire, sweeping down from their northern homes.

This invasion began with short programs of violence, like a small dog snapping at the flanks of a large animal, but eventually the attacks became more frequent, the barbarians stayed longer, and the small dog changed into a slavering wolf that rapidly devoured what was left. Resident populations were literally consumed and displaced, and a small group was pushed northwards and eastwards until they found themselves pushed against the shores of the Adriatic. They were confronted with a low lying, marshy, muddy shoreline opening out into a vast lagoon.

Desperation? ...Courage? ...Whatever motivation, the end result was that a population escaped from the mainland and sought refuge on a group of islands in the middle of this lagoon and its shallow and treacherous waters. So effective was this natural barrier that the Venetians never resorted to defensive structures, and they slowly consolidated this safety that they had stumbled upon. The waters of the lagoon were their protector and they were relieved of that tension in their lives. An elegance, refinement and reserve that bordered on aloofness settled on this population, and manifested itself in almost everything they touched.

Standing in front of San Zaccaria always makes me wonder about its builders. Unlike so many Gothic churches and cathedrals that screech at you from their flamboyant heights, San Zaccaria visually embraces the viewer, encouraging engagement of the intellect rather than superstitious awe. San Zaccaria has always occupied a place of prestige and even power in the Venetian world. In its heyday it was one of Venice's most prestigious institutions. It was founded in the 9th century when Byzantine influence was still strong and the

Byzantine court sponsored the first monastery, donating funds and skilled labor, but more importantly religious relics. Because of its age it was granted an endowment of land, some in front of the Basilica San Marco which was sold to the state for a huge profit in the 12th century. Its Benedictine convent was populated by only women from the highest levels of the patrician families and a famous abbotess was the sister of a Doge.

It is an amazing collection of classic columns and architectural motifs that could easily be secular rather than sacred. There is a confidence about this building that leads me to believe that its creators were neither cowed by external secular enemies, nor by the power of the Mother Church. It is constructed of expensive marble, and its builders took delight and pride in the fact that they had created such a unique place of worship. The original 9th century church underwent many restorations, but in the mid 1400's it was decided to demolish it and build another. This time much of the money for its reconstruction came from the Vatican. Rather than completely destroy the old structure, the new one was moved to the left, although some of its 'footprint' overlapped the old. The original architect Antonio Gambello began a Gothic structure, but had only completed the lower two zones of the façade when he died. The commission was given to Mauro Codussi who modified the design by softening the Gothic style with the addition of Roman arches. He preserved the tri-part division of the façade with the use of a system of decorative antefixed columns which reach up to crown the building with a magnificent tympanum, complete with oculus and massive cornices. While these are the normal ingredients of neoclassic architecture, Codussi manages to make this building distinctly and uniquely Venetian, somehow evoking the façade of San Marco.

It is this grand Venetian influence over a variety of architectural styles that tells us so much about the pride and confidence of the ancient Venetians. The architecture of Venice has been largely unaffected by the normal ravages of history, and capriciously or otherwise, has escaped the desecration that so many ancient cities have suffered. When we walk down the streets of contemporary Venice, we are walking past many external structures that have remained unchanged for 500 years.

I paid for the cappuccino, and with one last look at San Zaccaria, passed under the sottoportego back onto Riva Schiavoni and continued towards the Museo Navale.

In 1171, the sacking of a Venetian settlement on the Golden Horn polarized the already tense rivalry with Genoa, and Venice made plans for all out warfare. The Venetian administration ordered a gathering of war funds through a series of 'forced loans' and to facilitate the collection of these monies the city was divided into 6 parts called sestiere. If you consult a modern map of Venice you will see that these sestieri still exist. Each of these areas had a center that was once a single island or a cluster of them. San Marco is the ancient area of Rivoalto (meaning high bank) and the Rialto takes its name from it. Canaleclo became Cannaregio, Luprio was the area that became San Polo and Santa Croce. To the west of San Marco there were twin islands called Gemini and Olivolo an island of olive groves which was presumably important enough to warrant a fortified wall (the only one in Venice) and the sestiere Castello takes its name from this. Dorsoduro (hard back) is the only sestiere that still uses its ancient name. I have Venetian friends that tell me that in the days of their grandparents it was still possible to discern which sestiere you were raised in by your accent. Great rivalries sprang up between the sestiere and this internal competitive situation manifested itself in many ways.

Even though the divisions still exist, along with the ancient rivalries, walking down the Riva, looking across the Bacino di San Marco at San Giorgio Maggiore shining white in the thin morning sun, it occurred to me that modern Venice is actually a city of zones and boundaries that have no correlation to the ancient divisions. Tourists seldom wander far from the main "tourist areas", and there are parts of the city that are almost never seen by this visiting horde. The official number of tourists per year is counted at 15,000,000, but almost everyone considers this a very conservative estimate, and this is a subject of great debate. Couple this number with another estimate…the average stay in Venice by this mass of visitors is only 6 hours! The resulting picture is one that shows a very large group of people, on a tight schedule, determined to "see the major sights" of Venice. (They apparently don't have time to wander around!) The Venetians call us Foresti. In Latin foras means coming from outside The Venetian "foresti" is a variation on the Italian word "foreste"… coming from the woods or uncivilized … and after you watch a bus disgorge a group in Piazzale Roma, you don't take quite as much offense to the term.

The Museo Navale is a large, rather plain building, and if it were not for the enormous ships' anchors standing by the front entrance I'm not sure it would attract much more than passing attention. It is a building that sits back from the water's edge in an open campo, and the bridge that leads you over the canal running alongside it is decorated with the prows of marine vessels and a magnificent lion. This bridge is one of those unseen boundaries and as you cross it you realize that the tourist throng immediately thins and that you are walking with a very different group of people. You are entering the part of Venice where the Venetians live.

I turned left and walked along the Rio dell' Arsenale that runs alongside the museum to where the fondamenta opens into an irregular shaped campo that has a tall brick wall topped with white stone castellation as a backdrop. This wall is extensive and runs off in both directions, disappearing behind the encroaching buildings. They are the only fortified walls in Venice and they encircle and protect a large area of docks and warehouses that were extremely important to the function of the Venetian Empire. This is the Arsenale. It is thought that the word "Arsenale" came from the Arabic "dar sina", which means house of construction, but no matter what its source was, the Venetians gave the terminology 'Arsenal' to a number of languages, and presumably an English soccer team as well.

The Venetian Empire rose to its full power because of its naval superiority and prowess, and it was these shipyards that spawned their armadas. Here within these walls were foundries, wood yards, a rope making factory, sail making lofts, gunpowder magazines, even a bakery given over exclusively to the making of sea biscuits, and all of the other storage and production facilities necessary to build, maintain and outfit a navy. At the height of its production it employed 15,000 of the most highly skilled workers in Europe who, as difficult as it is to believe, could produce from keel to masts and sails, a ninety foot trireme every 24 hours.

A steeply arched wooden bridge spans the canal and deposits you in another small campo in the center of which is a large bronze flag pole. This is the official entrance to the Arsenale. The building itself is not architecturally commanding, but the decorations on it and in front of it are amazing. Here resides the greatest collection of lions in the city. In front of the building sitting like giant alley cats are a cluster of white marble freestanding sculptures that exhibit their disparate ages by the obvious difference in the sophistication of the sculptural skills used in their production. The more antique lions are dog-like and not quite believable, where their more modern littermates approach a regard for realism. The large lion looking down from the lintel over the entryway is worth a second look because, although he looks like so many of the official lions of Saint Mark that populate Venice, this one has some interesting differences...he is holding a book, but unlike all of the others that traditionally display the words "Pax tibi Marce" on its open pages, this book is closed and those words do not appear. The sculptor had obviously attempted to put a snarl on its mouth too, which to me falls short of that and turns into an almost wolfish grin. The lion was mounted here as a part of the rebuilding of these gates in 1460 at a time when the advances of the Ottoman Empire were fanning the flames of war in the Catholic Church and Venice was expected to play a major role in Christendom's stand against the Islamic invasion. Clearly this was not a time of "Pax" and I'm sure the closed book and aggressive snarl was seen as an act of resolve by all who looked upon it.

The walk from San Marco to here has literally been a walk along the front entrance of Venice. The grand churches, public buildings and Palazzi are oriented outward, presenting any visitor crossing the Bacino with an amazing view of sumptuous architecture and civic organization that has lost none of its impressive qualities. I wonder how many million photographic exposures exist of these views. Standing in front of the Arsenale, I look down to my left into narrow and dim alleys that lead to Venice's "back door". Most of the 15,000 artisans that worked in the Arsenale (they were called the "Arsenalotti") would have lived down there, and as I walk down past San Martino I wonder what their lives were like.

You only have to walk several hundred meters into this labyrinth to realize that it is just that…A labyrinth.

The alleyways twist and turn, following some pattern that completely evades my attempts at predicting their next move, and even though I spent a good deal of time with it last evening, committing my path to memory, I slide my pack off and get out my trusty map. I have a very good sense of direction and in truth don't feel even slightly lost. I'm looking at the map trying to discern an order of organization, and a couple of twists and turns of my own find me in the Campo Bandiera e Moro. Years ago I WAS completely lost when I stumbled into this small open space, and collapsed onto one of its park benches.

I walk over and reacquaint myself with the bench while trying to sort out what is chasing around in my head. The open map on my knees is not revealing anything to me, and I'm soon lost in the peace and reverie of this place.

In the 5th Century a group of refugees ran away to a shallow lagoon dotted about with tiny islands, some no more than muddy sandbars. Apparently it was noon on the 25th of March in 421 AD. You have to wonder about a group of people who will give you the inauguration date of their culture with such precision, but it's interesting that the Romans gave the same hour, day, month, and year precision to the beginning of their Empire and we are reminded that the first Venetians were the last of the Romans. What truly transpired was a slow population of these islands that took several centuries and an amazing amount of ingenuity to achieve.

The ancient Venetians needed to navigate waters that were often only inches deep and their boats evolved into craft that were light and lively. If you watch a leaf floating on water, you will have some idea of the dynamics at work. These waters often flowed through channels among the tall sea grasses and sedges, and the only way to navigate was to stand up to row. Fifth century descriptions of these early Venetians talk about the bond between the water and the lagoon's inhabitants and they were clearly an almost exclusively aquatic folk. Like their boats the earliest habitations were light and impermanent, flexing in the waves of wind and water that swirled through the lagoon.

They drove wooden pilings into the soft mud and tethered both their boats and their houses to them, but even as these buildings became more sophisticated, the technique of building on these driven pilings remained the same.

Weight was always a consideration to these structures that clung to the water's edge, giving easy access to their boats while leaving the open areas of the islands available for agriculture. These open areas were the fields...In Italian "campo"... and this name is still given to all but a few of the open spaces in Venice. These garden areas produced vegetables that were highly prized by a population that existed largely on sea food.

One of the most highly prized dishes of these Venetians was called Risi e Bisi... "Rice and Peas", a dish that was traditionally served to the Doge, or Duke, of Venice to celebrate Saint Mark's birthday on the 25th of March.

RISI E BISI

Take about 2 pounds of fresh peas and shell them. Keep both the peas and the shells.

Soak the peas in a bowl of cold water that has a tablespoon of flour in it for about a half of an hour. Then wash the pods and put them in a pot with water to cover them. Salt and simmer over a medium heat for an hour. Take a celery stalk and 8 or 10 sprigs of Italian parsley and finely chop them together.

Heat 2 tablespoons of olive oil and 4 tablespoons of butter in a saucepan, and when completely melted add 4 ounces of pancetta that has been chopped into small pieces. Sauté for 5 minutes and then add the chopped celery and parsley. Sauté for 5 more minutes and then add the peas that have been drained and washed. Cook for another 5 minutes. Add salt and pepper and then a half of a cup of dry white wine. Cover and cook over low heat for 20 minutes. Pour the water from the pods into a pot and discard the pods. Combine the water from the pods with 3 cups of beef broth and bring to a boil.

Pour the pan juices from the cooked peas into a heavy pot, and put the peas aside.

Bring these juices to a boil and add 2 cups of Arborio rice. Sauté for about 5 minutes.

Start adding the broth mixture to the rice a little at a time, stirring continuously until the rice has absorbed all but a quarter of a cup of the broth, then add the peas and the rest of the broth. Taste for salt and pepper and remove from heat. Add 3 tablespoons of butter and 4 of Parmigiano. Mix thoroughly and serve immediately. It's a wonderful dish filled with the sweet green tastes of early summer. The first crop of sweet green peas from the outer islands creates great excitement as they arrive in the vegetable stands of the central market.

We are told that there were 117 islands in the Realtine group, but it occurs to me that there could have been any number of connecting sand bars and surely the count differed from low tide to high tide. They learned to join islands by filling in the channels between them, and by digging some channels deeper they drained other areas.

The first thing the ancient Venetians had to do before they could build a city was to build the land on which it would sit. This activity served to manifest behaviors that marked the Venetians as very different from their neighbors, perhaps different from any other population. I am a landowner in Montana, and this has always seemed to me to be rather a silly term. The more I spend time on my property, working with nature, the more I am aware of the fact that at my very best I am a steward of the land. It has been here since prehistoric geologic time, and will be here long after I am gone. It is rather presumptuous to say that I own it, and I'm poignantly aware that it is not mine. The Venetians are not presented with this situation however, and in some ways can definitively claim ownership. They made it! The fierce pride of Venetians can perhaps be explained by this unique situation.

The fact that this was an empire without land also had a profound effect on its population. Life here in the lagoon was invigorating and unencumbered with the politics of the mainland. Because this useable land surface was so small, it could not be used as a weapon against the lower classes and the feudal system never took root in Venice. While so much of medieval Europe was under the yoke of the local landowning despot, Venetians enjoyed a freedom that was unheard of elsewhere.

As the early settlement took on a more permanent nature the houses became more substantial and after two disastrous fires in 1106 the wooden structures were replaced with brick and stone buildings. The small, red terracotta bricks called altinelle that were used to build most of these buildings have slowly weathered and oxidized over these many years, and they are now almost a rose pink, and it is this dominant color that surrounds the present day visitor to Venice.

Meander. The word slowly surfaces in my mind and immediately I recognize its relevance. These streets meander their way among the houses, just as I'm sure the ancient waterways moved among the islands. Perhaps I have found the organization of these streets? Leaving the campo I find myself walking slowly, allowing myself to drift down these alleyways, flowing into the next street, allowing myself to follow its twists and turns, sometimes to the right, sometimes to the left. I'm not consciously going anywhere…just forward.

Venice was one of the first cities in the world to have paved streets and street lighting, but even in the early 1400's when some of its grandest palaces were being built, most of the streets and campos were dirt and gravel. There were still large spaces of land given over to agriculture, and it was only in 1409 that the pigs of San Antonio Abbate were confined to their sties. Up until then they had wandered the streets as a sort of mobile garbage disposal unit.

My aimless wandering leads me past Santa Giustina to San Francesco della Vigna, and for some reason I decide to snap out of it and take up a brisk walking pace that pushes me through the sestiere of Castello and Cannaregio, back to San Marco. I meet Souheir at "our bar" which huddles in a narrow street that connects Campo Sant' Angelo with Campo San Stefano. The Venetians have apparently had a love affair with the beverage hot chocolate for a very long time, (they say that they invented it). Giacomo Casanova mentions it countless times in his long rambling autobiography, and it is clear that a cup of hot chocolate is considered the perfect drink to ward off the damp cold.

Venetian hot chocolate is rich, creamy and thick… Actually it's a lot like drinking a hot chocolate pudding! The whole lip smacking, moustache forming, soft blowing across the cup process is absolutely captivating, and I've become a hopeless addict. Over the past couple of weeks I've discovered a unique selection of hot chocolate flavors and have been slowly working my way through an amazing menu of them.

Today's flavor is white chocolate with pine nuts…Wonderful! Souheir and I are standing at the polished marble bar in our own little huddle created by the crush of people in this confined space. The clouds have covered the sun and a wind is blowing in off the Adriatic. It's cold out there and it seems that all of Venice has hurried inside to warm up.

She blows on her hot chocolate, which is peperoncini, and asks me,
"How was the walk?"
"Instructive..."
"In what way?"
"I think I'm finally getting to feel the pulse of this place"

She smiles at me and I reach across for a peperoncino kiss.

Chapter 6

FINDING THE RHYTHM

I enjoy the rhythms of the world that surrounds me. I'm a natural counter. I know the number of steps that I climb each day on the way to my office. I enjoy the regularity of life, not because it reassures me or because I feel like I'm in control, but because I'm always trying to work out my part in this cosmic rhythm. It demands quite a heightened sense of observation to see many of these rhythms, because they are so mundane and sometimes extremely slow.

Souheir and I live rather hectic lives and often our teaching schedules have us going on different paths that only converge in our home late at night. On days such as these we almost always spend a half of an hour or so in the hot tub which sits on its own deck adjacent to our house. There in the peace of 'our valley', wrapped about with hot water, under a canopy of stars that no city dweller ever gets to see, we tell each other about our day, or simply smile through the steam.

A small speck of faintly pulsating light begins to slide across the sky.

"Here comes the 11 o'clock satellite"

She laughs at me and says, "You say that every night"

"Well that's because it passes by every night. At exactly this time...And I like the fact that I know it's coming...that I have discovered its path across our sky."

Imagine how observant the ancients must have been to track the movement of the stars. To discover that there was a small group of them that did not follow the rhythm of the many. They were wanderers...The ancient Greek word for wanderer was planet.

Sometimes when I'm walking on the mountain behind our house I stop and sit with my back to a tree and just watch the forest move in the wind. It is just one large moving mass, but as you look more closely you see that each species of plant has its own dance, its own rhythm. It was these kinds of observational skills that I brought to Venice.

It's difficult to explain the difference that I felt as we arrived this time. In all of my many previous visits I had been quite adventurous and there were few places in the city that remained undiscovered. But, as I have said earlier, they were always short visits and I intuitively attempted to get the most out of my time. With four months at my disposal I hoped to discover the rhythm of life in Venice. For reasons that we never attempted to explain we took one route on the way to the Istituto Venezia, and a different one on the way home. It was not some time worn tradition of dragging one's feet on the way to school and skipping on the way home, but somehow the two journeys took on separate and very different qualities.

In the morning we travelled as a family pod, all four going to the same place. Walking anywhere in Venice predicates that you will sometimes be able to walk four abreast, and sometimes only in single file. The controlling influence is the width of the streets that you travel. There are many alleyways that are only a meter wide. Meeting someone approaching from the opposite direction demands that one of you stop and flatten against one of the walls. Strangers pass so closely, so intimately that you at once know if they are smokers, what their perfume or cologne is…what they had for lunch. And of course how do you pass so closely without saying "Buon giorno" or "Buona sera"?

The boys have never been enthusiastic about leaving their beds in the morning, and being in a foreign country seemed to have no effect on this behavior whatsoever.

Morning, therefore, is never a time of high energy exchanges and witty repartee. Everyone is civil and friendly, but there is no snappy conversation over coffee and toast.

Having consumed the morning comestibles we would pick up our bags and clatter down four flights of stairs to the street below.

In retrospect I realize that the moment of closing the street front door behind me became a special marker for each day, the moment that I made my daily commitment to this city. It was the moment that I took my first big breath of the outside air, and for some reason I always looked up at the old building above me. It was my first look at the sky, and this sliver of atmosphere peeping down between the crush of buildings needed to be studied carefully if I was trying to work out 'what the weather was doing'. Montana is not called the "big sky country" for nothing, and at home if I need to check the weather, I simply walk out on my deck and look into cubic miles of sky to do so.

In the heart of Venice, tight passageways through a maze of ancient architecture allow you to see very little sky, and you need to be in the campos, or on the outside Fondamente to be able to do it. I remember the mornings of misty rain most of all. Pulling the old door closed I would look up, allowing the rain to fall on my face.

"Looks like rain guys"
　　"You're an oracle Dad"
　　"Yeah…How do you do it?"

In the streets you are constantly exchanging space with others. You and a host of others are making your morning journey and there are never any streets that are 'empty'. You are always steering around fellow pedestrians, heading for that open space in front of you that will allow you to pass along the way that you have chosen. It's all feet and faces. There is no time for looking up or around and you must look where you are going; and more importantly, where others are going. You are searching for passageways between the people. What registers mostly in these constricted places is texture.

On wet days the older flag stones of the street are more obvious. They are smoother. Wetter, more slippery. If it's raining in Venice (and there is no month of the year when it doesn't), stay off the white stone which is used for decoration in the larger campos and the edging of the steps on many bridges. The white stone is much less porous than the grey, and there is always a film of water on it waiting for the unwary.

The street sweepers do an amazing job of keeping Venice clean and an early morning walk will reveal these folk with brooms that are incongruously long and archaic, rhythmically sweeping their way along the streets. The brooms are a single handle upon which is fixed a head of natural sticks and twigs, sometimes 5 feet long. It looks very quaint and "halloweenish" until you watch them at work. The long sticks and twigs reach into all of the corners and crannies and it is remarkable how efficient they are. In the rain, however, the trash sticks to the flagstones, making the job much more difficult. In heavy rain they don't sweep at all.

I'm constantly looking at patterns of flagstones, and have a hundred questions. Are they smaller in some streets for a reason? Where does this stone come from? I am fascinated by utility work that is undertaken by men in bright fluorescent orange overalls who have about them an air of purpose and pride in the job that they are doing.

The paving stones are numbered in chalk, pried up with long steel crowbars, and then stacked in piles awaiting the reconstruction of this giant jigsaw puzzle when the repairs are complete. The soil that is revealed is instantly attractive. Where in the central part of Venice would one go to actually see soil? It's an interesting question, and I'm taken by the stickiness of the mud that is in the trenches being dug. I expect the soil to be more friable; closer to sand, and smile at my discovery that the 'terra firma' is "firmer" than I thought it would be. All the work is done by hand, the most technologically advanced tool being an old dented wheel barrow, whose primary function seems to be the transport of tools to the worksite. They are skilled workers and these worksites are seldom active for more than a few days at a time and the inconvenience to pedestrians is minimized. I step over a small pile of flag stones, smile at the man with the long pry bar and head toward the opening into Campo San Stefano.

It's one of the largest campos in Venice, and the closest to our apartment, so we cross it daily in our travels. Like the valley in front of our house in Montana, this campo has become "ours" and my pace naturally slows as we enter, I presume out of some sense of comfort. This space has been used for an extraordinary variety of activities in the history of Venice; perhaps one of the most unexpected is that it was the venue for bull fights. The last one occurred here in 1802 and was marked by a disastrous collapse of the spectator stands. It is ringed about with a remarkable variety of trattorias and bars, which in better weather spread their presence across its surface with linen covered tables and clever retractable awnings. Today, however, they are like snails hidden in their shells, and their clientele stand behind steamed up windows drinking the morning cup.

The large stone sculpture of Nicolo Tommaseo, one of the heroes of the 1848 revolution commands the center of the campo and it elicits a smile from me as we pass by. The Venetian Republic strictly controlled the erecting of public sculpture, never allowing statuary that glorified individuals...even the Doge. No individual was more important than the State. The honorific sculptures of Venice only arrived after the demise of the Empire when Napoleon captured the city. I wonder if the disrespect often shown them is some latent reaction from times past.

Nicolo Tommaseo stands stoically on his raised plinth, the blockiness of his coat giving the figure an overall 'heavy' feel. As a reference to his literary prowess and studious habits a pile of books is stacked carelessly at the rear of the figure, connected as a form of support to the clunky coat. A Venetian student told me that the statue is called "Cagalibri" by Venetians...Because he is literally shitting books.

If you walk around to the rear of the sculpture the visual pun is oh so clear.

The old Gothic church of San Stefano chokes off the northern entrance to the Campo, and its rather dour exterior and equally dim interior give no hint at its outrageous history. This church has been deconsecrated no less than 6 times, each occasion because murder had been committed on its premises! San Stefano houses a number of Tintoretto paintings and has one of the most magnificent wooden ceilings in all of Venice. It is tucked so far back into the surrounding houses that its leaning campanile can only be enjoyed from the next campo north, that of Sant' Angelo.

We turn left at Tommaseo and exit the campo through its southern entrance past the church of San Vidal which is now the venue for musical concerts that are offered year round.   Adjacent to San Vidal the rear entrance of the gorgeous palazzo Cavalli Franchetti invites visitors into a large garden planted with deciduous trees and flowering shrubs. While such things are the norm in most cities of the world, here in this confined and finite space, it is a blazing sumptuous statement by a wealthy family flaunting such extravagance. The palazzo is now the home of the Istituto Veneto di Scienze Lettere ed Arti which is purported to have one of the finest libraries in Venice, and is often the venue for international meetings of both Academics and Politicians. Sitting placidly atop each major column of the palazzo's surrounding fence are a pride of some of the finest sculpted lions in all of Venice, and I never tire of looking at them. The principle façade of the Cavalli Franchetti opens onto the Grand Canal, and a great vantage point to appreciate its beauty is from the bridge that begins in the Campo San Vidal and spans the Grand Canal across to the Accademia.

There are only four bridges that span the Grand Canal and this is the one that is often simply called the Wooden Bridge. In an environment of decorative stone this wooden structure has an incongruous and temporary presence. It turns out that this is in fact the case, and in 1932 was erected as a temporary bridge. It was so well liked by the populace that they refused to have it changed. It was completely refurbished in 1986, and a supporting steel structure was cleverly hidden beneath it. We will watch an exchange of its wooden planking slowly take place over the coming months. It's a fairly steep incline, but is broken into low, wide steps that require a couple of strides before the next, and I find myself changing my pace to accommodate this rhythm. It is one of the favored vantage points of the city, and I don't think I have ever crossed it without finding a knot of tourists at its apex looking up and down the Grand Canal. It's a major thoroughfare and the traffic is a dense flow of pedestrians dressed in clothes as varied as my own jeans and jacket to the almost incongruous coat that is being worn by the matronly woman descending towards us. She is wearing a full length coat that appears to be constructed from an entire species of fur bearing animal.

Tamir, ever the champion of the environment, sidles up alongside of me.
"Did you see that coat?"
I nod. hoping he is not going to allow his outrage to find voice.
"That's obscene!"
"I know, but she's an old lady; let's show a little respect here."

He snorts and pushes on over the bridge in front of us. The wooden steps are wet and slippery, so descending to the other side of the Canal is done a little more slowly. On icy mornings, no one walks quickly over this bridge. Once across, we pass the entrance to the Accademia Museum and plunge again into the network of alleyways. I love this weaving meander that we take. The garbage collectors are wheeling their ingenious trolleys, stores are opening, produce is being delivered to the trattorie, linen to the alberghi, and kids are on their way to school. In all of this bustle there is always an old man walking an equally old dog. He seems not to be aware of the pace around him, and nods to the shopkeepers as they sweep the street in front of their stores.

Bridges, alleyways, under a sottoportego (Isn't that a wonderful word?), across the tiny Campo San Barnaba, past the floating vegetable stand, right over the bridge, and into Campo Santa Margherita and the Istituto Venezia. Puffing steam up the steps we enter the front doors with a couple of minutes to spare.

"Buon giorno Susanna!"

"Buon giorno Giovanni!"

We have become part of a family of fellow students. I just wish that I could repay such kindness with outstanding scholarship and linguistic skills. Each morning I awake at about 5 a.m. having a complete Italian conversation in my head. Within the confines of my cranium I'm brilliant. I wonder if it is ever going to come out of my mouth!

Four hours later the same family pod exits the big doors and stands at the top of the steps. We can see out over part of Campo Santa Margherita and look down at a steady stream of pedestrians wrapped about in winter clothing moving through the thin cold sunlight, all making a beeline for something. There are no strollers here.

"'Bye."

"See you."

Tamir and Tarik drop away quickly down the stairway in front of us and Souheir calls after them.

"Dinner is at 7:00…Don't be late!"

The words pass over their heads and I wonder if they even register. The boys pass through the old metal gates and are gone, each in a separate direction. They are heading for lunch with friends, adventures? We never know. Tarik is 17 and has made friends with students from the University quarter. He is a college student himself, and it's been fairly easy for him to fit in with a group that, being international, makes the language barrier less daunting. Tamir is 15 and most students of his age are Venetian and involved in high school. This is a much more difficult demographic and consequently he has made few friends in this group.

However, he has insinuated himself into a very special group of "Venetians" who are street entertainers, musicians, mimes, and his most favorite of all, a young Bulgarian man who wheels around an ingenious, completely self-contained marionette theater.

Sometimes on family walks, we will find ourselves in some remote part of the city and pass by a street "salesman" hawking all manner of products from small creatures created by filling a balloon with a paste of cornstarch, to handbags and fashion accoutrements, purporting to be brand names from some of the world's leading fashion houses,

"Ciao Tamir"

It's a deep, almost booming voice from an incredibly tall and handsome black man who is standing over four leather bags displayed on a white sheet of fabric on the ground in front of him.

"Ciao Jamal"

They shake hands in a complex bumping of knuckles and slapping of palms and then Tamir falls back in step with the rest of us. I ask him, "So who is that?"

"Just a friend"

I look across at Souheir. She smiles back her "don't ask me" look.

So... each afternoon Souheir and I are abandoned on the steps of the Istituto and have the whole afternoon to pass in any way we choose. Today we amble across the campo to a small supermarket where we buy a bottle of wine, some bread and pasta and then retrace our morning path back to San Barnaba. Just beyond the sottoportego is our favorite pizza shop. It's a small negozio where two-thirds of its interior is given over to the production of pizza, and one third to the customers who stand at benches (actually shelves) that are attached to the walls of this tiny space.

"Buona giornata!....Che vogli?

It is one of the cheeriest places in town and we are greeted like old friends each time we come here. The choices are all wonderful. The traditional meats and cheeses that we know in the US, but beyond that, marvels such as eggplant (melanzane), arugula and tomato. Most of the customers are students and there is a great feeling of fraternity here. The pizza is served on a single pie shaped piece of cardboard, and you buy it one slice at a time. If you arrive after 2:30pm the place is jammed with high school students who seem to need to stand in much closer proximity to each other, and judging by the volume of their voices, all have hearing loss. Incongruously, the pizza changes too. When the kids arrive, the cook quickly twirls up a couple of pizzas that have as a topping French fries! It's called pizza patate...And of course I tried it. Really putrid! Think McDonalds meets Pizza Hut and you'll have some idea. It's ambrosia to these young folk, however, and the two pizzas disappear instantly.

Today we choose to once again retrace our steps and cross back to Santa Margherita where we stop for a while at the fish market and buy a kilo of small clams. They are a principle in one of our favorite dishes:

SPAGHETTI VONGOLE (CLAMS, COCKLES)

In a large pan brown one large chopped red onion in olive oil. Add a can of crushed tomatoes (fresh even better), 2 cloves chopped garlic and peperoncino (You choose how hot you want it...In Italian arrabbiata...angry). Salt and pepper to taste

Cook on medium heat for 15 minutes.

Meanwhile wash vongole and soak in a pot of fresh water.

When the sauce has cooked for 15 minutes, drain vongole and empty into sauce.

Cook until all shells open (discard those that don't).

Serve over al dente spaghetti.

You put everything into your mouth. Suck the vongole out and spit out the shells onto a side plate...Delicious...And a lot of fun to eat.

We continue our slow walk along Santa Margherita, crossing over the bridge at its northern end into the little campo of San Pantalon where the old façade shows its mostly closed weathered wooden doors to passers by. The ceiling of this church has one of the most remarkable cycles of painting in all Venice and any time I bring a group of students here they exit in stunned silence. The church, however is only open for limited hours and many who come to see its marvelous interior are confronted by closed doors.

Continuing our stroll, we pass through a series of narrow streets, past one of Venice's most famous pasticceria (pastry shop), and after passing under another sottoportego, emerge at the rear of the magnificent Gothic church of the Frari. As you walk down the side of this enormous old church, you pass a bakery that produces calzone that is famous citywide. They are displayed to pedestrians on huge trays that hang out into the street. Our favorite is the funghi (mushroom) and we divide one between us and continue our walk, munching and smiling. I'm not sure that I could actually give you directions from this place to where we want to go. As is the situation in so many of the 'Passeggiatas' around the city, you just have to know where you are going. I'm heading for the Grand Canal; and the vaporetto stop at San Toma. Even then you have to know where the small alleyway runs down to the traghetto stop, for that is where we are bound. As I stated before, the Grand Canal is spanned by only four bridges along its entire length. Tourists are careful to cross at the correct bridge, for there is nothing more frustrating than being able to see your destination on the other side of the Grand Canal, and having no way of reaching there other than a long hike back to one of these bridges. However, a system of water ferries cross the canal at a number of places, enabling locals to cross with a great deal of freedom. These ferries are called Traghetti. They are a form of gondola with a deeper draft and are propelled by two oarsmen, one fore and one aft.

They cross the Canal constantly during daylight hours. The cost of a ride is 50 centesimi and you pay the oarsman as you step aboard. Venetians never sit down but ride across standing up just like the tiny bow legged lady with her shopping cart who is standing in front of Souheir and me. As the boat pushes off from San Toma and begins its water strider dance across to the other side she never shifts her feet nor her balance for the 3 minute ride, and it is clear that she is as comfortable here on the water as she is walking down the street. We climb out on the other side, thank the gondoliers, and move off down the long narrow alleyway. A few more turns and twists and we emerge in the northern end of Campo San Stefano! The first time that I led Souheir this way she had no idea where we were, and as we entered the campo she said,

"How did you do that?"

"Magic!"

Our bar is the next on the left and we have to go in to continue our research on the flavors of hot chocolate. We stand at the bar chatting to the barista, a young woman who is enthralled by our stories of Montana mountains. We're 'locals' now and they serve us munchies and potato chips for nothing. It's easy to while away a half an hour over a cup of Orange Rum chocolate.

We saunter across the Campo Sant' Angelo with the campanile of San Stefano beetling above us at a decided lean. I wonder aloud to Souheir if the real estate value of the property towards which this tower leans is less than on other side of the tower! We laugh and turn into an alleyway that is two hundred meters long…And you can touch both sides of it with your hands for its entire length. Over a bridge, under a very dark sottoportego smelling of cats and who knows what, and then we are at the rear of La Fenice, the great opera house of Venice which just happens to be in the backyard of our apartment on delle Veste. Ascending the stairs is always done without talking, and we arrive at our front door slightly out of breath. Souheir is putting away groceries and I'm hanging up my backpack and getting out my homework.

"I'm going to read for awhile", she says "What are you going to do?"

"I'm going to finish my homework and then go for a walk. You want to come?"

She knows I'm still exploring the city one street at a time and instinctively allows me the space to do so.

"No, I'll wait for you to return and then we'll take a little passeggiata before dinner.

A page of verb conjugations and I'm at the front door letting myself out into the street

"Which way today…?"

Chapter 7

MESSING ABOUT
IN BOATS...

"There is nothing...Absolutely nothing, half so much worth doing as simply messing about in boats..."

These words spoken by Rat to his friend Mole in "Wind in the Willows" have always resonated within my head in an upper class English accent. Now, however, I'm pretty sure that Mr. Rat was a Venetian.

If the weather was not good, or time was short, I would simply leave the apartment, take a left at the front door, and then the first right, and retrace the footsteps of our first hour in Venice. The alleyway dead ends at the same wharf that we arrived on, a quiet little pocket out of the weather, and away from pedestrians. There I would watch the boatmen of Venice maneuvering and manipulating their craft with such skill. The Venetians really do know how to "mess about in boats". It's almost as if a Venetian without a watercraft of some kind is not quite complete.

The obvious part of the story that I have told so far revolves constantly around a body of water called the Lagoon, and its entryway into the Adriatic Sea. It was Venetian mariner skills that brought the trade goods back to the Mother City and from there transshipped them to the rest of Europe. They became the world's best boat makers, and their great shipyard, the Arsenale, the blueprint for a hundred navies. The tourist or visitor moves effortlessly on a system of ferry boats that function with such efficiency and punctuality that most of us never really come to grips with the fact that this is a titanic organizational effort. Every tour guide will at some time parrot the phrase, "Everything comes in by boat…and goes out by boat", without even beginning to explain how complex this activity is.

The little wharf at the end of San Moise is empty of people and activity for most of the day, but always has a cluster of vessels moored to it. Sometimes they are stacked alongside each other, their hawsers connecting one to another. Sometimes they are all tied to the wharf with their own bow lines.

It would be a great stretch of anyone's imagination to label me a "mariner", but like Mr. Rat I too 'mess about in boats". My boats are a plastic kayak and an inflatable rubber raft, both of which I use in the rivers and lakes of northwest Montana. I love to row…Even think I'm pretty good at it; and there is a natural affinity that I feel with all vessels and their pilots. Armed with this affinity I began to enquire about the boats of Venice and was bowled over by an entirely new vocabulary. Most of the vessels bear names that still reflect the ancient Venetian dialect and I was soon awash in words that I had never encountered. Pupparini, Caorline, Mascareta, Sandoli, S'ciopon, Topi.

The topi--literally the rats--are the heaviest boats that frequent the canals of Venice. They are a large dory-type vessel that taper towards both the stern and the bow, where most of their midships are given over to cargo space. They are seldom crewed by more than two sailors and are driven by powerful engines that burble their presence through their water exhaust. It is this distinctive sound that usually signals their presence. The steering mechanism which seems almost archaic and consists of a long tiller connected over the stern deck to a large rudder, is extremely effective and is often manipulated with a leg or foot while the captain is doing other things with his hands.

They are the workhorses of the canals and can be seen moving cargoes as varied as ice cream and building materials through the maze of waterways. Some are quite specialized and have earth moving buckets attached to them, and in many cases are equipped with hydraulic cranes which can reach onto the docks and wharves to pick up their cargoes. These sturdy vessels are maneuvered into seemingly impossible spaces, with such panache and skill that I simply never tire of watching. All boating activity seems to be accompanied by the "Venetian cool", where everything must appear effortless, characterized by great economy of motion, and above all is absolutely intentional. You are always sure that the boatmen are aware that they are on show, and their audience is treated to a constant act of bravura. In all of my boat watching I have never seen a collision.

Today the garbage collectors are running late and I'm treated to the entire spectacle of the loading. Each morning we take our bags of garbage downstairs and leave them in the entryway back against the wall. This garbage is collected daily by men and women clad in smart light grey industrial uniforms who ring the doorbells and call "Garbage" into the intercom. They are then given access to the entryway of the building and they load this garbage into large two-wheeled aluminum carts that are lightweight, maneuverable, and narrow enough to pass through all but the smallest passageways. The collectors are in small groups usually commanding four or five carts and each group is accompanied by a large garbage boat which moves through the canal system, staying as close as it can to the collectors and their carts. When these carts are full they are wheeled to the boat. In the front of these carts is attached a set of small wheels on the end of a long bracket which allows the collectors to 'walk' them up and down the steps of the bridges. The garbage boat has one crewman and he operates a hydraulic crane that is fitted with a special arm that picks up the entire cart and swings it over the central cargo area where a covered hold has a single rectangular chute rising from its center. The cart is lowered onto this chute which activates a spring mechanism in the bottom of the cart. The entire bottom of the cart opens into two trap doors, and the contents are disgorged instantly. When the cart is lifted up, the doors snap back into place and the cart is returned to the waiting garbage collector. The entire process takes about sixty seconds!

With a low throaty exhaust note the garbage boat moves slowly along the canal to the next loading point and I'm returned to my reverie in the quiet of the canal. Most of the vessels that pass by are powered by some form of engine, usually small outboards. A "license to drive" in Venice is only required if the boat has an engine with a capacity that exceeds five horsepower and many small craft putter quietly by, leaving behind the telltale blue smoke of these small engines. Many of these small craft are wonderful examples of wooden boatbuilding skills, and many are simply utilitarian constructions of fiberglass and aluminum. Whatever their construction, it is simply my nature to wonder where they are bound.

Boat ownership among Venetians does not parallel the automobile ownership of mainland Italians, but I was continually surprised by the number of folk that I met who actually owned a boat. My observations lead me to believe that if they are going shopping at the local supermarket, average Venetians do not use their boats. So the question of "where were they going?" became more of a conundrum for me. During the winter months their boats are used for utility hauling, much like we would use a pick up truck in Montana, and on several occasions I accompanied our landlord as he delivered television sets to his other apartments. The heat of summer comes with its contingent crush of tourists, and I'm sure that many of these boats are simply used to run away to quieter parts of the lagoon where the peace of nature beckons.

However, it is just as obvious to me that there is such a bond between the water and Venetians, that they simply have to be on it, and the "messing about in boats" theory seems entirely reasonable to me. Public transportation in Venice has become something of a "cash cow" for the city coffers and the price of a thirty minute ticket (which in most cases is only a single ride) is now 7 Euros. I have been told that two-thirds of this fee is actually a form of 'tourist tax' and is shared among the many architectural restorations that are a constant in the skyline of modern Venice. Wherever these funds are spent, and whatever justifications are offered up for this fee, it places public transportation in Venice among the world's most expensive. I am continually absorbed by the consummate skills that the crew of these ferries display. Just like the rest of the world's public servants, the drivers and conductors (which I presume translates to Pilot and Crew) of the Venetian transportation system run the gambit from pleasant and helpful, to unfriendly and combative. However, the attitude that this job is actually beneath their skills and dignity which seems to pervade so much of the public sector of the Western world is not apparent. Think of the bus conductor that takes your ticket, all the while affecting an air that lets you know that he is grossly overqualified for this job. The Venetians in these positions work with pride and great skill and they are held in high regard by their passengers. Remember they are boatmen among other boatmen and as such are always under expert scrutiny, and their activities are always affected with that 'cool" that I spoke of earlier.

A ferry powers up to one of the many fermata (bus stops) and at the last instant the pilot cuts the power to the propellers and allows it to coast. As it slides gently alongside, the conductor throws a heavy rope (hawser) over a set of metal cleats. With the boat still in motion he twirls this rope around and knots it with a half hitch, all of this in one wonderfully arabesque motion. The pilot then returns the power to the props and this 'sucks' the vessel up against the dock. The rope groans and creaks and the boat comes to a halt. The gateway is then slid back with more of that same bravura, and the conductor calls out the name of the stop. People get off. People get on. The gate is closed; the pilot reverses the props, the rope slackens, the conductor twirls it free from the cleats, forward power is applied…It's an amazing piece of choreography, and if you ride this system every day you come to know the 'dancers'. They all have their own little flair that they add to this process, and I found myself actually having favorite conductors. These jobs, both pilot and crew, are shared among the sexes and it is not unusual to see women performing these skills.

If you ride the public transportation around the lagoon and its islands you will encounter four kinds of vessels. Most tourists will arrive at Piazzale

Roma and catch a ferry down the Grand Canal. The vessel that will transport them on most occasions is a vaporetto. These are sturdy steel vessels that were originally steam powered, hence the name. They now use diesel engines that, like so many of Venetian craft, have a distinctive voice. There are two sizes to these craft, and if you visit in the summer when the tourist throng is present you will be riding in a larger version. Most of the seats are to be found inside the central cabin, but there are a few that are outside on the stern deck and a few more up alongside the wheelhouse which is in the front of the boat. Separate from these, there is an open space that runs from behind the wheelhouse back to the main cabin, and the entry gates of the vessel deposit passengers here. Even when there is plenty of space inside, some folk choose to ride outside standing up, and in all but the most inclement weather, this is my choice. The views to either side of the boat are uninterrupted where I prefer to be out in the salty air; but it also gives a great opportunity to watch the crew at work.

Another vessel that plies some of the Grand Canal, but mostly circumnavigates Venice, connecting it to some of the closer outer islands, is a smaller more sleekly designed boat called a Motoscafo. These vessels have a few seats on an open rear deck, and only a small open area behind the high wheelhouse. They are narrower than the vaporetti, and are designed for greater speed and more stability in rougher 'outside water'.

If you venture further out into the lagoon, out to Burano, Punta Sabbioni, Lido and back to San Zaccaria, you will ride the largest of all the public vessels called Motonavi.

Some of these are quite large with multi deck levels that carry hundreds of passengers. A very important piece of information is that they are the only public vessels that have a bathroom on board!

The fourth set of vessels at work in the lagoon is run by a separate company called Alilaguna, and as the name implies they go around the lagoon. The company uses an assortment of boats, but most are smooth, sleek fiberglass launches that are some of the fastest boats on the Lagoon. Alilaguna connects central Venice with the Marco Polo airport and passes through the Lido and Murano.

For the day tripper or short term visitor to Venice, the public transport system is nothing more than a way into, and out of the city. It is usually accompanied by a high degree of confusion; and if you are carrying a bag, a sense of outrage because you may be charged an extra fare for your luggage. For many visitors, then, these are the only two journeys they will make using these boats.

However, riding the boats of Venice rapidly became one of the most important elements of our daily Venetian life, and each of us eventually had our own way of using the vaporetti to move about the city. Because of the length of our visit and the fact that we had a permanent residential address, we were eligible for a special public transportation pass called an Abbonamento. This pass allows, for a very nominal fee, unlimited use of all vaporetti, a discount on the Alilaguna, and use of autobuses on the mainland in and around Mestre.

So for the tourist who is watching the depletion of his Euros as he 'boats' around Venice and wonders how the locals can afford it...The answer is... They don't! The truth is that the locals seldom pay ANY of the prices that tourists are dealing with.

Sometimes after four hours of language immersion my head literally hurts and I have an almost uncontrollable urge to hurry through the Istituto doors so that I can stand on the top of the glorious stack of stone that is its' staircase and gulp down the cool air of Campo Santa Margherita. Today is one of those days and I'm the first outside, waiting for the boys and Souheir to join me. We have a special task to accomplish today and the boys are not happy that they can't do their normal 'disappearing trick'.

"Where are we going Dad?"

"We have to go through Campo Santa Margherita to the Railway Station."

"What for?"

"We need to get ID photographs taken so that we can use them to apply for the Abbonamento"

"The vaporetto pass?"

"Yes"

We cut across the campo, but just as we pass out of the northern end of it we find ourselves in front of the little bakery that makes the most amazing snack, small loaves of bread that have olives baked inside them. A green loaf and a black loaf.

I look across at Tarik,

"You know it's criminal to pass by here and not get a couple of them"

"I was just thinking the same thing…"

I toss him my wallet and he is inside in seconds.

Shaking her head Souheir enters the conversation,

"You three are hopeless addicts"

Tarik emerges through the throng of students and with a theatrical flourish begins breaking off large chunks of this warm wonder.

"Your Mother doesn't want any"

"I didn't say that! Here, give me a piece"

We are laughing and stuffing bread into our mouths as we continue on our way.

The low profile of the railway station can only be described as incongruous when compared to the entire fabric of Venetian architecture, and as we cross the Ponte degli Scalzi it juts square and somehow fascist onto the Grand Canal.

Inside we are quickly employed in first finding enough one Euro coins, and then working out the instructions that are displayed on the screen of the tiny photo booth.

"I can do this. I've just come from a four hour class in Italian. Of course I can read this!"

It's fairly obvious that I'm attempting to convince myself as much as Souheir, who leans across me and depresses the button with the Union Jack on it.

"Or you could just read it in English!"

The words miraculously are reorganized into the English language

"I hate you"

She smiles a treacly sweet smirk at me and withdraws.

Given that the machine allows the user to make as many 'retakes' as desired before making the decision to depress the 'print' button, it is truly remarkable how horrible the small black and white photographs that have just slopped into the 'complete' tray are.

"I don't look that bad do I?"

I get nothing but giggles from the three of them. But wait; who is this bug eyed, curly haired woman who just showed up as another strip is regurgitated by the machine? I'm not spending more money so we take our photographs and descend the broad steps of the Railway Station. We are crossing back across the Grand Canal, and are walking towards Piazzale Roma and the office of ACTV, Venice's public transportation organization.

"Who'd have thought that the damned machine had a fish-eye lens?"

"That's just your nose Dad!"

The complete process of filling in forms and making payment has taken less than ten minutes and we are standing in Piazzale Roma looking at our temporary abbonomentos. The official version, laminated cards bearing the disastrous photographs, will arrive in the mail at some time in the future.

"You can now ride any vaporetto as many times as you want"

The boys look up from their cards.

"Anywhere?"

"Yes"

"Can we go now?"

"Yes"

They are gone, immediately becoming part of the crowd that is moving aboard a number 2 vaporetto. Down the Grand Canal and then who knows? It is now safe to say that we will never know where they are from here on. Souheir and I take a ride to Murano for lunch...Just to make sure the pass works.

Many of the routes of these public vessels are a circuit and circumnavigate the main cluster of Venice's islands. All of them have a system where boats travel in opposing directions. To facilitate this there are two 'bus stops' at every 'station' one for each direction. They are floating docks which are partially enclosed and are connected to the shore by gang planks that either slope up or down depending on what the tide is doing. Tourists sometimes have difficulty in working out in which 'stop' to wait, and a common question from visitors is how to work this out. As rudimentary as it sounds, I find the best way to explain the process is as follows: You first need to know what direction you want to travel in. Each of these stops has a large map of all of the routes in Venice to help facilitate this. Once you have worked out your direction the rule of thumb is that when you are standing looking at the water, the stop on your right will be the one to go to if you want to travel to the left. And vice versa. But just as you complete this explanation I then have to point out that some stops actually only have one stop!

The service is extremely punctual and timetables are marked in minute increments.

I quickly learned that I could be quite creative with even mundane travel. Let me give you a small scenario. If I wanted to travel by vaporetto from Sant'

Elena to Arsenale and I take a vaporetto that is going toward San Marco, it is a ride of two stops and it should take about ten minutes. But if I take a vaporetto from Sant' Elena going in the other direction, that is going away from San Marco, I literally have to go all the way around Venice to arrive at the Arsenale. A ride of many, many stops that will take almost an hour. If you are in no hurry and the sun is shining, I can think of no finer way to spend an hour. A fact that many visitors never quite understand is that eventually all of these vessels will return to the place where you originated your journey. If you are completely lost, just stay on board, eventually it will deliver you back to where you started!

Our 'moment of truth' came one afternoon as we were exploring Murano's back streets. The weather had taken a rather sudden turn for the worse and, umbrella-less we were making our way through driving rain to a vaporetto stop. Murano has a well provisioned supermarket that is hidden behind a large gateway that opens onto Fondamente Cavour and we followed Souheir as she splashed into the courtyard that is its front entrance.

We decided that we would do some 'major' shopping to keep us inside, warm and dry, and then the four of us would catch a vaporetto back to San Zaccaria when the weather improved. It sounded like a good plan.

We shopped for too long (they have an incredible cheese selection), and acquired way too many things. (Do you know how many different shapes of pasta these places have?)

The end result was that we spent too much time in the supermarket and now each of us was carrying two loaded bags. It was dark as we came back out onto the Fondamente and the weather had actually deteriorated further. Even in the confines of the canal, large waves were buffeting the floating vaporetto stop and we literally had to sit down for fear of falling down. A motoscafo appeared out of the darkness, dense with rain and spray, and we staggered aboard and slid onto wet seats. Very few people were aboard, and nobody was standing up. We headed off into the dark, bumped our way through the main canal of Murano and then began to cross open water towards San Michele. Waves began to break over the bow of the motoscafo and the seaworthiness of the sleek steel boat was quickly revealed as it ploughed its way toward Fondamente Nuove…And then the journey entered its own time warp and seemed to be interminable. The windows were completely fogged over but we were aware that large dark water shapes kissed the other side, sometimes alarmingly high up the side of the boat. I'm not sure that I would have seen much more from the deck, and I eventually lost any idea of where we were or where we were headed. I thought that I recognized some of the lights as we surfed our way past what could have been the Giudecca, but truly I was completely lost and just settled back into the seat hoping that something positive would come of this little adventure. It was not a happy moment…We were cold, wet, tired and ostensibly lost.

There was a change in the pitch of the waves as the motoscafo began to lean left, and through the swirling wetness, the lights of San Marco sparkled at us. The motor changed its song and we were bumping into the vaporetto stop at San Zaccaria. Boat and dock were like two arguing dancers and banged and ground against each other. The crewman threw the rope loop three or four times before he could lasso the steel cleats, and then it took a long time before a knot could be tied and he motioned us forward, helping each of us and our bags onto the gangplank that was heaving in front of us. When the vessel released from the dock, the plank danced even more erratically and we staggered slowly toward terra firma and Riva degli Schiavoni. Water was running down Souheir's face and the boys had that long suffering look they wear when their parental units have dragged them through an experience that they didn't appreciate.

"Did you know where we were going Dad?"

"I knew we were supposed to end up in San Zaccaria…But I was lost most of the time"

"That was scary!"

"Yeah, but don't you think it's amazing that even in this weather these boats are totally reliable?"

We had excellent cheeses and salami stashed in our bags and we hurried through the wet shiny streets to home where we could plunder them.

And so the vaporetto system became a major part of our daily lives and we were as relaxed on these vessels as we would have been in our own car driving down a Montana road. Some of my favorite images from our life in Venice come from experiences aboard vaporetti. Cutting back across the Bacino di San Marco from the Giudecca at night gives you a view of the lights of the Piazza and Palazzo that you will never forget. Add the atmospheric mystery of fog to this and the result is absolutely magical.

Our favorite trattoria is on the Giudecca, and evenings of food, wine and wonderful conversation were always concluded by catching the last vaporetto back to San Zaccaria. Souheir and I would huddle in the vaporetto stop at Palanca, a small structure gently bobbing in the night on black water that reflected the lights of the Zattere. In the winter months it was always cold, a moist wind slicing down the Canal della Giudecca and we would always wonder if we had "missed the boat", and how complicated it would be to get home if we had. The same graffiti mocked us for the entire time in Venice and we would sit looking at large scrawled letters which read: "I hate your hate".

On Valentine's Day, after a particularly spectacular meal, we were doing our 'normal thing'.

"Do you think we missed it?"

"No…It will be here soon."

And sure enough, it's lights gently moving with the gentle swell, the vaporetto cuts a long sleek curve across from Zattere and slides up to the Palanca stop.

There are very few people aboard and we sit outside because tonight there is aqua alta (high water) and it's fascinating to watch the water lapping up and over the fondamente as we travel down the Giudecca. Souheir snuggles onto my shoulder and pretends to sleep and we slide into the Zitelle stop. No one gets off or on and we simply "bump and go". The Vaporetto travelling in the opposite direction is reversing its engines waiting for us to depart. The boats pass within inches of each other, the exchange of dock space a seamless dance. As they pass each other the pilots flash the large search light mounted on the bow of each vessel...Just once, and then they are past each other. We are smoothly moving through aqua alta toward San Giorgio, I have this beautiful woman sleeping on my shoulder and the lights of San Marco are twinkling their welcome across the Bacino. These are magical moments that I will carry with me for the rest of my life.

Let's go back to the little wharf at the end of San Moise, because it was here that I made so many discoveries about the boats of Venice.

One late afternoon I found myself back at this small dock simply watching the reflections as they danced across the water and was startled out of this reverie when a small boat slid almost silently by me. The only sound was a slight dipping sound as oars kissed the surface of the water and then moved rhythmically forward to repeat the action. It was a craft that I came to know as a Sandolo and was built entirely from a wood that shone with a deep golden glow, highlighted by mahogany at the gunwale. It was bejeweled with a marvelous array of brass screws that glistened against the wooden accents. The oarsman was an ageing man who was standing as he stroked long oars into the water and then back out. An effortless, seamless motion that allowed his arms to literally fold across his chest as he drew the oars back, and then to open in front of him as he moved his weight forward to propel the small boat away from me toward the Grand Canal. Our eyes met for a moment. I smiled. He simply allowed his head to nod forward a little more on the push stroke. I began to haunt the canals that had small boats moored along their fondamente so that I could watch the oarsmen set up their craft and observe their rowing techniques. Small vessels can be propelled with one oarsman and two oars, or two oarsmen with one oar apiece. In all situations, the oarsmen are standing.

The most unique vessel of Venice, one that has become its signature in a rather clichéd way is, of course, the Gondola. This vessel is rowed by a single oarsman with a single oar and is one of the most sophisticated craft on the planet. Modern day gondolas are just that; modern. There are few of them left that are very old. In fact, in 2000 the Mariners' Museum from Newport, Virginia created a stir when they sent a gondola that had been donated to their collection back to Venice so that it could be refurbished authentically. It turned out that the gondola was likely the same one that was built for Robert Browning in the late 1840's, and predated any gondola in Venice. The life of a gondola is traditionally somewhere between 20 and 25 years, and after that, they are simply discarded, and a new one is built to replace it.

Design sophistications have continued throughout the life of this vessel, and the shape of a 20th century gondola is quite different than a 19th century version. All of these boats had to be narrow, of shallow draft, nimble and sleek, and above all, comfortable for passengers. The canals of Venice dictate many of these requirements, and their clientele the rest. The boat building techniques are consistent throughout, and the construction techniques used on these craft largely unchanged for centuries. They are handmade and consist of about 300 separate parts made from 8 different kinds of wood...Fir, oak cherry, walnut, elm, mahogany, larch, and lime.

In times past the elm trees would be trained so that their branches yielded timber that was already formed into curved lumber... Up until the early 20th century gondolas had a covered cabin that protected their passengers both from the elements and from prying eyes. These cabins, called "felze", evolved from little more than fabric stretched over a frame, into a substantial wooden enclosure complete with doors and windows that had an ingenious system of slatted openings that could be closed for privacy (the Venetian blind!). If the gondola was to be used for prostitution (and this was a famous and classic use for these vessels) it had to display a red light at its stern. (Now you know the origin of the 'red light' districts).

In the 19th century the gondola was still a symmetrical craft, but as their use became more and more focused on the interior canals of Venice, and they were not used to cross long stretches of open water, they were designed asymmetrically so that they only required one oarsman.

And the gondoliers that pilot them are some of the finest oarsmen alive. The physics of the oar is governed by a rather rudimentary set of principles. The oar is held to the gunwale by a device called an oarlock. The oar is rotated about this point which becomes a fulcrum when the force from the rower is transferred to the water. The oarlocks in my boat are bronze cradles that allow my oars to slide laterally outwards from the boat at that point, but don't allow them to move fore or aft along the gunwale.

The oarlock of the Venetians is a thing of wonder however. They are called Forcole and are fashioned from hardwoods from as far away as Albania. I found only three active workshops where these remarkable devices are still made. One in the Arsenale area, one close to San Zaccaria, and the last one close to the Frari. I began to make weekly visits to one of them to watch the production process. The forcole are beautiful, abstract forms and it is literally impossible to describe one of them because they are subtly different from each other and it would be like asking me to describe a Henry Moore sculpture, curve by curve, hole by hole. I use this analogy purposefully, because while these forms have evolved over hundreds of years to incredible utilitarian sophistication, they are also spectacular acts of sculpture and are as easily appreciated as objects of art, as a functional maritime artifact.

It was the sculptor in me that resonated most with these wondrous forms, because I had never rowed a Venetian craft in the Venetian style, and had therefore no empirical sense of its function. This purely sculptural attachment rapidly changed as I began to understand the cultural and historical ramifications that are the story of the forcola. Once again in the simple process of exploring a single element of Venetian life I was led into a complex story that reached back to a misty arcane history and the swirling waters of the lagoon. Why do the Venetians stand to row? Standing to row is probably a natural posture when moving through shallow waters that have reeds and rushes obscuring the narrow channels, for how else could the rower see where he was going? It is reasonable to assume that this technique is indeed ancient and was predicated by the natural elements that were present when the first inhabitants moved into this area.

A major expression of being "Venetian" revolved around maritime prowess. They built the best boats, they built the most boats, they rowed them further and faster than anyone else. Where they lived, how they lived, their commerce, their military prowess, their food sources; all of this married to the waters that flowed about them. Indeed every year on Ascension Day, the Doge would be transported by his illustrious barge, the Bucintoro, to the Lido at San Nicolo which opens onto the Adriatic (it was called the Gulf of Venice) where he would perform one of Venice's most important ceremonies called the "Sposalizio del Mare".

He would cast a wedding ring into the waters and recite the following:

"We marry you, O sea, in a sign of true and perpetual dominion, asking God to protect those who travel by sea."

It is interesting to note that when they were the supreme maritime force of the Adriatic and Mediterranean they accomplished this with vessels whose principal form of propulsion was the oar...lots of them! The Venetian word for oar is 'Remo'...plural; 'Reme'. The famous Venetian Triremes were powered by 3 rows of 15 oars on each side of the vessel...90 in all. These large vessels were absolutely lethal, travelling at remarkable speeds, with great maneuverability. They were used to outmaneuver an opposing vessel, eventually swooping down on it to strike it amidships from the side. The rowers on the trireme would propel it at maximum speed and the helmsman would literally drive its bow (rostrum or beak) through the enemy ship often cutting it in half where it sank immediately.

However, this navy almost never spent an evening at sea, and bivouacked their way along the coastlines of the Adriatic and Mediterranean. Simple, single sails were used as a supplement to this manpower, but the complex sail systems of multi-masted vessels had yet to be invented, and even when they were, the haughty Venetians disdained such vessels. They were not great sailors... They rowed. Venetian craft bristled with forests of oars, controlled by oarsman of remarkable skill and prowess. It was this skill alone that established Venetian maritime supremacy.

Their vessels eventually benefited from the invention of the maritime compass in 1275 and the rudder in the early 1300's, but even as the trading vessels became larger, the warships still depended almost entirely on oars for propulsion. Whether it was a superiority complex or just austere conservatism, the Venetian decision to stay with rowed vessels would eventually cost them dearly. Remember too, that they were extremely efficient in the production of boats and simply may not have wanted to change a 'good thing'. At the height of the Arsenale production in the 16th century, 100 galleys were produced and outfitted in a two month period of time.

The Venetian navy controlled the waters of the Adriatic and the Mediterranean that connected Europe with the Orient and Asia and the city of Venice became the focus of this trade. Sumptuous and exotic goods flowed into the Northern countries through the city of Venice...It was a monopoly that the Venetians exploited to the maximum...Life was good.

Meanwhile the Portuguese, English and Dutch, who were excluded from this trade were exploring all possible innovations. No one had made the journey around the West coast of Africa, not just because it was a daunting task, but because maritime technology had not evolved enough to produce a vessel that could accomplish such a trip, and one can only imagine the depth of the Venetian dismay when the envoy to Portugal reported to the Doge on the 27th of June in 1501 to tell him of "the truth of the voyage to India" completed by Vasco di Gama.

And so it is not too much of an exaggeration to say that the providence of the Venetian Empire was powered by the stroke of an oar.

Each one of these oars required an oarlock or forcola, and these devices proliferated in both number and application over the centuries. A vessel without a forcola could not be rowed...The comparison to an automobile without a drive shaft is appropriate.

If the number of gondole was truly as high as 10,000 then that number alone would have kept many craftsmen busy both making and repairing oars and forcole. However when we also take into consideration all of the vessels that transported food and commodities, it becomes clear that the group of craftsmen that were called Remieri had a pivotal part to play in the day to day life of the average Venetian. They formed their own guild in 1307 that allowed them to control standards and quality, and to share the sophistications of their craft. In the 1770's the forcole underwent a major change and the beautiful elbow like curve called the Sanca became a part of its design. It is this curve that allows the rower to row backwards, an extremely important tool in the tight and narrow canals that are the back streets of Venice.

I find it difficult to believe, then, that this essential group of craftsmen almost became extinct and in fact arrived at a point in history where there was only one of them left.

Giuseppe Carli was the last Remer in Venice. He was born in 1915 and apprenticed under both his father and older brother. When they died he inherited the last oar and forcola workshop in Venice which is a wondrous medieval building tucked away in a tiny alleyway not far from San Zaccaria. Carli in his turn, apprenticed two young Venetians...The first of them, Saverio Pastor left to start his own workshop in the Arsenale area, where it still is. The second, Paolo Brandolisio was still very young when in 1987 Carli died and there was some concern that he may not have been ready to take over the workshop. Quickly he established that he not only had learned well from his Master, but was also a highly skilled wood worker.

With great friendliness and patience Paolo allows me to drop in whenever I want to, and I have spent a great deal of time watching him work. The ancient workshop has two large skylights which cast a cool silver light on a white stone floor that has been polished smooth by centuries of footsteps. The floor is always littered with shavings and chips and the smell of wood is everywhere. Oars are stacked against one end of the workshop and ancient templates and forcole in every stage of completion hang from the beams and shelves. Everything is covered in sawdust which seems to constantly hang in the air, moving slowly through the shafts of light slanting down from the skylights.

Using the skills and the ancient patterns of the Masters before him, Paolo coaxes these elegant, almost serpentine shapes out of raw blanks of walnut, cherry, pear, apple and maple that he has selected. Logs are quartered, the bark and sapwood removed and then left to cure for up to 3 years. They are the dusty amorphous shapes tucked back into the corners and along the base of the far wall.

The magnificent oars of Venice are long and smooth, with clean lines that sweep from the handle, which has no notches, grips, ropes or other devices for engaging the forcola. It is custom made to the exact grip of each gondolier, down to the slender blades that are fashioned to the preference of the gondolier. Paolo makes nothing that is not custom designed for a particular individual, and each work is a sculpture. No two will be identical. The process of customizing the forcola and oar requires that the oar fits into the groove that is literally "bitten out" of the head of the forcola. This groove is called the "morso". The shaft and the blade are made from different woods, and when they become worn, Paolo is clever enough to replace the blades on a shaft that may have seen many years of work ...All in the hands of one loving individual.

Gondoliers are constantly bringing their oars for this refurbishment, and a great sheaf of them leans against one end of the workshop. Little has changed in this ancient workshop. There are few power tools, and Paolo uses some hand tools that I have never seen before, so it is not difficult to imagine yourself in this place hundreds of years ago. It is here that I feel a connection to a Venice of great antiquity, but every time that I say "Ciao" to Paolo and step back into the narrow alleyway I have an almost ominous feeling that what is happening behind the thick walls of this ancient workshop is slowly sliding away as the crush and the noise of the twenty first century approaches.

Chapter 8

...TOURISTS!...

We have reached a point in this storytelling of mine where it needs to be moved from the children's section of the library. I want to talk about what I call "Venice's fuck you factor".

There seems to be little agreement between the various sources that calculate the number of visitors that Venice receives each year, but none of them would disagree with me if I made the statement that it numbers in the millions and millions. This statistic is not a new phenomenon. As the Venetian Empire established itself on the foundation of maritime commerce it actively generated the concept that all things 'flowed' toward it.

Its ships sailed out into the Adriatic and Mediterranean where they encountered Oriental, Asian and African cultures that sold them all forms of goods and foods that had never been seen in northern Europe. These goods were shipped back to Venice in large convoys of merchant vessels that were protected by Venetian war galleys. Some of these convoys contained as many as five hundred boats, and in a good year there were as many as six convoys. These enterprises generated huge amounts of money and it was said that a boat loaded with pepper and other spices was more profitable than if it were loaded with a cargo of pure gold. In the 1370's all maritime enterprises came under the control of the state and the speculation that produced huge fortunes in earlier times was halted.

Until then many merchants borrowed heavily to outfit their ships, and waited in great anguish for their return, for if they sank or were raided by pirates this could be their financial ruin. If they returned to Venice their fortune was assured. This speculative nature was an accepted way of life and it should come as no surprise that the world's first casino, the Ridotto, was an invention of this city. This gamble with trade is the stuff of great stories, and William Shakespeare fashioned his "Merchant of Venice" on such a situation. Once these cargoes were unloaded in Venice they were then sold to a wide variety of Europeans, both from the mainland and parts further north. These northern traders often had a permanent presence in Venice and could be said to be the first tourists. The Venetians for their part were involved in a duplicitous situation where they understood the value of this trade and actively protected these foreigners in their midst all the while attempting to remain aloof from the rest of the world.

The Venetian currency was the "ducat" which they produced with typical Venetian regard for quality, knowing that if it was to be well received it had to be of consistent high quality. The Republic mandated stringent size and quality specifications for their coinage and vigorously enforced them. The ducat quickly displaced the Florentine florin as the preferred currency of Europe. Visitors who enter Venice from across the Bacino di San Marco, Venice's front door, are treated to the architectural splendor of the Doge's Palace and San Marco, but directly adjacent to these buildings sporting columns that look like stacks of coins, is the Mint of Venice. Money and power...Perhaps money as power?

Along with a trusted currency, the visiting merchants were protected by rules that forbade Venetians from overcharging them. Overlying all of this commerce was a profound sense that if all trade was regulated it would be fair. The Venetians were also renowned for the consistency of their weights and measures used in all transactions.

If you stand in front of San Giacomo, close to the current central market, you can read an inscription carved into its edifice. It reads:

"Let the law be fair for those who trade, let the weights be true and let the contracts not be corrupt."

This was clearly an empire that lived not from the income of its possessions, but from the profit of its trade. But don't ever lose sight of the fact that the trade was protected so that the profit could be made. Another inscription that is often found in many Venetian documents is, "Divitis et Honoribus"...In wealth and honor! No matter what controls the Venetians applied, however, it is clear that the rest of the world considered them to be extremely shrewd businessmen who expected premium prices for their trade goods. Until the

African route was opened, the Venetians had a complete monopoly on this trade, and had no compelling reasons to drive anything other than a hard bargain.

As this trade increased, its successes were mirrored in the number of foreigners who visited Venice, and it was not long before another merchant class evolved.

This group of merchants tailored their business to the foreigners who visited their city.

Alberghi and locande (hotels and hostels) proliferated at an enormous rate and this industry employed a significant percentage of the population. Stores selling food, clothing and crafts grew at an exponential rate. In 1661 there were 4,422 shops...In 1712 there were 5,267...by 1740 there were 5,904. This number of shops reflects a reliance on visitors, for surely there weren't enough Venetians buying such goods.

Many contemporary Venetians and writers far more erudite than me lament the decline of Venetian culture by telling us that it is becoming a Disneyland, a theme park. While this comparison is becoming a little overused (just as I am doing here), it resonates with many Venetians who are slowly seeing the character of their city change.

This city has seen the rise and decline of some great industries, some of them innovative and profound. Fifteenth Century Venice produced some of Europe's finest books. Between 1481 and 1501 two hundred and sixty eight printeries produced more than 2,000,000 volumes. She has been a major producer of soap and of silk and woolen products, but by 1700 these industries were all but nonexistent. Is it possible that those once employed in these disappearing industries found new employment in a tourist industry? All of this is a rather roundabout way of saying that this "tourist industry" has a long history in the city of Venice, and it has evolved along with the rest of the city's industries, often filling in the spaces left by a commercial failure. Is the lament then that this industry has become too successful and powerful?

Giving directions in Venice's labyrinth of canals and streets is almost impossible and we would often joke with each other when retelling our daily excursions at the dinner table,

"You go down the street until you get to the glass shop on your left...Turn right at the mask shop and then left again at the next glass shop, just across from that other mask shop!"

So how many glass shops, mask shops, trinket stands, do you need in a city? This question can only be answered by calculating the number of people who are prospective customers...Apparently millions and millions of them.

Having millions and millions of visitors clearly is a logistical nightmare, but it is also an enormous source of wealth. A giant empire that siphoned luxury goods from distant lands into its markets, that encouraged the immigration of highly skilled craftsmen into its factories, that was a major contributor to the markets of its European neighbors, has slowly devolved into a living museum that survives almost entirely on the industry that caters to its visitors. Once again the Venetian duplicity emerges as they go to extraordinary lengths to encourage a trade that they constantly complain about!

Please don't think for a moment that I have no sympathy for their situation. One only has to stand in the crowds of Piazza San Marco on a sunny July day for a short time before you begin to understand that something has gone seriously awry. How do you deal with that many people? The Venetians tend to treat tourists as if they were some kind of magic bean crop. They spring up without any cultivation, can be treated with complete lack of care, and if you cut one crop down it magically reproduces itself instantly. The stream of tourists that traipse through Venice is apparently endless, and while Venetians may profess to hate this phenomenon, it is the source of almost all of their income.

I've just walked across from Campo Santa Maria Formosa, down to the Riva degli Schiavoni, cut across the Piazza San Marco, and am heading for the Calle 22 Marzo. It has rained almost all day and the top of the Campanile is barely visible through a descending fog. The bells begin to boom, their wondrous sound slightly muffled by the saturated air, and I realize that I'm actually earlier than I thought. It's about 35 degrees Fahrenheit, my feet are wet and I'm chilled to the bone. In Calle 22 Marzo I notice that a little bar that is just around the corner from our apartment is open, the yellow light of its interior casting a long warm slash on the wet stones of the street. I open the door and move into the warm interior. I'm the only customer and a husband and wife stand behind the bar. They answer my "Buona Sera" cursorily and continue with a discussion about one of their family members. Finally she asks me what I want, and I ask for a hot chocolate. She begins a series of fluid movements that bring cup and saucer together and then the steaming viscous brown liquid is moved across the counter to me.

I thank her and hold the cup in both hands while I sip my chocolate. It warms both my hands and my insides this way. I attempt a discussion with the woman who simply nods when I tell her that it is cold out there. She nods again when I add the fact that it is the moisture in the air that makes the cold so penetrating. I give up and return to the chocolate.

I'm finished, ask for "il conto" and she pushes a small cash register receipt across the counter to me. Three Euros and fifty cents. I can get a cup of hot chocolate in the Campo Santa Margherita for one Euro fifty! I decide to tell her that I think this is expensive. She looks at me in a way that lets me know that she knows it's expensive…And then just shrugs. As I pay her I'm toying with the idea that I will tell her that this is a "primo and fino" situation, my first and last cup of chocolate from her establishment. I am completely defeated, however, by her demeanor that tells me quite clearly that she couldn't care less.

She doesn't have to cultivate me, because tomorrow there will be hundreds more new tourists who will also only visit her bar once…And the day after that, hundreds more.

Of course such attitudes are not universal, but what I've described is not an isolated incident either, and many visitors to Venice leave with less than positive feelings about how they were treated.

Souheir and I decided that if we were going to spend four months In Venice we would attempt to somehow shed the tourist persona. We had arrived for an extended visit and were determined to rise above the fractious relationship that so many Venetian merchants seem to have with tourists. We were of course 'Foresti', but I wondered if they would allow Foresti into their world without treating us as if we were a part of the marauding horde. We decided that we would find a bar and a restaurant that we enjoyed and felt relaxed in, and then frequent them as often as possible in the hope that we might eventually be considered 'regulars'.

"Our Bar" is in the narrow calle that connects the Campo Sant' Angelo with Campo San Stefano and is on the route that we regularly followed returning from our language classes. The first afternoon that we breasted up to the marble bar and asked for four cappuccinos we were served with civility and the normal barista expertise by a young woman whose dark eyes seemed to focus somewhere behind us. We drank our coffee at the bar and discussed the morning's class. Asking for the bill we were told that the coffee was two Euros and twenty cents per cup, and she took my money with the smallest wisp of a smile. When we left the young woman returned our goodbyes, but was busily involved in the constant cleaning that seems to be a feature of Venetian bars.

Our next visit was much like the first, but by the end of the week the girls behind the bar smiled when they saw us coming, and even asked where the boys were if they were not with us. At the beginning of the third week as the young woman barista passed us our coffees, she placed small biscotti in each saucer and smiled at me. It was as if this was the first time that she had actually looked directly at us and there was genuine warmth in her greeting. As she pushed the coffees toward us she said,

"So what are you doing here in Venezia?"

She was patient with our poor Italian, and was clearly interested in our story, taking special delight in the fact that we lived in the mountains of Montana. She called over the other barista who, it turned out, had a fair command of English and the conversation became a little livelier. At the end of this, as we were paying for our coffee we were told that they cost one Euro and fifty cents each! And that was the price we paid for the rest of our time in Venice. We had crossed some invisible barrier. I cannot say with any certainty what this barrier is, but I think that it has something to do with the fact that most Venetians who work in the service industries of stores, restaurants and hotels deal with tourists who arrive for a brief stay, sometimes as little as a few hours, who make little or no effort at understanding or accommodating the complexities of Venetian life, and who very often speak no Italian.

And remember there are millions of them!

It is a matter of "them and us", and I wonder if the cool demeanor of the Venetians is not some form of a protective device. Of course the quick counter to this comes from we 'Foresti' who would remind the Venetians that if they are actually in a service industry, then civility and friendliness should be a part of client expectation. Unfortunately with a teeming horde behind you, if you complain about service or quality, or price; or anything, the average Venetian simply shrugs and waits for the next Foresti to take your place. There always is one who will. The interesting thing for us was that as our technique of visiting the same bar and restaurant allowed us to finally "be seen" by the Venetians, we in turn began to see all Venetians, not just those who befriended us, in a different and infinitely more positive light.

I had spent a good deal of time watching the gondoliers at work and had developed a sincere admiration for their skills and commitment. They are a direct and continuous link to the past glory of Venice and most visitors have no idea what is required of them to hold their positions. In the early mornings I would watch them cleaning and polishing their gondolas, calling back and forth in Veneziano, a dialect almost entirely incomprehensible to me, and realized that it was like watching actors preparing for a performance. Many of these men would stand on small bridges with their gondolas moored nearby and proposition passing tourists to see if they would like a ride. The call of "Gondola…Gondola" is a major part of my memory of Venetian sounds. On many occasions I would watch tourists react and reply in indignation, often angrily waving them away. Every time I was asked by the gondoliers, I always made a point of smiling directly at them and saying "Thank you…But no".

Their response was a small nod, sometimes a returned smile, always an exchange of respect.

We discovered two restaurants that we liked across on the Giudecca and began to frequent them regularly. Because the boys are pizza aficionados we settled on the one with a pizza oven and it became a place we visited at least once a week. It seems to me that we were looked at differently simply because we had taken the time to escape the tourist crowds and even though we were often the only Foresti in the entire establishment, the welcome was warm and genuine from the time of our first visit.

What slowly changed as we took on the role of 'regulars' were subtle things. The waiters who we came to know by name would stay longer at the table, encouraging conversation, apparently deciding to become a major support in our acquisition of the Italian language. Complimentary wine would often be sent over to our table, and on several occasions dessert.

When we entered and were being sat at our table they would begin to tell us what food the chef had cooked that was especially good, or fresh, or often seasonal. I have never tasted Seafood Risotto (Risotto di Mare) that is even close to the beautiful silky white primo piatto that I think I ate every time we visited. We were often the last to leave and this almost always resulted in an exploration of the Italian spirits that were lined up in their multi colored bottles behind the bar. I learned the difference between Grappa and Grappa Vecchio in one of these exchanges and could still feel the difference as we rode the vaporetto back to San Zaccaria! One of the owner's brother visited from Umbria, bringing with him some homemade salami. They insisted that we take one home, and on our next visit were clearly thrilled with our enthusiastic response.

It is a May evening, which happens to be our last in Venice, and also Tarik's 18th birthday.

"So where do you want to go for your birthday dinner?"

There is no hesitation.
    "Across to the Giudecca of course"

The night is warm and we stand on the deck of the vaporetto which is filled with day tourists on the way back to the Tronchetto and their cars. The crush of the summer tourist season is beginning. At Palanca we disembark and walk down the Fondamente to "our" restaurant. It is filled with people! Apparently the horde has descended, and as we stand in the doorway can see plainly that all of the tables are taken and they are even serving people at the bar and a few tables outside on the Fondamente...

"I'm sorry Tarik, but it looks like we are out of luck tonight"
    He nods and we begin to turn away.
    Just then Antonio returns from serving a table outside.

"Ciao Ragazzi!"

We tell him that it's our last night and that it is Tarik's birthday, and that we understand that the restaurant is overflowing. He ushers--actually pushes--us back into the restaurant, calls loudly to a young man in the rear, and immediately chairs and a table are being moved into a space that didn't seem to be there a couple of minutes ago.

With the flourish of a matador he swishes a table cloth over the table, deals knives and forks like playing cards, and then turns to hold the chair for Souheir.

As we sit he leans conspiratorially close to Tarik and says,

"Buon compleanno…the cozze are marvelous tonight!"

It's been a wonderful evening, we are the last to leave, and everyone is standing outside on the Fondamente exchanging hugs and good wishes. I have never ever been involved in such a relationship, have never been treated with such warmth and friendship from a restaurant…But I wonder how many of Venice's visitors ever get to see this side of these wonderful people?

I have no satisfactory way of concluding this chapter, because the situations and problems seem insoluble. It is at some level simply true that the Venetians have conducted commerce of every kind at the levels of "Them and Us" for centuries and it is inconceivable that this will stop. On too many occasions they stood alone in an inhospitable world, and the instinct to hold themselves aloof and separate is still strong in their culture. However, they have created a monster whose proportions seem only to grow as the tourists of the world descend upon them. This monster brings them both misery and succor, for the city obviously depends on the wealth that these visitors leave behind. But what of the quality of life that Venice's residents surely have a right to expect? They are in fact, watching their city turn into Disneyland.

There are many ideas that circulate among the intelligentsia and students… Some so radical as to call for the destruction of the causeway that now connects the city to the mainland. I am not well enough versed in this subject, nor is it my place to offer up an opinion, but my heart feels the genuine anguish of this situation, and I try to remember this when confronted with unfriendly storekeepers and exploitive merchants.

I live in what has been called "the last best place", and this has served to increase tourism as folk visit to see if in fact it is true. Tourism is a major industry in my world too.

In the heat of the summer when the streets of my small Montanan town become clogged with traffic, and we can't get a table at a restaurant, it is not uncommon for we locals to speak disparagingly about "Damn tourists!".

Chapter 9

CARNEVALE...

PALAZZO BARBARIGO

I spent most of my childhood growing up in a small country town in southern Australia, and as a consequence reflected the mostly British values that permeated the local education, legal and political systems. The fact that my parents were Londoners added emphasis, and I absorbed prejudices and misconceptions with ease and even enthusiasm. On November the 5th

we celebrated Guy Fawkes Day with bonfires and fireworks, never for a moment aware that in England this was a midwinter celebration, while we in the southern hemisphere were choosing to light giant fires and scatter incendiary devices during the dry months of our summer. It took many bushfires before the Australian government realized the folly of such pyromania and banned the celebration. I consider myself one of the "lucky generations" that knew about this northern celebration.

When I arrived in the US I had barely even heard of Halloween, and certainly did not know what it entailed, so the first October 31st that I spent here was a night of learning for me. I had never worn a masquerade costume, had never painted my face, never worn a mask. I was repeatedly told that the kids did it mostly for the free candy, but that was obviously not true, and it certainly did not explain the enthusiasm with which adults entered into the process of "dressing up". Over a period of years I have watched with great interest as my children embraced this festival, and have been co-opted into helping construct all manner of implements and accoutrements to augment costumes. I have only on two occasions donned a costume myself, and have to admit that while I certainly enjoyed myself, my performance lacked the abandon that was shown by others who had a childhood of training.

All of this is a rather rambling way of letting you know just how unprepared I was for Venice's great festival called Carnevale. Deriving its meaning directly from the Latin meaning "farewell to meat", this festival is celebrated in all parts of the Christian world in preparation for the pre Easter season of Lent.

The Venetians, however, add their own signature to the way they celebrate the festival, and it seems that the world comes to watch them don their magnificent masks. The wearing of masks is a long and treasured tradition of the Venetian people who historically encouraged their use in the everyday life of all levels of society. They have always lived at "close quarters" with their neighbors and perhaps the need to become incognito comes from a society that was simply too confined.

The first use of masks in Venice was documented in 1268, and by the 14th century Venetians were permitted to wear a mask for almost 6 months of the year. The very speculative nature of their commerce made gamblers out of most of the merchant and upper classes and it should come as no surprise that the Venetians institutionalized these games into yet another industry. They created the world's first casino called the Ridotto. A place set aside strictly for games of chance played for money...Gambling.

It was customary and at times compulsory for the players within the Ridotto to be masked, where it was a "leveling" device, where a player's influence of class or wealth could not be used.

As difficult as it may be for us to believe such behavior in present day Venice, it was absolutely common to encounter masked people almost anywhere within the city on any day of the week in the Venice of the 1500s. This was just another tool that could be used to withdraw oneself...To remain aloof. One of Napoleon's first edicts after entering the city was to ban the use of masks, a punitive act aimed at removing the screen of secrecy that the Venetians so famously hid behind. He also banned many of the Venetian annual festivals, because most of them entailed the wearing of masks.

Carnevale went through a series of revivals and it was only in 1979 that it was restored to its current fame. And what is its current fame?

"Madness...Complete madness. If at all possible I try to be out of the city"

I'm talking to Matteo about what I should expect in the coming weeks of Carnevale. He is the Director of the Language School, a sophisticated young professional who speaks a number of languages. I have no answer, so I simply smile at him and shake my head.

"No, I mean it John...It is madness!"

And in a way he was correct.

I was trying to pay attention to all of the subtle changes that slowly crept into the life of the city in the weeks before Carnevale, but in truth there were just too many of them, and when the roaring tide of revelers stampeded across the causeway, all lemming like and masked, it was too late to do anything but run or join in.

I think Matteo ran…We decided to join the throng.

The mask shops, which are everywhere, were already in "high gear' when we arrived early in January so we had no way of knowing that they had been stocking up for this season. There are always plenty of masks in these stores throughout the year, but the variety and number on the shelves in preparation for Carnevale is truly impressive.

A more obvious sign for the events ahead occurred one Friday on the Molo, (the Fondamente in front of the Doge's Palace) when a barge began to unload enormous amounts of scaffolding and platform materials. The large flat barge had a huge yellow crane on one end of it and it looked like some giant bird slowly building a nest, as it picked up piles of pipe and fittings and placed them carefully on the wharf where the gondoliers usually sit. It then unloaded a small forklift that was the same bright yellow color as the crane, which immediately scurried around like some chick of the mother bird and began to trundle the bundles into the Piazza San Marco. By the end of the day a huge pile of material surrounded by a tidy chain link temporary fence sat quietly outside the Correr Museum. Nobody seemed to take any notice of it and it stayed that way for a week.

Another colorful cargo showed up on the same wharf about a week later. It was a cluster of objects constructed from sky blue plastic. Portable toilets! I thought that this was an ominous sign, but reflecting on my own difficulty in finding places to pee, realized that this was a resource that was certainly going to be necessary if Venice's population was to be boosted by a crowd. The two weeks preceding the festival were filled with frantic activity. The pile of scaffolding in San Marco was miraculously teased into a giant proscenium arch stage that reached towards the surrounding roof tops. In most of the campi small kiosks were being constructed, the end result being an encroachment on what is already limited open space in the city.

The Campo San Stefano lost its wide open feel and the statue of Nicolo Tommaseo; Cagalibri; was quietly shitting his books into a circle of gaily colored booths. In the tiny Campo between San Vidal and the Accademia Bridge two small booths that were obviously going to serve food were being coupled together and in Campo Santa Margherita a stage was constructed from very "space age" looking aluminum tubes. On each side of it two towers of speakers reached upward and it was obvious that the quiet of the surrounding houses was going to be severely shattered by anything that came out of this giant collection of woofers and tweeters.

In the final days leading up to the opening ceremony the population of the city slowly swelled and many of the restaurants and bars that had previously been closed, opened their doors in expectation. It was clear however, that not all vendors embraced this strategy, and the fruit and vegetable store that sold its wares from a boat close to Santa Margherita closed; its decks scrubbed clean and strangely empty except for a sign that read, "Chiuso per due settimane". Perhaps they were related to Matteo.

The ranks of the street performers doubled and then tripled, with imports from every part of Europe, and our evening walk became a smorgasbord of music, juggling acts, puppeteers and ever present mimes. Most of these mimes wore robes, gloves, and hats of white, painted their face the same color and pretended to be statuary. It's surprising how effective some of these performers were, and I never tired of watching them at work. One of these performers attempted a new approach and his face, hands and clothing were all of a metallic dark cast iron color. He would sprawl on the steps of the bridges with a bottle of the same color, affecting the posture of an inebriated sculpture. I'm not sure everyone quite understood his act, however, and when the crowds became really dense, puzzled tourists found themselves stepping over his prone body, not sure if they had disturbed some artistic activity or a local vagrant.

No matter how many of these activities we watched and participated in during those days leading up to the festival, nothing could have prepared us for the opening ceremony and festivities. We had visited Venice a couple of times during the summer months when tourism is at its height, and quite frankly had made the decision to never visit again during this period, because the density of such crowds does not interface well with a family that chooses to live on a quiet mountainside in Montana. I don't know what multiple the crowd on the opening Saturday was in comparison to the summer throng, but we found ourselves in a crowd many, many times larger than we had ever seen.

I attempted to work out the difference between Carnevale and summer crowds, and it quickly became apparent. In the summer you are a part of a group that has come to Venice to look at it, to be a participant in that almost tragic dance of the tourist. You will buy things that you will never use, eat food that you don't like, perhaps even buy silly clothing, hats, caps, T-Shirts, that will remind you of your trip in a very un-serene Venice. As a group, these tourists have only one thing in common, and that is their trip to Venice. The Carnevale crowd comes to Venice to be looked at! All of us had somehow made a multifaceted commitment to fun, food, wine, music, dance, and above all…Anonymity. There were eventually more people on the street wearing masks than those not, and yes, I joined in with an enthusiasm that was new to me. The commonality of the crowd was immediately infectious, the dominant sound laughter, and the city literally did not sleep for two weeks.

"Volo di Angelo"

"How do you spell that?"

"Dunno…"

Tamir looks up from the book he is studying.

"It means the flight of the angel"

"Read what it says"

"At 11:00 am on Saturday the Angel flies from the campanile to the Piazza San Marco. The Angel is a young woman specially selected for this privilege"

"She flies?"
    "I was in San Marco last night and they have a rope from the bell gallery on the Campanile down to the stage in front of the Museo Correr"

"They are going to lower her on a zipline?"

"It says here that this magnificent spectacle harks back to ancient times when a specially chosen maiden was lowered to the Piazza below to signify the beginning of Carnevale."

I asked Matteo what he knew about this event.

"I've told you it is madness."

I'm nodding even before he finishes the sentence, so it's obvious that I want more.

"They take some terrified girl to the top of the Campanile, dress her in an Angel suit and slide her down to the Piazza below."

"And this is part of a tradition?"

"Who knows…maybe a new tradition…but this poor young thing will be dangled over a huge crowd…Half of whom turned up just to see if the rope will break!"

Clearly we have to be a part of the crowd and have decided to arrive early so that we will get a good view of this spectacle. We leave delle Veste at 10:20 am and only barely make it into the Piazza by 10:55. The crowd is as dense as any that I have ever been in and I admit to feeling a little apprehensive. This is a lot of people in a fairly confined space. The entire crowd is craning their necks upward at the enormous stack of red bricks topped with a white stone temple; the Campanile or bell tower to the Basilica of Saint Mark which sparkles gold and somehow oriental in the background.

There is movement on the second tier of the bell gallery and two small feet are being dangled over the edge. A dilemma of etiquette unfolds and seconds later we are all looking up the dress of the Angel. Would the polite thing be to look away? Apparently none of us are polite, because now all eyes are on the Angel (or at least her underwear). More movement…Two stiff, strangely tasseled wings fold outwards into space and then with a slight drop which sends a shiver all the way down the rope to the stage, a female form is suddenly dangling from a harness that is attached to her shoulders. A gasp which quickly gathers into a roar comes out of the crowd below. We are yelling too. The giant speakers blast down at us a powerful orchestral version of the Hallelujah chorus of Handel's Messiah.

The Angel is stiff with fear as she spins slowly in a clockwise arc and it is clear that she has no control over this movement. For the first 50 meters of rope she is as stiff as one of those small dolls that are made from a clothespin. The music swells, it is huge, we are still looking up the dress of the Angel. She begins to believe that she is safer than she feels…Opens her arms; the wings move backwards.

I'm a believer!

How authentic is this? How corny is this? I don't know...and care less. I'm captivated...We are all clapping and clapping. And the Angel descends all the way to the stage. She is released from her harness and whisked backstage, presumably to change her underwear. I'm smiling at Souheir who might be giving me that "You are so easily impressed" look, but I don't care.

The aftermath of crowd control; or its lack thereof, is predictably chaotic and it is almost an hour before we can climb the stairs back to our apartment.

After we climbed the stairs we spent a quiet time over a simple lunch while we made plans for our next excursion. The boys disappeared and only reappeared late into the night. We had been told that at 3.00pm there would be a large procession arriving from the other end of the city, and that it was something that we 'should not miss", so Souheir and I sat drinking some white wine in the front room, wondering what would be a good time to "wander down to the Piazza San Marco".

The noises swirling up from the streets had not changed since the morning, so we knew there were plenty of people still in town, but even as we stepped out onto Delle Veste we encountered more people than we had ever seen on "our" little street. Turning into the 22 Marzo we were swept up instantly in a seething mass of people and slowly bobbed our way into San Marco. On each side of the proscenium arch of the huge stage, two enormous masked Gullivers leaned on faux marble columns, leering down at we Lilliputians in the square. The stage took up a considerable part of the Piazza and this simply served to compress this giant throng into a smaller space. Souheir and I ducked under the arches of the Procuriate Nuove, made our way down to the Molo, and arrived there just as the procession topped the bridge of straw. Perfect timing!

It had begun in the old part of San Pietro, passed down Via Garibaldi, and then along the Fondamente to San Marco.

I am left with a flurry of images and impressions, and even recalling it from this distance does not give it any better form, so I offer this kaleidoscope...

There were musicians playing instruments of ancient design, drummers beating drums, dancers dancing. Every age and level of a society long passed was represented, each person wearing costumes that were perfect down to their shoe laces, or buckles.

When you're in Disneyland, you always know that's where you are. This was authentic in a way that I have never felt before. A Princess with three ladies in waiting passed by, beautiful and serene and mysterious. In their hair they wore garlands of rose buds. I was looking at them as the water of the Bacino reflected the afternoon sun across from San Giorgio, sending the pearls in their hair into a sparkling dance. I could smell the roses. I was smiling, smiling. Young boys dressed as pages, one leg of their hose orange, the other blue. Everywhere people in costume, some period, others great flights of fantasy. Concoctions of feathers and lace and shimmering fabrics. Eyes looking through masks. Photographers everywhere... Little groups of grand costumes posing in front of the Doge's Palace and San Marco. Leaning against columns. Spectators sometimes posing with them. A man dressed in the ceremonial robes of the Doge, with his hat of office, the Corno, pulled down over his ears, white hair and beard immaculate, flowed by with his entourage and people literally bowed down before him. Young women were carried on boards on the shoulders of gondoliers, accompanied by soldiers in armor that had clearly seen action in some ancient time.

This procession walked into the Piazza San Marco and up onto the stage where they were introduced to the crowd who roared its delight. The giant sound system allowed the commentators to introduce each participant and two huge television screens that had been erected in the Piazza enabled the crowd to see the close up details.

We stood and watched as the procession left the stage and stayed on to watch a number of popular bands give a concert, then slowly wove our way through the crowd back to San Stefano where we bought the Carnevale treat, frittelle. They are deep fried pastries which have a variety of different fillings that are rolled in sugar. Souheir and I cut back to delle Veste behind La Fenice, and even our "secret way" was jammed with people. Licking sugar off my fingers before I pushed the key into the lock, I had a profound feeling that I had not gone to be a spectator at some event. Rather that I was a participant...that I had been a part of something. Upstairs, Souheir and I sipped limoncello and waited for the boys while playing a game of remembering our favorite costume.

Chapter 10

COMMEDIA...

Carnevale occupied our waking hours for the next two weeks, but before I continue with that part of the story I need to introduce you to a new character that spent these two weeks with us, and whose sharing of the "madness" enriched those memories.

We had invited our friend David to spend a couple of weeks with us, and because David is an actor with an interest in Commedia and the theatrical use of the mask, he wanted to experience Carnevale.

He is a great deal of fun to be with and a very relaxed traveler. However, David came with an agenda, had done a good deal of research before his arrival, and knew what he wanted to see. Commedia Dell' Arte was basically an unknown art form to me when he arrived, but by the final days of Carnevale I was a complete convert. We spent the next two weeks in an absolutely changed city, and realized that for whatever reasons, we were changed too.

Our days continued with much the same routine as they had before Carnevale, even though many streets and campi were filled with stalls and stages, and we realized that we sometimes chose routes through the city that would avoid the crowds. Our conversations focused on the previous night's adventures and of course, what tonight's might be. There was something going on in some part of the city every evening and it was always difficult to find information as to their quality or content, and at times even when they were supposed to start. As a result we found ourselves wandering from one side of the city to another in search of these venues and of course became a part of the masked horde. Much of the entertainment was pretty mediocre and even amateur, but in among these were events that were of such power and magic, that I'm sure I will remember them forever.

The ancient Venetian Empire, a city state literally floating in the center of a vast body of water had a population that was unlike any in Europe or for that matter the world. Because there was no land surface to lever the peasant population with, the feudal system simply could gather no traction and an entirely different organization of people came to be. This was a merchant mariner society and its population grew in step with its maritime and trading successes. At times the population exceeded 180,000 inhabitants which meant that there was literally very little space between people. While the patricians and merchants controlled both the political and financial purse strings, and occupied the upper structure of this population, the vast majority was working class.

Ever since Roman times ruling classes have known that it is important to keep this large portion of the population happy. A major tool used to achieve this was entertainment. Remember… "Give them bread and circuses"? You, dear Reader, can decide whether the creation of Carnevale was a Machiavellian ploy by the ruling class—or a spontaneous flowering from within the working class—Whatever is the case, the Venetian masses took great delight in many forms of entertainment and in typical fashion, have left their mark on many entertainment art forms that are now found worldwide.

Opera was begun by a small group of erudite intellectuals in Florence, but it was in Venice that it blossomed into the major art form that stormed through Europe. The number of opera houses in Venice exceeded those in most European cities and in Venice it became the entertainment of the masses. These masses did not reflect the refined intellectualism of opera's founders and the form quickly changed to suit their tastes. Opera Buffa was born in Venice. It was funny, bawdy, sometimes lewd, and the working class was its major supporter.

This same leveling effect took hold in theatre too, and Commedia Dell' Arte has most of its roots in this city. In some ways, commedia is the antithesis to formal theatre. It is largely improvisational where a troupe of actors plays specific stock characters that are recognized by their costume and the mask they wear, but also by their character traits. Il Capitano is full of swagger and braggado, constantly leading with his ample codpiece, sword always at his hip...but he is a coward and everyone knows it. Arlecchino (the source of harlequin) is a fool...but a shrewd fool. He spends a great deal of time in contorted acrobatic positions and sports a strange stick which consists of two palings tied together that make a loud noise on impact. It is a "slap stick". It is a finite cast of characters and each has a part to play. But what part? Each character possesses what is called a "lazzi"—basically a stock way of responding to a series of stimuli or cues. The cast "writes" the plays, but this is done in the loosest of ways and the characters simply improvise their way through a basic plot. No two performances are the same even though the basic narrative of the story remains the same. The script of such plays can read as follows:

"Il Capitano and Arlecchino enter and do something funny..."

The plays the working class enjoyed told stories of young lovers, miserly fathers, clowns with lots of acrobatic moves, and stories that related to their contemporary life. Many of Shakespeare's plays--Romeo and Juliet, Two Gentlemen of Verona, The Tempest--have so many elements in common with ancient Commedia plays that it seems likely that he either personally saw them or was told about them. Commedia dell' Arte is no longer strongly represented in any part of the world, but here in Venice there are a number of companies who are committed to continuing this ancient theatre form that in all probability had its roots in these streets. During Carnevale there are two Commedia troupes who perform two separate "plays" and repeat these performances 3 or 4 times over a 7 day period. David is determined to see each performance and we plan our activities around the schedule that the tourist Bureau in San Marco has given us. We set off from delle Veste toward the Piazza San Marco at about 3pm with the knowledge that we have time for a "Spritz" before the advertised commencement time of 4pm.

The Piazza is filled with people in the masks and costumes of "day trippers" who seem to display a dogged determination to create their own carnevale, no matter that there are few official activities during the daytime. They seem more like a group of kids who are out trick-or-treating, and the costumes reflect no attempt to replicate the fashion or history of this city...Unless you give credence to the fact that Batman and Spiderman belong everywhere.

We move back into the warren of streets behind the Museo Correr where the maze is dense enough to discourage the large crowds, find a small bar and order two Spritzes. The French and Austrian occupations of Venice marked the end of the Venetian Republic and the many changes that they wrought are seldom discussed with anything but disdain by present day Venetians. The drinks that glow deliciously orange in front of David and me, seem to be one of the exceptions to that story. In the Austrian/Bavarian regions to the north, white wine is mixed with carbonated water to produce a light thirst-quenching summer drink. They call it a spritz. Like most things Venetian, the local version has some unique characteristics. The Venetian spritz begins like its northern relatives, but adds the local ingredient of amaro, which means bitter.

SPRITZ—(VENETIAN)

1/3 glass white wine
1/3 glass soda water
1/3 glass Aperol or Campari or Select

Venetians all seem to have their own preference for this drink and it is often served with 2/3 prosecco and 1/3 aperitif and garnished with a variety of fruits and olives. Aperol is an orange based aperitif and gives a golden richness to the color of the drink. It is also less alcoholic than the Campari and Select which are a red liqueur. It's an afternoon drink, and as the weather warmed, became a part of our daily routines.

David and I sip the spritz, chew on the orange slices, gnaw the green olive down to its pit, thank the bartender and move back toward San Marco. The Piazza is filling up with noisy revelers and we make our way across to the Piazzetta that runs down the side of the Palazzo Ducale—the Doge's Palace.

There, backed up to a column of the building's side colonnade is a small wooden platform protected from the crush of the crowd by only a few metal barriers and we take a place in the center where we can lean on them…front row seats! The platform is about 5 feet above the ground which means I can easily see beneath it, and the first thing that catches my attention is the fact that it is held together entirely by ropes that are cleverly tied in what can only be the knots of a mariner. Along the back edge of the stage hangs a curtain with an opening that will allow the actors to enter at center stage…On each of the other sides a flight of simple steps connects the stage to the ground so that the actors will be able to access the stage from any of its four sides.

There is a simple drum kit with a collection of percussive "noise makers" set up in front of the stage and a young woman is adjusting the stool and preparing to take her place behind it.
"Here come the actors!"

David is intense and excited and I realize that I'm expecting him to explain this event that is unfolding before me. We can look directly beneath the stage/platform to see the group of actors who are in costume, talking and organizing props. Costumes hang on a simple rack, and it is clear that we are going to be able to see them make any changes. "It looks to me that they are probably going to play multiple parts".

"Is that normal?"

"Yes…These troupes were made up of only a few actors, and while key players like Il Capitano and Arlecchino may remain in their character for the whole play, the rest of the cast will play multiple characters".

The drummer begins a long drum roll finishing with a clashing cymbal; the curtain parts and an actress wearing a long dress that is pinched at the waist with a bodice that forces her breasts upward into a wicked cleavage, takes center stage.

"Signore e Signori…"

I can easily tell you the story that was acted out over the next 30 minutes. What is impossible for me to tell you is how I came to know that story. What followed was a play that was acted out by a troupe of five people plus the percussionist. The girl never wore a mask, but was nominally the narrator when not playing the part of the damsel in distress. All of the others wore masks made of leather and David would tell me the name of the character by simply recognizing the mask. They changed masks and costumes directly behind the rear of the curtain, right on the street where we could see them beneath the timber supports of the stage. In a different mask they moved and spoke in a new way and I was surprised at how quickly I came to know each character. I have fairly good comprehension of spoken Italian, but became aware I missed some of the colloquialisms and references to current events, and then realized that the dialogue was not always in Italian. There were little asides in French that a small group to our right noisily appreciated, and the unmistakably guttural sounds of Veneziano were liberally sprinkled throughout. On several occasions English was spoken, and each time I was so earnestly looking for foreign words that it took me several seconds before I recognized them.

Each move and verbal exchange was an exaggeration, an overstepping of the obvious. Overacted? I don't think that's how I would describe it; I found the whole thing captivating and felt that it was wonderfully acted. I laughed and smiled through the complete performance and could feel the actors playing to me as a part of that polyglot audience.

That audience was only about 20 people deep and beyond that circle the activities in the Piazza San Marco continued as if we weren't there. The actors continually called to the folk in the square but obviously could only be heard over a distance of not more than 30 meters, their voices swallowed up by the rest of the Carnevale crowd. The troupe stood as a group on the small wooden stage, clasped hands and bowed to the crowd. They then removed their masks and bowed again. As the masks came away from their faces, something like a veil fell away with them. People, just real people were revealed and I had the feeling that we were now in a different time/space. These actors now in front of me belonged in this time; the characters behind the masks from a history long passed.

"Well?"

"I don't know what to say...I'm stunned!"

"Me too."

"David, they were just so good. I'm still not sure how I understood so much."

"How many languages?"

"I'm not sure. Four at least."

"And that is consistent with historic Commedia dell' Arte. Even within Italy there were so many regional dialects. Historically Il Capitano probably spoke

Spanish. Dottore in a Bolognese dialect, and Arlecchino in Veneziano...They could entertain anyone... Anywhere."

"Well they certainly entertained me."

We pushed through the crowd toward delle Veste where we would retell this experience to Souheir and the boys.

Carnevale unfolded, day by day and we found ourselves becoming more and more selective in our choice of events and venues. Tarik came home one evening and told us that his friends from the University were rehearsing a large and extensive piece of choreography that was to be danced on the center stage of San Marco. It was advertised as "A Night of Fire" and the central story was being written and staged by one of Tarik's friends. The evening was cool and blustery and a low fog hung heavily over the Piazza when the troupe took the stage. There were about 40 young people involved in the performance and, in what seemed fairly typical for many Carnevale events, they went through a series of "false starts" before the lights, music and dancers were finally in some form of syncopation. It was a classic story of two young lovers forbidden by their families to consummate their passion. It could have been Romeo and Juliet until the last act when they were set upon by a group of large insect-like monsters. It wasn't great dancing—or even moving. It wasn't a clear narrative and was pantomimed to a rather eclectic hip hop collection of music. But it was a pyromaniac's delight! The "dancers" carried torches and swung balls of fire on the end of ropes. The monsters had long arm-like extensions which were wrapped around with material that could be soaked in a flammable liquid. There were even some on stilts, which of course, had flammable elements.

The main thrust of the stage which extended into the center of the Piazza had been covered in about 4 inches of sand and had obviously been prepared to play some part in this pageant. A strong alcohol smell wafted down from the stage and an oily smoke had begun to flow over the stage apron, down to the audience.

"It's a sterno fest!"

David was clearly enjoying himself, but I was beginning to think that our "front row seats" might become something of a liability. Dancers stood close to the arch of the stage carrying or wearing costumes and props that were soaked in fuel, and as they passed down onto the stage they were "ignited" by a pair of stage hands who were clearly enjoying themselves.

They danced their part in the story and then when they "ran out of gas" circled back to the rear of the stage to be refueled and then repeat the process. One of the "returning dancers" was not quite extinguished and as she cycled back to the rear of the stage managed to ignite a waiting dancer who suddenly was ablaze before his cue. He was standing close to another dancer who also burst into flames, then another and another until the entire group awaiting their cue were all merrily ablaze. They were standing too close and had to move out onto the stage to avoid burning each other.

"Shit"

"Oh dear"

David is howling with laughter, Souheir is telling him to behave himself, I'm slowly backing away from the barrier we have been leaning on. The stage is filling with flaming, frantic activity.

"They're really on fire now!"

"Stop it John!"

The show must go on…and it does!

The lovers surrounded by blazing monsters are pushed into the part of the stage covered in sand—A ring of fuel has been soaked into this sand and as the lovers cling to each other, a monster extends his insect-like arm and touches it to the sand. A whoosh, a blue wall of flame. They can't possibly have rehearsed this part—The two lovers are lost behind a wall of flame about 10' high! The monsters are reeling backwards.

"I bet they didn't keep their eyelashes through that..."

David is right; there is now a distinct smell of burning hair coming from the stage. The crescendo of music that is supposed to be the finale does not signal the end of the action, however, and it is clear that the stagehand with the CO_2 fire extinguisher who is busily extinguishing everyone is a piece of welcome improvisation.

The two lovers come to stage front and take a bow. The crowd is generous. We are just happy to see them alive. Juliet may not have acquired a complete afro, but her hair is definitely frizzy!

"Great show Tarik..."

"Did they actually practice with fire or was this the first time?"

David and I are still laughing. Souheir is being protective.

"Stop it you two."

We begin to control ourselves but then, in the middle of an empty stage in the middle of the Piazza San Marco, a blue circle of flame springs up out of the sand with a muted whooshing sound and sends us off into gales of laughter.

There were several memorable concerts on the list of events that unfolded over the next few days, but finally we woke on Fat Tuesday to the sure knowledge that "it" would all end tonight. If you are a "day tripper" to Carnevale in Venice, I'm sure it is a wild and exciting time, but we residents just wanted our city back. Wanted the litter out of our streets, the quiet of our evenings returned.

The final concert from the grand stage in Piazza San Marco was not memorable. It was populated by too many Italians with hand held microphones and some rather mediocre music, but the crowd was huge, debris and bottles impeding every step you could take and giant pictures of harlequins and masks were projected high up the walls of the Campanile. It was one last frantic, hedonistic effort, but I felt it lacked conviction; the players in the game were reaching exhaustion. The finale was to be a fireworks display at midnight, and Souheir and I spent a couple of hours in a small bar waiting for the appointed hour.

At 11:30 we made our way across the Piazzetta to the Molo and stood at the edge of the fondamente where the gondolas are moored. Front row seats again.

At midnight, large speakers hidden in the darkness above the roofs of the large official buildings that crowd down to the water's edge, burst forth with music and announcements that the display was beginning. The crowd flowed out of the Piazza toward us and it was soon obvious that the possibility of ending up in the Bacino was quite real. The fireworks were mounted on three large flat barges that were anchored about half way to San Giorgio and I could barely make out the shapes of men moving about on these low dark vessels.

I have seen a number of quite grand fireworks displays in my life, but I can honestly tell you that what unfolded in the next 30 minutes eclipsed all of them. I didn't know that individual explosions and starbursts could be orchestrated to every note in a piece of music, and Vivaldi blared across the water to be met by synchronized pyrotechnics in ways that I never dreamed were possible.

The water of course reflected all of the fire in the sky above it, bouncing and repeating each constellation as it was released. It seemed to go on and on and the crowd which was raucous and boisterous in Piazza San Marco was transformed, and there was a stillness in it now that was perhaps due to the fact that we all had our necks craned toward the sky.

And then came the finale. Huge explosions of colors and fusillades of squirting flames shot fanlike across the water. All syncopated to John Lennon singing "Imagine". The crowd sang along swaying from side to side with a oneness that was palpable. And then the last star raced to meet its reflection and was swallowed by the water of the Bacino.

I'm smiling at Souheir, and the crowd is shaking off its torpor and is beginning to move. It seems folly to attempt to cross the Piazza and I tell Souheir we should make our way down to the #1 stop at Harry's Bar. I'm sure that the bulk of the crowd will go the other way. I was wrong.

So many people. The crush is almost unbearable and I can no longer hold Souheir's hand. We are being squeezed onto the narrow bridge crossing from the Giardinetto and it is clear to me that this has the potential to go very wrong. I'm not enjoying this, I am now no longer moving of my own volition but am being carried along by the sheer force of bodies. Souheir is still with me, but there is fear in her eyes. On top of the bridge, this flow suddenly stops and somehow the crush on my body increases. I know that in so many other places and cultures this would be the signal for violence. I try to reach Souheir's hand, but can't raise my arms.

Somewhere behind me in a very accented English, someone begins to sing.

"Imagine all the people…"

It is like a shudder running through the crowd and we all pick up the tune and begin to sing. I look across at Souheir. She is singing and smiling. The fist that had clenched us together slowly releases and we flow across the bridge to the vaporetto stop. Most of the crowd was attempting to ride down the Grand Canal to Piazzale Roma. Souheir and I sat almost alone waiting to go in the other direction.

"That was a pretty crazy situation"

"Were you scared?"

"Of course"

"And then they just started singing!.."

She snuggles up to my shoulder and smiles to herself.

God I love this city.

Chapter 11

CITY OF CHURCHES...

Any day spent in Venice will be a day decorated with the glorious sound of bells. Bells sound at all times of the day and are not rung randomly.

They mark the time of day at a secular level when the clock tower in the Piazza San Marco strikes, but it is the bells marking sacred intervals that weave through the streets and canals of districts far from the tourist center. These are the bells of the local churches and surely if Venice is a city of bells it is therefore also a city of churches.

Depending on who's doing the counting and whether the church is active, deconsecrated or damaged, a count of all of the churches of Venice including those found on the many islands that are the Venetian satellites, will add up to a nice, round 110 "ish". As I continued my quest to walk down every street, the largest number of questions that would form in my mind always revolved around them.

Sacred architecture is treated with less caprice than its secular cousin and as it became clear that the oldest structures of the city were churches, I became engrossed in their exploration.

It is possible to trace the ascendance of architectural style by walking around Venice and recognizing stylistic elements in every building you pass. In some ways Venice is a giant historical laboratory where architectural time has been slowed if not stopped entirely, and we are treated to outstanding examples of living architectural styles that have long since disappeared from the rest of the planet.

Very few of Venice's secular buildings are standing the way that the original builders left them and it is consistent for younger generations to simply change existing architecture to accommodate new styles and ideas. One must remember that "new" in the context of Venice means an era sometime before 1800. Most of the Palazzi that front the Grand Canal do just that. They often have a front that is quite different from, and often inconsistent with, the rest of the structure that reaches back from the water entrance to the streets beyond.

I don't want to leave you with the impression that none of the churches have been refurbished and rebuilt in response to architectural fashion, rather to tell you that many of the structures that remain consistent with the original intent and design of the original architects, are sacred structures.

"So why do you want to find the oldest building in Venice?"

"Because it'll be a starting point. I'll be able to see what the architecture was in the beginning…and then I can follow subsequent styles right up until the 1800s"

I have commandeered the table in the front room and it has been covered with books and notes for about 3 days now. Souheir is asking questions that are ostensibly about architecture, but I know she is actually asking,

"So when are you going to get this crap off the table?"

"I've compiled a list of churches and the sequence in which I want to visit them. Would you like to come along sometimes?"

"Where are you going first?"

"Well it's a bit of a toss up…But I think I'm heading to Torcello first."

It's one of our favorite places, and she smiles.

"Would you like some help clearing this stuff of the table?"

"Er…sure…thanks."

San Giacomo di Rialto (called San Giacometto by the locals) is often listed as the oldest church in Venice, and it probably is the oldest in the city center where it is tucked away in a campo that you enter just over the Ponte Rialto, surrounded by a seething mass of stalls selling tourist junk. This tiny church is one of the easiest to miss in all of Venice and I'm sure many, many people have no idea that they have passed it by. Its style reflects classic Veneto Byzantine influence and is easily recognized as archaic among the many later churches, but Venice did not begin here at its current center (these high banks of the Riva Alto). It grew from the mainland towards the islands out in the center of the lagoon, and the early Venetians almost certainly crossed the sticky mudflats of the northern lagoon to the small island of Torcello to build their first church.

The walk to the Fondamente Nuove vaporetto stop passes by a remarkable array of stores which sell flowers, funerary statues and headstones. Fondamente Nuove is where many embark to go across to Murano, but the first stop along that journey is San Michele, Venice's cemetery, and it makes perfect sense that these shops cluster as close as possible. Cutting back behind the beautiful little church, Miracoli, you quickly enter a long, narrow calle, Calle Stella, which makes a straight line to the water's edge. It's an interesting walk because not many of Venice's streets move in such straight lines, but the real interest to me is the way the shops seem to organize themselves.

As you enter the calle, the first stores encountered are ateliers where stonemasons produce funerary sculptures and headstones. A few meters along the narrow way, you begin to encounter the flower shops, and the first of these deal in artificial representations made from a variety of plastics and fabrics. Continuing toward the fondamente, the next group of shops sell only silk flowers and a singular floral scent accompanies these often clever counterfeits. It is not until you are in the last few meters of the calle, where the wind can be felt as it blows across the lagoon, that you encounter glorious displays of "real" flowers and their varied perfumes.

Turning left onto the fondamente you are greeted by two of Venice's premium gelaterias. Souheir and I walk slowly past the last of the flower stands and up over the Ponte Dona which has been wonderfully restored. On the other side is the vaporetto stop where we will catch a boat to Burano, one of the larger vessels that work the waters of the lagoon called an "autonave".

There are large and small autonave, but all are much longer than the vaporetti or motoscafi. They are often multi-decked, have a capacity for hundreds of passengers and most marvelous of all…have a toilet on board!

We are heading for the tiny island of Torcello where we will start this scavenger hunt of sacred buildings. The large vessel crosses in front of San Michele and cuts a smooth arc as it curves toward the floating "bus stop" and Souheir and I shuffle with other Venetians toward the loading door. We are "locals" now and know that waiting politely is not the way. As any vessel approaches, this commuter shuffle is somewhere between excitement and impatience and I always smile when I become part of it. The little old lady in the fur coat who was sitting quietly guarding her Dolce e Gabbana shopping bags over in the back corner is now miraculously at the front of the pack (for it is never a line or a queue), and I marvel at the fact that even through the depth of the dark fur encasing her, you can still feel her bony elbows!

With a flourish of hawser knots, and the swish clang of the gate, we are welcomed aboard, Souheir and I push quickly through the cabin and out onto the small rear deck where we commandeer two seats. It is our favorite place to sit and it is only in really inclement weather that we stay inside the main cabin.

It's a cool day and the low cloud that is almost a fog bank hangs low over the lagoon which is a slightly undulating mirror the color of putty. We just sit and watch the city slowly sink into the horizon. The church of San Michele which always seems dangerously close to the water's surface slides by, and we bump into the stop at Faro on Murano. It is not until we pass this island with its tiles shimmering in the heat waves of its many glass works, that we speak.

"It's this open space that I miss."

We are mountain people and are used to large open spaces. I smile at her.

"Yeah…I just feel like I want to take a deep breath when I get out here."

Islands in various stages of habitation and abandonment pass by. When? Why? How? They present so many questions, most being the kind I know I'll find few answers to.

"You don't have to know about everything, you know."

She's teasing…But how does she know what I'm thinking?

We disembark at Burano and then walk quickly along the fondamente to where a vaporetto is waiting. The boat takes us across a small expanse of water to Torcello and about 10 minutes later we are standing alone on this tiny little island in the middle of mudflats that stretch to the west and the north as far as you can see.

The walk from the vaporetto stop to the other side of the island and the church that we have come to see is one of my favorites in all of Venice. Winter has a firm grip on this landscape and although the grasses still cling to a semblance of green, all trees except the few cypress are stripped bare and brown… Grey is the dominant color. The fondamente that follows Canale Borgognoni has recently been refurbished and we walk on a complex carpet of patterned bricks, the sound of our footsteps rolling over the edge across the still waters of the canal. We pass a large house that seems to be sleeping behind its closed shutters, a half dozen cats doze on the front porch. The canal dead ends at the small bridge called Ponte di Diavolo (you just have to wonder how it received such a name); we cross it to stand in front of the Locanda Cipriani. This exquisite restaurant and hotel counted Ernest Hemingway, Winston Churchill, even Queen Elizabeth among its patrons.

We pass on down the gravel path past a couple of boarded up tourist kiosks into an open area that is the entrance to Santa Maria Assunta. The small church founded in 639 when this part of Italy was still firmly under the rule of the Byzantine Empire stands lonely, almost forlornly forgotten, and everything about it is arcane and mysterious.

At the height of its importance, Torcello was the home to 20,000 residents and this tiny church played a pivotal place in their daily lives. The population of Torcello is less than 80 today and I wonder about the size of the church's present congregation. The pressures that moved the early Venetians further into the lagoon rendered Torcello an outpost, and this precipitous fall in population was hurried along by malarial mosquitoes that flourished in the surrounding mudflats.

I stand holding Souheir's cold hand in mine and we say nothing as we look at the cluster of buildings that has opened before us. I've been here many times before, but never on this errand, and I am almost overcome by the feeling of inadequacy. I don't have the training, and I'm not clever enough to find what I'm looking for amongst this clutter of architecture. It's like standing in a boneyard trying to visually reconstruct animals.

I don't know why, but the collection of buildings is profoundly feminine. The passage of time has not been kind to her. The church was modified dramatically in the 9th and 10th centuries and the current structure dates from 1008. However, there are no rocks to be found in these muddy parts, and almost all of the materials from the 739 version of the church have been recycled into the existing structure.

Santa Maria is an ancient basilica form, meaning that it has a high central nave flanked on each side by lower aisles, each roofed over with terracotta tiles which have weathered to a beautiful rose color. Its simple brick façade is interrupted by a portico or porch that cuts entirely across it and then connects it to another small church which was built in the 11th and 12th centuries. Santa Fosca presents a tantalizing façade and roofline which intimates that something quite different is going on over there, but I force my attention back to Santa Maria and we move toward the ticket office that is its entrance.

The first sensations are olfactory. You can smell the wet of the outside world wicking up through the floors. The air is heavy and cold, and my first exhaled breath hangs in a little cloud of condensation... Over all of this is something else.... It's what ancient religion smells like. Tens of thousands of candles... How many kilos of incense? ...Gardens of flowers? ...Cadavers beneath the floor?

Plain brick walls reach up to the three ceilings of the roof, the central nave covered by what looks like an upturned boat as if the roofers were on loan from a Venetian shipyard. Looking to the right down the central nave, I am transfixed by the altar screen or iconostasis and its finely carved marble panels. You feel that these panels were not made for this place and guess as to their origin; they seem oriental to me. The panel with the two drinking peacocks is instantly my favorite.

I'm visually wrestling with what seems to be a construction site in the apse behind the altar, when I become aware of the giant Madonna looking down from the conch above. I've been holding Souheir's hand the whole time and without thinking, squeezed it tightly as I look up. She looks upward too; nodding her head and smiling,

"Oh my!"

"She takes your breath away every time, doesn't she?"

This giant, "pudding basin"-headed Mother of God hovers in the gold of the mosaic covering the hemisphere above the apse as she has done since the 13th century, and there is an inescapable sense of nurture that emanates from her. She holds the Christ child, who at this time was still depicted as a sort of mini adult, and is therefore filled with his own precociousness. The Madonna, however is real and the look that she projects to all who enter is mysteriously warm and engaging even though a tear is clearly shown running down her cheek. I look up at the giant Madonna, this kindly soul, and am absolutely convinced that this little church belongs to her.

The floor is a complex blanket of colored marble tiles of various sizes and shapes that has taken on an organic character as it pitches and undulates in response to the muddy earth below, and I wonder how long it has been since it conformed to any sense of "flatness". We walk down the center of the nave and stand in front of the altar which is fashioned from an ancient Roman sarcophagus, and look beyond it into the apse. Santa Maria Assunta unfortunately is an example of what archeologists call "repristinization" This is when they enter a building, find its oldest elements, and then strip away everything that is younger than these. This concept never takes into consideration the fact that sacred buildings are churches, that churches are nothing without their congregation, that it will change continually, and that architectural and artistic elements will be added and modified. They are evidence of its life and each represents a moment in the church's history. The stripping away inevitably eviscerates the building and often what is left is truncated and incomplete.

The mess behind the altar is the end product of such a process and I wonder if the archeologists simply reached a place where they realized they had gone too far; or if some kindly soul stepped in and said "Enough".

We wander back to the opposite end of the church where an enormous mosaic cycle depicting the end of time breathes down on us. It is a truly remarkable work if for no other reason than its scale. It's a huge work that culminates in Christ welcoming the blessed into heaven and condemning the damned to hell. I'm smiling.

"What's so funny?"

"Well, when you use the written word and you tell someone that they should not commit adultery, the end product is just a sentence. However when you use imagery; symbols, to tell the same lesson, you end up with an image that many would find pornographic...like that one there..."

I point to the cluster of figures on the right side of the mosaic and she smiles back at me.

"I've noticed that the artists depicting hell seemed to have more fun than those showing the blessed."

Turning for one last look down the small church, I nod at the Madonna and realize that I am quite chilled. The cold simply adds to the loneliness of this place.

We pass no one as we retrace our steps back to the vaporetto stop and I wonder how many visitors the lonely Madonna receives each day.

⁓

Leaving the vaporetto stop at San Basilio, we cut across a small campo and follow the Rio di San Sabastiano which is bordered by a waist high brick wall until we encounter a bridge that leads across to a small rather plain church presenting a façade which offers not even the slightest hint of what might lie beyond rather strange half glass front doors. It is San Sebastiano, and Souheir has heard me talk of it.

"This is the San Sebastiano you're often talking about isn't it?"

"It is…But we are not going in there today."

"Why?"

"Because it's out of sequence…I'm trying to do this in chronological order."

She rolls her pretty eyes theatrically. We cut down beside San Sebastiano, cross a rather awkwardly shaped campo and walk down the side of another church; Angelo Raffaele.

"This one?"

"Nope."

Cross the bridge in front of the façade and then left down another walled canal and we are clearly entering a secluded almost forgotten part of the city. From the rear, we skirt around the campanile and stand in front of San Nicolo dei Mendicoli. The church is oriented so that this northern wall should contain its main entrance, but a strange porch or portico is attached to the lower section of this wall and an ancient iron grating serves as a fence to keep us out. This was a very common feature of many churches in the 1400s especially those of the Mendicant orders. These porches were built so that the poor and indigent could sleep there with at least a roof over their heads.

"The entry door is down the side here. Come I'll show you."

Souheir follows me down the side of the small church and we pass through a double door system and stand looking at its glowing interior. This church still wears all of the changes and decorations that have been lavished on it over its long history. Great cycles of painting and sculpture all contained within gorgeous gilded frames gleam down from the walls and ceiling above the nave, and there is a feeling that can only be described as coziness that seems to have settled in this place.

"This is the church that was used in the movie 'Don't Look Now'."

"With Julie Christie and Donald Sutherland?"

"Yeah…he was hanging from that ceiling right there."

"It was being restored?"

"In the 1970s this whole place underwent a major restoration. It had been badly damaged in the 1966 flood. This was one of the first restorations by the British "Venice in Peril" fund. I think they raised the floor by about a foot."

We have been talking quietly, and because we are the only people in the church, are not bothering anyone's devotions. A caretaker has appeared from the gloom at the altar end of the nave and is walking toward us and I'm sure we are going to be asked to be quiet. However, with a smile and slowly enunciated Italian, he asks if we would like to see one of the Church's treasures. We accept his invitation and he continues past the altar, through a small door and then begins to climb a flight of stairs. At the top he opens a door and we step into a kitchen! We are clearly in his apartment; there is something cooking in a pot on the stove and laundry is drying on a rack under the window. He motions to continue following him and we pass through a bedroom and up another flight of stairs. He unlocks a door and we are in a small attic space that is lit by a skylight that has been cut into the terracotta tiles of the roof. Once our eyes accommodate the low light, we see what it is that he wants to share with us.

The remnants of an ancient fresco are illuminated by the silver light shafting down from the roof. St. Francis and two angels fight for space on the wall that has been bisected by the later addition of a chimney. The brickwork has been removed, but the space that was within the chimney is totally black, the painting beneath the soot irrevocably lost. I have a host of questions, none of which are escaping the logjam that's the translation process in my head; but the man is nodding knowingly.

"Si. San Francesco…Questo fresco E molto vecchio…duecento…dalla chiesa vecchia"

He genuflects as he speaks and Francis, stolid in a lifeless art that certainly predates Giotto, stares upward into the shaft of light. Locked away up here in his garret with his attendant angels, I wonder how many visitors he receives. How many people even know he's up here? The attendant genuflects one more time and reverently closes the door behind us as we leave.

Back in the beautiful church below, I am still speechless and the attendant is warmly shaking my hand.

"Mille grazie, Signore…Mille grazie."

He is still smiling and nodding as we leave San Nicolo. Souheir and I walk back up along Rio delle Terese looking for a bar. We need a cup of coffee and a place to sit...somewhere we can verbalize what we have just experienced.

Francis is featured in the next church too. The two largest gothic churches in Venice were raised to glorify God by relatively new monastic orders that were started by two of Christianity's most charismatic priests: Dominic and Francis.

The medieval period is often referred to by church historians as the Benedictine centuries, and Benedict of Narsia who lived from 480 to 547 had an enormous influence on the church and its place in society for the next 500 years. In his book "The Rule of Benedict", he writes 73 chapters that embrace his concept of balance, moderation and reason, but also goes on to give instructions of how to build, organize and most importantly, to administer monasteries that serve both the spiritual and physical needs of their congregation. Because they had to be self-sustaining, these orders (it's an accepted fact that Benedict himself was not attempting to create such an order) were never very large communities, and were mostly rural. To enter most orders, an Initiate had to present a dowry of some form and this too restricted both the number and the social class of those entering the clergy.

Francis in 1210 and Dominic in 1266 established orders that were committed to the poor and disenfranchised. They were Mendicant orders. They begged and lived off the charity of their congregation. Because they accepted anyone into their ranks, even the poorest could join and the resultant change rocked the church, but also had profound socio-political ramifications on the secular world as well.

Both of these religious orders grew in numbers that exponentially outstripped all other orders very rapidly. Their organizations were characterized not only by large brotherhoods, but enormous congregations which would need correspondingly large churches. These two new dynamic orders which committed to ministering to the lowest classes of society in mostly urban areas, literally sprang up overnight. They presented unseen and unprecedented problems to the Papacy that scrambled to control them. Less than two years after the death of Francis, he had been canonized. What they couldn't control in life they did in death. He was "their" saint now, and through him they controlled a vast workforce who were not only skilled artisans, but more importantly, creative entrepreneurs in the emerging mercantilism that would fuel the Renaissance.

Venice, being the most mercantile power perhaps in all of Europe, recognized the potential that these orders might achieve and acted accordingly. In 1234, Doge Jacopo Tiepolo gave the Dominicans land for a grand new church. This land was nothing more than mudflats that were often covered by high tides on what was then the city's northern perimeter. In 1236, the same wily old Doge gave the Franciscans some equally soggy real estate on the edge of San Polo.

No other religious groups could bring such a workforce with such zeal to projects like these. No other religious groups could harness the engineering and construction skills that these sites demanded from within their ranks. The Franciscans and Dominicans got their giant new churches. Venice grew in size as these lands were reclaimed. Her populace was given vast employment opportunities and ownership in a truly egalitarian endeavor.

⚏⚏

If you were on skis, the path you take from the vaporetto stop at San Toma' to the Frari would be a slalom course! It weaves first right and then left and continues to go back and forth until you are emptied into a small open space squished up against the eastern wall of a huge church. This is Santa Maria Gloriosa dei Frari. Tiepolo's land grant of 1236 actually gave the Franciscans more water than land. He ceded them a tract of land that contained an old abandoned monastery alongside such watery soil that it was called Lake Badoer. The industrious Franciscans went straight to work, demolished the monastery, drained the lake and by 1280, had erected a small church. In the next 50 years they insinuated themselves among the lower classes that populated this area, and as the fortunes of these people rose in these successful times; so rose the fortune of the church. The building program for the grand church was officially begun in the 1330s and the Franciscans immediately revealed their entrepreneurial prowess by literally "selling" parts of the structure to individuals and fraternities. A specific family might donate the money for one of its massive columns…a guild or group of tradesmen for another… All of this activity buoyed by the massive workforce of the Franciscan brotherhood. Its official name is Santa Maria Gloriosa dei Frari— (Frari being a Venetian compression of Fratti—brothers); however it has always been known lovingly as the Frari…the Brothers.

In a rather strange building program, the transept and apse were built first and were completed in 1361. The campanile which is Venice's second highest was completed in 1395, and the nave extended and finished in 1415.

The smell of coffee from the corner bar is so tantalizingly powerful that I only have to look at Souheir and she is nodding and opening the door.

"What is it about their coffee?"

"It's always so good…"

We are sitting at a tiny table looking out the window at a brick wall that extends in all directions literally out of our sight. The bricks; altinelle is the Venetian word; have weathered to beautiful pastel shades of rose and there is a softness about them that is almost organic.

"How many bricks do you think there are in this building?"

"I'm sure they number in the millions."

"Where did they get that many?"

"I presume they made them on this site…there would have been no shortage of clay…".

We leave the coffee bar and walk down along the wall until we reach a well head in the center of a small campo. Leaning on its smooth Istrian marble rim, we look up at the campanile towering above us.

"Why are those big white stones included in the structure of the campanile? They look random like there's no reason, no pattern to them."

"I hate it when you ask questions like that…I don't know…and I can't find anyone who does."

I fall back on my best imitation of a Jesuit priest.

"It's a mystery my daughter…"

Entering the Frari by its front doors is a breathtaking and completely theatrical experience. No matter how vast the exterior may seem, when you enter, the interior seems to be larger, and most of us don't have much experience with such a space. The central nave opens to a space about the size of a football field before it is interrupted by a decorative wall pierced by an arched central entrance. As you proceed towards it you feel insignificant, even inferior. Enormous and extravagant tomb structures climb the walls of the side aisles, their presence incongruous with the simplicity of the building.

They don't distract us however; we have made this walk before and we continue on task. The far end of the nave (with the emphasis on far) is illuminated by stained glass windows which pierce the walls of the apse, and bathing in this glorious light, a large painting, predominantly red and gold, rears over the altar. The uppermost point of the frame of this painting is curved in a semi-circle and as we walk forward, the curve of the painting and the curve of the arch over the entrance come together. Exactly. For a brief moment (and if you stop walking, for as long as you want) the painting is perfectly framed in the doorway.

We continue walking and climb two steps to pass through this entrance into an enclosed choir. The individual stalls for the chorister monks are decorated with wood inlays (intarsio) and are worth a separate trip to appreciate them.

The glowing gorgeous painting beckons us on and we walk through the choir to stand before it in the only part of the church that has pews. The painting is a work by Tiziano Vecellio (Titian) who was still quite young when he painted it in 1516. It is a painting of the assumption of the Virgin and is reverently and comfortably called the "Assunta" by all Venetians.

Representing the moment at her death when the Madonna is transported directly to heaven, Titian presents the unfolding of three separate spatial orders. At the bottom of the painting in secular space that is an extension of the space we are standing in, the disciples cluster in dark tones and reach up as Mary ascends. Thomas' hands are outstretched to receive her girdle. The Madonna has broken free and is in an entirely new space and, surrounded by attendant angels, reaches for the bright light of heaven above her. Tucked into the half round uppermost point of the painting, and its entirely sacred space, God, like some giant delta winged kite, glides in to receive her.

"If you bring binoculars, you can see so many of the details that are not obvious from here...What look like clouds around the Madonna and God are actually little cherub faces..."

"Really? Oh you're right; I think I can see them now"

The "Assunta" literally transfixes the viewer and we stand in front of her for ten breathless minutes. This is the experience that we came for and, because we are not tourists and can visit whenever we want, we retrace our steps. We don't walk the few feet to the chapel at the right of the altar and look at Donatello's "John the Baptist" resplendent in his (in my opinion) over-restored state. We don't enter the door into the sacristy where one of Giovanni

Bellini's finest works glows jewel like in its dim light. We don't wander up and down the side aisles and the six chapels to gawk and wonder at the tombs of doges and great artists...Doge Giovanni Pesaro, entangled among giant, black African men carrying sacks of what looks like flour, and skeletons and fantastic creatures, not quite dragons nor wyverns, that screech at the viewers below. We don't stop at the tomb of Titian, where a compendium of every classical architectural motif known to man has been used, his magnificent "Assunta" cleverly carved in bas relief in its central part... Nor that of Canova, incredibly a giant pyramid. This most ancient motif somehow looks way too modern for this building.

We just walk quietly hand in hand down the vastness of the nave towards the front doors.

"Oh...There's something else I want you to see!"

I have stopped about halfway down the nave and am looking up at the brick interior of this giant space. The same altinelle are present on all the interior walls too.

"Walk over to the part of the wall that reaches down to the floor...And have a close look at the bricks."

Hands in pockets she approaches the wall and then stands in front of it for a few minutes. She turns and is shaking her head and smiling, walking back to me.

"My God...They're all painted...they're not real! The entire interior of this church is faux brick?"

"Yes...Imagine how many men it took to do that. In some ways it's the most impressive feature of the whole building...A bazillion painted bricks...Painted by how many workers? How many little Franciscan Brothers scurrying around on scaffolding? Each brick is a signature…It's how they own this church."

--※--

I never tire of cutting from one side of this city to the other. The route imprinted in my memory is testament to my hours of wandering, and if I'm honest it makes me feel Venetian. I know that's not possible…That only people like Matteo are "cento percento Veneziani", but when I'm weaving down tiny streets and under dark sottoporteghi, I know I am connected to her in a special way.

A quick traghetto across the Grand Canal, a serpentine path through some of my favorite narrow streets and 15 minutes later we are standing on the little ponte which leads across Rio degli Mendicanti into Campo Zanipolo. In front of us is the giant façade of another Gothic church that gives its name to this Campo. It is Santi Giovanni e Paolo.

"How do they get the Venetian word Zanipolo out of Giovanni e Paolo?"

"Maybe some of the early parishioners were Welsh! Honestly, I don't know, I find most Veneziano pretty impenetrable…"

Zanipolo presents a boxy structure that is obviously similar to the Frari, but beyond that basic external structure the two cathedrals have very little in common. Doge Jacopo Tiepolo gave the Dominicans this land 2 years before he made a similar grant to the Franciscans; and the Dominicans entered into a reclamation and building program equally as industrious as their Franciscan brothers and the church was dedicated in 1430.

The façade of the church is the end result of a series of design ideas over a period of time. The upper part bears a strong resemblance to the Frari, the same circular windows and rooflines almost interchangeable. However, the bottom half is another story altogether, and is unlike any other church in all of Venice. About halfway down the façade the brickwork becomes uneven and rusticated as if it was prepared to receive a finished stone facing. This has never been added however, and the rough textural brickwork has weathered to a darker color than the rest of the brick façade. A series of six blind archways are set back into the lower wall and in four of them reside white marble sarcophagi—In one of these stone coffins resides the body of the old Doge who made the original land grant, Doge Jacopo Tiepolo. Inside the church you will find the tombs of 25 more doges.

To complete the architectural mayhem of the façade, a grand central doorway was added in the 15th century and its cluster of beautifully proportioned columns flank a grand door with its overarching tympanum. Passing through this door is as equally theatrical as the Frari, but in a very different way.

"It's bigger isn't it?"

"It certainly feels that way…but look further and tell me why…"

"It doesn't have a choir like the Frari?"

"It used to have one…but after the Council of Trent in 1560, the Vatican decided to make churches more open. The congregation was not to be separated from the altar, so they moved it."

Zanipolo seems to be brighter and more open than its cousin the Frari, but it also has some very different elements that contribute to its character. Even at first glance, it is clear that there has been a continuous and ongoing decoration process at work here. The fact that 25 doges are buried within its walls speaks to the prestige of this church. Tombs reflecting the architectural styles of the day stretching from the Gothic beginnings of the church right up to the

Baroque, decorate the walls and side chapels. There is no attempt at centralized harmony here, and architectural and sculptural elements are presented in glorious discordancy. In a smaller space one can only imagine the sense of disorder this might generate, but there is enough space in this vast interior to allow all of these competing elements to exist separately.

We walk slowly down the central nave toward the altar, our footsteps echoing in this vast space, a walk of wonder. It takes no stretch of the imagination to turn the columns at each side into giant trees, the gorgeous light shafting down from the windows above into sunlight peeking through the canopy of the forest...

I point to a large painting hanging in an alcove to our left.

"Him again..."

"Titian?"

"Nearly"

"What does that mean?'

"It's a copy of a Titian...Called the "Death of St Peter Martyr" It was said to be one of his finest paintings... Was installed there in 1530 and for 300 years people came to venerate and copy it. Napoleon of course stole it and had it transferred to canvas...But even after that tragedy it was still revered by the art world. It was being cleaned in the Rosary Chapel just down there on the left in 1867, when a fire broke out and destroyed it. That painting is a copy that was made for one of the Medici in Florence... Mr.Titian had the two most prominent and prestigious paintings in the two most prominent churches in Venice...No small feat."

"I don't think I like it"

"It's not my favorite either...But too many folk effusively praised the original; so I just presume this copy falls a long way short of it"

There are more pews here, intimating a larger congregation...Fresh flowers that speak of a sense of pride and love of this space. On each side, tombs of doges and wealthy patrons hang on the simple brick walls (faux, just like in the Frari), some showing the antique sculptors' battle that they lost trying to produce horses and men, others the enlightenment of the sculptural discoveries of the Renaissance, and finally the lugubrious bravura of the Baroque as it oozes its presence into the church.

On the left there is both the Sacristy and the Rosary Chapel; the latter a repository of some remarkable Veronese paintings. We spend some wonderful moments as the only people in this intimate space, and we each choose a favorite painting.

The high altar of Zanipolo is said to be the work of the baroque genius Baldassare Longhena and literally creates its own wind with the movements of its luscious elements.

"Over the top?"

"With the addition of a kitchen sink, it would be…"

"That's the only thing missing!"

We both squirm in front of the reliquary containing St. Catherine's foot and then turn and retrace our steps up the center of the church.

"Oh my!"

We turn to retrace our steps up the center of the church and are now confronting for the first time, the inside of the west wall—the front wall of the church. The huge tomb of Doge Alvise Mocenigo takes up two thirds of this wall right up to the round oculus window. The rest of it is given over to members of the Mocenigo family, including Pietro, another doge.

"You get the feeling that they would really have liked to have this on the outside. It's like they've turned the church inside out."

Outside we look up at the equestrian sculpture of Colleoni (which will find a chapter of its own, dear Reader) and decide to walk back to the Fondamente Nuove and catch a "slow boat" home.

᪥

The Mercerie is a street that runs from San Marco to the Rialto and its history has always been that of a street of shops. At the San Marco end it takes its name from the giant clock tower that it passes beneath and is the Mercerie dell' Orologio, then changes its name to the Mercerie di San Zulian as it passes this church and then becomes the Mercerie di San Salvatore as it enters the Rialto area.

I almost never walk this street as I have little interest in the high fashion stores that line it with a seemingly endless wall of glass, behind which astronomically expensive clothing and footwear are displayed... No interest at all in becoming a part of the tourist horde that is often compressed into it. However, Souheir and I have almost completed the journey from San Marco to the Rialto, and so far it has been a pleasant stroll among groups of people who, even as they cluster in front of the more appealing windows, are not blocking the progress of those of us who wish to continue walking. We are heading for San Salvatore, Salvador in Veneziano, and its high brick wall appears on our left just before we get to a campo of the same name.

There is actually a side door that opens directly into the Mercerie but we walk around the front and climb the steps up into San Salvador. Standing just inside the front entrance looking down the central nave, you are immediately aware that this is not the same theatre as the two Gothic cathedrals that we previously visited. In the Frari and Zanipolo, you are insignificant. The human form is simply swallowed up into the vastness of those spaces. God is a long way above your head and you get the feeling that he isn't looking down. You arrive as a supplicant in the hopes of an occasional glimpse in your direction, and ant like, await his response.

San Salvador is from another time. A time of enlightenment...It is a classically Renaissance building built by men who subscribed to a new measure of godliness...the intellect. Begun in 1508 by Giorgio Spavento with subsequent contributions by Tullio Lombardo and Jacopo Sansovino, this church owes much of its architectural vocabulary to the great Florentine, Filippo Brunelleschi. It is not a small church, but its organization is such that you never feel completely overwhelmed by it. Clearly this is a place to come for a conversation with God. The central nave is actually created by joining three Greek crosses together which creates three separate chapels on each side rather than continuous aisles. Above the intersections of these three crosses rise three domes with lanterns that flood a cool, ambient light into the interior.

The architectural elements of the interior, rather than being hidden, are revealed, even amplified by the use of a cool grey stone (called the pietra serena...the serene stone) in contrast to white stucco surfaces. The pietra serena is used in the vaulting and columns and in most of the three dimensional decorative forms, and the white stucco fills the pillowy forms of the domes and the cool flatness of the side walls.

"If you stand still and look down the length of the church, you'll find that your eyes begin to follow the lines of the grey stone and they lead you from element to element until you've followed them from one end of the church to the other."

"I like the way it loops from one column to the next...What's that painting down there?"

She is pointing toward the large work that is bathing the central altar in an unworldly light.

"That's Mr. Titian at work again...Come, let's go and have a look."

We walk down the center of the nave and stop in the space that opens before the altar. The floor is pieced together with geometric shapes of polished exotic stone, the overall design a giant star. The center of this star is actually a circular hole in the floor which has been covered by a thick glass insert, so that we can stand on it and look down into the crypt of the earlier church built in 1177. Condensation clings to the underside of this glass oculus and the concept of a "floating city" reasserts itself once again.

Titan's "Transformation" does not sit placidly above the altar however, and reaches out to gather our attention. Painted in 1560 when he was no longer a young man, it possesses the power of a lifetime's skills and once again we find ourselves speechless in front of this man's work. It is not the huge canvas that the "Assunta" is, but we are standing closer and the experience is somehow more intimate. There is an obvious looseness to the brushstrokes that was not present in his earlier works and the Christ figure swirls through space that is illuminated by his presence… Light and form somehow stirred together.

Souheir moves against me, almost leaning; I reach across and squeeze her shoulder.

"And as if that isn't enough, there's another Titian over there in that side chapel…"

Turning to move toward it, we are confronted by an enormous sculpted monument that occupies the entire end wall of the right transept.

"What's that?"

"That, as they say, is another story…"

"In nome di Deo e buon profito" was often written in the front cover of the ledgers of the Venetian merchants. "In the name of God and good profit" Religious zeal? Or was their religion actually commerce? Whatever…This mercantile empire spread itself throughout the Adriatic and Mediterranean seas and along their shores. The Venetian merchants were the "linchpin" between the Orient and Europe and they cultivated this position with great energy and protected the attendant privileges with a fierce jealousy. Very early in their mercantile history they established warehouses in foreign ports so that Venetian merchants could conduct year round trading to stock them. When the trade convoys arrived they simply had to load the cargo and leave. Over time these outposts became larger, the Venetian residents became more assimilated with the locals, and small colonies of ex-patriot Venetians were sprinkled along the trade routes. It was only a series of small steps beyond this that allowed the Venetians to actually establish their own trade centers which they often fortified, and the Venetian empire began to acquire the one thing that they did not have in their watery home. Land!

By the 1400s they had outposts from Istria to the Levant and often were the controlling governance in many places far from La Serenissima. Cyprus was a large island that developed its own bounty of natural resources, but was also close enough to the Orient to reflect those influences in almost everything Cypriot. It was the pearl in the necklace of Venetian trade centers that strung down the Adriatic and across the Mediterranean.

The Cypriots had their own monarchy and in 1468, James the Second came to power. He actively sought a queen that would help increase his power and prestige; and of course his wealth. The greatest source of this wealth came from the trade with Venice which was principally controlled by the powerful Cornaro family that had been trading exotic goods out of Cyprus for many years. The family had produced four Doges and they offered up their youngest daughter Catarina as a queen for the Cypriot king. This union was a great moment for both families. James married Catarina by proxy in 1468 when she was only 14 years old and they consummated this with another wedding in 1472.

The Queen of Cyprus was now Venetian. It is difficult not to cast a jaundiced and cynical eye over the next part of the story. Catarina quickly became pregnant and James died just as quickly, and under strange circumstances. Catarina continued as regent and gave birth to an infant James, who died under mysterious circum-stances just before his first birthday. She was now absolute Queen of Cyprus, and ruled the Island from 1474 to 1489. There is plenty of evidence to verify the fact that this "rule" was quite superficial and that she was simply the puppet for a group of powerful Venetian merchants. However, she seemed to have been a rather pleasant being, and the Cypriots began to look to her as their real monarch. Once again some dark and mysterious moves were made and Catarina was forced to abdicate and sell the administration of the country to Venice in 1489. Dressed in black, she was said to have cried all the way from the capital city Nicosia to the coast where she was shipped home. She was allowed to keep the title of Queen of Cyprus, and was given another, the Daughter of Saint Mark. Kept at an estate in the little town of Asolo she cultivated a court of intellectuals and artists. She died at 55 and if the portrait by Gentile Bellini is any indication, was a dour and unhappy woman.

"This sculpture shows Catarina handing over her Kingdom to the Doges"

"She doesn't look happy"

"I'm sure she wasn't"

We use the side door to exit and are immediately swept into the shopping throng of the Mercerie.

⁂

Sixth century Venice was about the same size as Murano, a remarkable fact that I never tire of telling. It illustrates the tenacity of the ancient Venetians, the drive to make their mark on the earth's surface, the in-credible energy that they used to create a home…And it often explains the contemporary geography of the city. Fondamente Nove can also be found spelled and expressed as Fondamente Nuove, and it is this newness that has my attention. We are standing on the Western most point of this Fondamente looking into the Sacca della Misericordia which is a harbor filled with boats patiently working at their hawsers like dogs chewing on their leashes. This harbor seems to take a bite out of the precious land mass of Venice, but its true story is both unexpected and instructive. Rather than being removed from a land mass, it was simply never created as one. In other words, the structures along Venice's northern shore are on new earth, laboriously filled in by 16th century Venetians, and the Sacca was left as the lagoon it always was. This entire northern shore was being slowly and inexorably moved out into the lagoon. There is evidence to suggest that land covered with water; (literally submerged land) was sold before it was reclaimed. It's as if the ancient Venetians were so comfortable in their watery home that they barely made the distinction between land and water; indeed Venice was as much water as it was land.

A short walk from the Sacca and we have passed under a long and rather dank sottoportego, taken a left turn down-what for Venice-is a remarkably straight calle, and have reemerged on the Fondamente Nove directly across the canal from where we started several minutes ago. I can literally throw a tennis ball to where we started out!

Our morning walk is directed along the Fondamente Nove toward another on my list of churches, and as we turn right down Salizzarda de la Spechiera, the edifice of a large white church presents its profile...And immediately this becomes a part of the conundrum of the building, because the profile of this church is all that can be viewed from a distance. A major element of any religious building is its exterior, because it sets the stage for an approaching worshipper. In this chapter, dear Reader, I have spent time telling you of my personal responses to architectural elements that were designed to make me feel small and inconsequential and others that were welcoming and encouraged my intellectual involvement. The church I am approaching is yet another Santa Maria Assunta (although few of its visitors will ever know that, because it is known to the world simply as the "Gesuiti") and has been built in what historians call the Baroque style. This style is characterized by the use of classical elements that are usually populated by many free standing figures often in rather dramatic and at times flamboyant poses.

Classic Greek and Roman structures almost always dominate a vista. They are designed to control their surroundings and draw attention to themselves from afar. The walk up to them, and then into them, was often as important a part of the experience as what was awaiting the visitor in their interiors. The great strength of Andrea Palladio's triumvirate of buildings is not just in the unique and masterful shaping of San Giorgio Maggiore, Zittelle, and Redentore, but in the fact that they sit on the Fondamente of the Canale Giudecca or the Bacino San Marco and can be seen from across a wide expanse of water. The boat ride across to them is breathtaking, and in the case of Redentore, the climb up the front steps is one of the most theatrical activities I know. You expect to be greeted by angelic forms just inside the door! Having said all of this…What about Gesuiti?

It has all of the elements to accomplish the theatre and grandeur of the Palladian trio…Beautiful white marble fashioned into every known classical element. The façade is resplendent with columns and pilasters and cornices with triglyphs; the giant truss form of the entablature, perfectly balanced on all of this. Above that, a crowd of monumentally scaled figures, most of them winged, stand with their wings back; like seagulls leaning into a strong wind. And to what end?

Gesuiti is squished into the tiny space of the Salizarda de la Spechiera that makes a concession by becoming slightly wider as it passes the church. It is impossible for the viewer to step back and see all of these elements presented in a single view, and in a kind of architectural myopia you almost instantly stop looking. It's certainly not invisible…But just as certainly, cannot be viewed.

It is cool, and low clouds serve to filter the morning light so that it becomes the wonderful silver, ambient illumination that Venice so often wraps around herself. Souheir and I step through a door that has been cut into a larger door almost as an afterthought, and we pass through a short space and an even smaller door before we enter the church proper.

"There you are."

I gesture, like this is my gift to give, and she smiles the sweet smile of the recipient.

"This is one of Venice's most important Baroque churches…"

Our eyes are slowly accommodating the low light of the interior, and even though I resist, the word "gloom" comes immediately to mind.

"Are all of the surfaces decorated?" She is craning her head upward to a ceiling that is rich with stucco, gilding and large inset paintings. The floor and walls are all polychrome and pattern and the dominant theme leaves the viewer with the feeling that the interior has been wrapped in damask. The dark green of the central floral pattern is repeated in the floor and eventually the altar.

"Go over to the wall and tell me what you see close up…"

"You just like sending me across churches to look at bricks and things don't you?"

"Well, your responses are always so wonderfully theatrical…and I can't help being the teacher…"

She walks across the nave to the nearest wall where the floral damask motif appears to be frescoed over its surface and begins to shake her head from side to side and as she turns back to me and says,

"All of those patterns are inlaid green marble!"

The entire place is one amazing piece of stone intarsio. The painted bricks of the Frari and Zanipolo gave us insights into the sheer volume of their brotherhoods, but these walls are about opulence, wealth, and all of its attendant power.

We walk slowly down the nave and stop at the marble balustrade that closes around the area of the altar. The floor in front of us takes on the guise of a carpet and marvelous oriental patterns in surprisingly bright colors have been created by inlaying wonderfully exotic stones. This carpet flows up the steps to the altar; the patterns uninterrupted by its sinuous climb.

"This is modeled after the altar in St. Peter's isn't it?"

"Yes…it can't be anything else."

Giuseppe Pozzo designed this magnificent baldacchino blossoming above us, but surely he was inspired by Bernini. The four spiraling columns of the supports have been fashioned from some remarkable green stone and a recent restoration reveals depth and luster that are inescapably impressive. We turn to look back down the nave and it is somehow a different space.

"So this is the Jesuit's church?"

"Yes, this version of the church dates back to only 1728 and was actually based on their mother church in Rome."

We pass back down the way we came and approach the front door.

"Mr. Titian is in here as well you know."

"Where?"

I point to the last chapel on our right.

"Over there."

"I was looking for vibrant colors"

"It's a night scene…A nocturne"

We are now standing in front of a large canvas that is set back into a dark niche. The first minute in front of this painting is spent waiting for your eyes to accustom themselves to the gloom of the poorly lighted niche, and it comes as almost a shock to many viewers when they realize it's not just a matter of poor lighting and that the painting is in a darkened corner of the Gesuiti, but it is depicting an event that is happening entirely at night. It's a grisly scene of the martyrdom of St. Lawrence who is being forcibly held down on a brazier by two burly torturers whilst a third tends to the fire that is burning beneath him. Lawrence reaches up with his left hand ostensibly to the light of God which pierces the blackness of the night clouds, but the narrative becomes clouded here, for behind him, standing on the steps of a large classic building (looking remarkably like the exterior of this church) are a couple of onlookers that he seems to be acknowledging. The scene has three light sources that can't quite compete with the darkness that seems to consume them. The light of the brazier illuminates the foreground and the principal actors of the drama, two strange metal baskets of fiercely burning coals, held aloft on long poles, (one by the apparent doorkeeper of the classical building), blow in a wind that adds ever more drama to this horrific scene; and the light of God pierces down from above. It is a strange painting.

   She turns to look at me as she asks, "So what do you think of it?"

…and I know she is "fishing" for my reactions before she gives up her opinion.

"You're allowed to dislike it you know."

"No, I just want to know what you honestly think of it."

"Why?"

"Because it's so different from everything you've shown me that he has paint-ed...really from anything that I've seen in Venice."

I stand looking up at this dark and somehow foreboding painting and real-ize that for all the times that I have stood here, I have never answered that question.

She is looking intently at me, those beautiful dark eyes shining in this low light, and I know I have to answer.

"It's too secular...There are too many overtones from a narrative other than the religious story it purports to tell. It's not just about the horrible death of this saint..."

"So what is its story?"

"Perhaps that's the reason that I struggle with it. I don't know what the story is. I don't know anyone who does...Not convincingly...And I think that's what old Titian intended. You can't get very close to it, but I'm sure that unlike Tintoretto who works up from a layer of dark, sometimes black, Titian covered a painting beneath with this cloak of night; he consciously hid things. I'd love to peel some of this dark away and see what might be hiding beneath it. The three soldiers standing to the right are obviously in Spanish armor. The red flag has the black eagle of the Habsburgs on it. The painting is said to have been completed in 1558, which is a year after Philip of Spain, one of Titian's grand patrons, defeated the French at the battle of San Quentin. Why put that in the painting? Because of the Jesuits? Was he sucking up to Philip?

What about the three figures in the background? I've always thought the two on the steps were Lorenzo's parents! I have no idea why. The guy in the doorway is what? An angry neighbor who's being kept awake by all that screaming? The statue of the Madonna holding the smaller statue…?"

I make my best "I don't know" grimace.

"…and she's standing on top of what appears to be a Venetian wellhead…He's telling a story that I'm just not clever enough to understand."

We stand for a long time and the fury of Titian's night buffets around the frame of the painting while the cold stillness of the church seeps into our bodies. I am gripped by a long, uncontrollable shiver.

"I'm cold…let's go get a coffee."

We exit Gesuiti and stand in de la Spechiera looking to the right where a small bar beckons, but I pull Souheir to the left and stand down on the street looking back at the door. "I came through here one night when the wind was sucking the rain off the lagoon and directly down this street. It was dark and wet and I stopped right here and thought that if the Gesuiti was the building in the background of the painting, then this would be the very spot of Lorenzo's death. The wind was howling, swirling down the street and just for a moment I "felt" that painting."

Souheir snuggles up against the warmth of my coat and smiles.

"Coffee or hot chocolate?"

⚍⚏

The vaporetto ride from San Marco Valdarosso to Salute is one of the shortest distances between stops in all of Venice's water bus system, yet in those brief minutes spent between the two floating fermate, passengers are treated to one of La Serenissima's most breathtaking vistas.

San Marco Valdarosso is the stop at the end of the Canale Grande where it empties into the Bacino of San Marco, and while waiting for the next service, you can view perhaps the most theatrically perfect architectural view in the world. On the other side of this expanse of water, Andrea Palladio's San Giorgio Maggiore floats in its creamy whiteness. I'm always surprised at the small intake of breath that occurs every time I look across at it and today is no exception. I pan slowly to my right bringing my focus back to the low, squat and rather muscular building...the Dogana, or Customs House which is commanding the last piece of Grand Canal embankment as it points into the Bacino. On the rooftop of this narrowest part of the building a magnificent sculpture, resplendent in a coating of gold leaf, shows two gigantic male figures hoisting the globe upon their shoulders while a third female figure said to represent Fortune holds a shield or a piece of fabric aloft while delicately balancing on her left foot. She pivots on this foot as the wind catches her shield and turns her, and she becomes one of the most beautiful weathervanes on the planet.

As I watch, she turns slowly, extending her arms and the shield to point down the length of this triangular shaped building and beyond. Beyond is our destination, and an almost incongruously complicated organization of classical and fanciful architectural elements are combined to create a building that raises itself above the Fondamente of the Grand Canal and culminates in a vast leaden dome that looks down onto the squat form of the Dogana. Madonna della Salute, St. Mary of Health, has occupied one of the most theatrical sites of Venice since 1681 when it was built as an act of gratitude for deliverance from the horrendous plague of 1630-31 when 46,000 Venetians perished.

The familiar sliding, clanging sound of the vaporetto gate comes from behind us as we move up the steep sloping gangplank and onto the small campo in front of Salute. Souheir turns and speaks quietly to me.

"That means the tide is out...right?"

"Yes…the steep angle of the walkway?"

We smile at each other aware that we are sharing our wonder for this city, and continue across the open space to the set of steps that surround Salute. She is counting out loud as we ascend.

"…three, four, five, six"

…And stops on the final one that opens out onto another smaller space in front of a door.

"Any significance to that number?"

"Almost certainly; there's some degree of numerology in almost every architectural element in sacred buildings…and no, I don't know what that significance is."

We pass a woman dressed in a long green woolen coat who asks in perfect English if we will give a donation to the Church. I tell her "no" with my politest smile and open the door for Souheir. Apparently it is not polite enough and the woman switches to Italian to pass some disparaging remarks our way. However just as we pass through the vestibule of the door we are confronted with a sign telling us that the people who are asking for money outside of Salute are not a part of this Church and that visitors should not pay them. The fact that the sign is in English and has no Italian counterpart indicates that the locals are not being singled out for this treatment.

"So what was that about?"

"The redistribution of wealth I presume."

This is not the theatrical entrance that I had planned and we both sort of amble off to the right, following the architecture as it unfolds for us.

There is no central nave and the focus of the church seems to be ambiguous. It is clearly a circular structure so the natural focus of the interior is the center of the building. There is an inner circle that is open to the massive dome beetling above, from which is suspended the longest lamp chain element that I know of. Directly below this centralized chandelier, a plaque marks the center of a complex decorative, inlaid floor of many colored marble.

Inscribed on the plaque is "Unde origo inde Salus"... "From the origin comes Salvation"... And I am yet to receive an explanation of this verse that makes sense. This inner circle that takes up probably a third of the entire interior floor surface is cordoned off and the congregation stands at rope barriers looking into this empty space. Arranged around this circle an octagonal organization allows for an array of small chapels, and directly opposite the main entrance the space is elongated to accommodate the church's central place of worship.

"So do you want me to go over and look at the walls or something?"

Souheir is smiling and I walk over to her and show her my watch

"No, but we've arrived just in time. I want you to listen to something."

Salute is one of Venice's most active churches and services occur throughout the day. The afternoon mass is usually accompanied by music from the organ that is a part of the altar in the main Chapel. Almost on cue the amplified voice of the officiating priest calls to the small congregation that has assembled, and the music of the organ begins to wind its way upwards to the dome above us.

It's an astounding unwinding of sound that flows into the spaces of this vast building, resonating within its concavities, bounding off its columns and pilasters...An unworldly sound that, once it hits the apex of the dome above, trickles back down like waves on a beach that once tossed onto the sand, retreat to the ocean from which they came.

It's as if one sound passes through another and the aural effect is not easily described in words. Standing close together we allow the sound to wash around us and it's one of those moments when no words should be spoken; so we just smile at each other.

For a 3 euro entry fee we are allowed to enter the Sacristy where some of the church's art treasures are housed, and the functional restrictions of this circular building are revealed to us. To access the Sacristy we have to walk down a very narrow and poorly lit passageway that curves along the main interior wall. It is not especially disorienting, but I can imagine that individuals who have anxious moments in confined spaces would not be happy here.

At the end of this "secret passage" we are greeted by a man with one of Venice's friendliest smiles, who takes our money and directs us toward a table that has interpretive sheets in multiple languages explaining the artwork on the ceiling and walls. Tintoretto is represented by a painting, the "Wedding at Cana", but once again our friend Titian steals the day. The sacristy altar piece is adorned with his representation of St. Mark enthroned, receiving a panoply of saints, one being St. Roch who is the patron saint of plague victims. The painting can be viewed at close proximity and we stand for a long time enjoying this intimacy.

"This is really a little hidden treasure trove, I'm always amazed that there is no one back here. You almost never have to share this experience with anyone."

She smiles and nods, we say goodbye to the man with the friendly smile and slide back down the curved passage and out into the body of the church where a Bach fugue is feeling its way around the interior architectural elements.

Once outside we walk up and down the Fondamente trying to take in as much of the exterior as can be seen from close quarters.

"It's amazing how many different architectural elements have been crammed onto this building."

"And this is Baroque?"

"Quintessential Baroque...Over the top Baroque...This church had a huge effect on other Baroque structures throughout the world. It was truly revolutionary. The architect Longhena knew that he was breaking new ground...A circular structure that was holding up a crown. An army of grand scale figures, huge and exaggerated architectural elements...I mean look at those giant volute, spring forms...What are they about? What function do they serve? It's all decoration."

We both smile up at the giant wedding cake of a building and then walk slowly over to the vaporetto stop.

Chapter 12

AN UNEXPECTED MOVE

"John…we 'ave a problem…a little one…"

Claudio is sitting at his desk. It's not a large desk; just your average garden variety normal sized, not enormous desk. However it takes up about a third of the office that it is crammed into. All of this a rather complicated way of letting you know just how small this office is. The boys and I have walked over from Veste and occupy the other two thirds of the office space and stand in front of Claudio with our hands in our jacket pockets. It's cold outside.

"Just a little one…"

Claudio is the rental agent or landlord of a number of Venetian apartments and ours is one of them. He emailed about an hour ago asking us to drop by.

I 'ave made a problem…mistake, and must move you to another appartamento."

"When?"

"Domani…tomorrow if possible."

He smiles as he says this and it is clear that he sees no problem confronting us with such news.

"I find a very nice apartment…much bigger than the one you now 'ave…and I make you a very good price."

"Where is it?"

"In Sant' Elena…What do you think?"

For reasons not entirely clear to me I look at the boys, who both nod their assent for this unexpected change of address.

"So how will we do this?"

"I bring my boat tomorrow…pick up your bags and take you to Sant' Elena. A good idea yes? What time you ready?"

"How about noon?"

"Noon?"

"Yeah…noon."

"Noon?"

Claudio is obviously a little confused by my answer, and begins making gestures with his hands moving them about his head, obviously describing a hat or some head covering.

"Noon…sorella…a sister…Noon?"

The three of us are instantly laughing.

"No...that's a NUN. Noon is mezzogiorno...midday!"

"Really? I thought that Noon was a sister of the church."

We are now all laughing and Claudio jumps up from his desk and shrugs into a dark overcoat.

"Come...we go 'ave coffee!"

The next 24 hours were spent cleaning the delle Veste apartment and packing suitcases. We were promised a preview of the new apartment, but that proved too much for Claudio's organizational skills and the next day found us standing on the little dock that we had first used in our inaugural Venetian disembarkation. A fine rain was swirling its way into a canal that was steely grey and glass smooth. We were homeless, had no idea where our new apartment was, and were uncharacteristically calm about the situation.

The sound of an outboard engine preceded a small wooden boat that made its way toward us. Claudio hunkered down in the stern wearing a rain slicker.

It was immediately clear that there was no chance of all of us getting into this cockleshell, and once the bags were aboard, only Tarik could fit into the small bow seat.

"You take a number 1 vaporetto and I meet you at Sant' Elena. San Zaccaria, Arsenale, Giardini...and then you get off in Sant' Elena. We will wait for you...ciao, ciao!"

They disappeared in a cloud of bluish colored smoke and the canal instantly reclaimed the silence.

"Well, that went well. We are now homeless, have no possessions and our oldest son has just been kidnapped by a pirate!"

As much as she tries, Souheir can't quite get a sense of levity into these words, and I know that she is more than a little anxious about this adventure.

"Come on, we better hurry if we are going to get there to meet them."

It was huge! Large kitchen, two big bedrooms, separate dining room, big bathroom, and two outside patios; all on the third floor! Souheir was very happy; the boys had tripled the size of their bedroom, and I couldn't stop walking through the large glass doors to stand on the patio to look down at grass…and a couple of trees.

Sant' Elena is one of the latest additions to the land mass of Venice. It is now Venice's westernmost point, jutting out into the lagoon, the last vaporetto stop before reaching the Lido.

Legend holds that in the 8th century a ship returning from Constantinople with the relics of Saint Helena entered the lagoon, but ran aground in shallow waters near San Pietro di Castello. The sailors off-loaded the entire cargo including the relics and floated free, but when they returned the relics to the boat, it became enmired again. They considered this a sign that the saint wished to remain on this spot and in 1028 the Augustines erected the first chapel that would house her remains. Subsequent religious orders continued this building project and in 1439 a grand church and convent were completed and if you walk along the Fondamente that runs down the side of Lo Stadio— the football stadium—and take a left you will be confronted by this rather simple, but beautiful old church that is largely forgotten by Venetians, and seldom visited by tourists. Its tall campanile now competes for the sky with 4 giant towers of lights that illuminate Lo Stadio, they however are mute, and this wonderful old structure sounds the hours of the religious day with beautiful sounds from its glorious bells.

Napoleon plundered this old church of all of its possessions and in 1810 it was deconsecrated.

In the 1920s, a reclamation process was begun and the sand bar was backfilled and connected by 3 bridges to Venice proper. Twentieth century Venice began to build apartments to house their population. Sant' Elena became the place to have an apartment. It was higher above sea level than most of the city and aqua alta had little effect. The streets were wide...and straight...and a forest of trees had been planted.

In 1930, Sant' Elena was reconsecrated, her relics were returned, and the church was restored to its present state.

So had we come to the thriving modern hub of Venice's bedroom community?

The Italians are among the longest-lived of all Mediterranean peoples and among them the Venetians live the longest. Clean maritime air, a diet that is largely seafood and the constant exercise of climbing bridges and stairs are said to be the contributing factors at work here. And most of the young, nouveau riche Venetians that moved into Sant' Elena in its 1950's heydays... are still here!

The collective age of the residents of just our apartment building was about a million years! We were the only young family in the neighborhood and there was little hope of becoming invisible in this environment. It was wonderfully quiet and the chance to walk among trees on actual grass a luxury unknown to us in our Veste days. However there were often times when we actually wondered if we were talking too loudly when we were inside the apartment. Souheir passed an edict that said there would be no eating of apples after 8:00p.m as she was frightened the crunching would wake the neighbors!

The vap stop at Sant' Elena became our fermata and we quickly generated a "nodding" acquaintance with fellow travelers. Our great discovery was the bar and pizzeria that was on the corner of the first building that we encountered after walking from the stop through the tree filled park on the way home. It is staffed by one extended family, and we quickly established friendships with father, mother, daughters and their husbands...Even the family dog. Morning coffee on the way to class, afternoon spritz, evening beer and pizza...We seldom passed by without dropping in and we became Giovanni and Susanna in a group of locals.

It wasn't just Sant' Elena's wide streets, (almost boulevards by comparison with the calle of most of Venice) and vaguely Neapolitan architecture that changed our outlook on Venice...Not just the fact that I could walk beneath trees and over grass. Sant' Elena is removed from the heart of Venice; a suburb of the old lady; and this distance supplies a perspective that made me look at La Serenissima with new eyes. The lagoon laps at three sides of these reclaimed islands and its presence is always a part of every day. When the winds howl in from the Adriatic they whip these waters into considerable waves and I spent many mornings standing on the Fondamente feeling the pulse and power of this water as it crashed ashore.

Standing at the vaporetto stop each morning, we looked across this expanse of water to San Servolo the ancient sanitarium for the mentally infirmed of the upper classes, across to the Armenian island of San Lazzaro degli Armeni and finally to the long line of the Lido stretching south to the horizon. And each day this water had a different presence. Each day it reflected a different light; and a different story awaited us as we walked onto the floating fermata. Some mornings the water was mirror smooth and placid, others it tossed the dock around in such ways that we didn't descend to it until the vaporetto was making its final approach. On September 11th in 1970, a motoscafo left Sant' Elena with a contingent of passengers and began its 5 minute journey across to the Lido. Halfway there it was struck by a series of freak waves and a small tornado and it sank, killing several on board.

The lagoon was, and is, Venice's protective barrier against the outside world; it was the primary influence that made Venice a maritime power, and living in Sant' Elena allowed me to see this defining element in an entirely new way.

Our commute to school each day was always by boat and standing on the open deck we would watch the vista slowly open before us as we leapfrogged from fermata to fermata along the Fondamente that runs all the way down to San Marco.

The Giardini planted by Napoleon in his attempts to gentrify the city passes by on the right and San Giorgio slowly gathers height on the left until just after the Arsenale stop you can look across the Bacino and without turning your head see all three of Andrea Palladio's churches. San Giorgio, Zittelle, and Redentore each rise above the buildings of the Giudecca to bid us Good Morning; and each day I remind myself that such a remarkable view is simply a part of my everyday life. After San Marco, the vaporetto enters the Grand Canal and it's like entering a burrow or tunnel as the city closes around and the presence of the lagoon is left behind.

Between Sant' Elena and the Lido the small fortified island of San Andrea acts like a cork in a flagon of wine and controls the entrance from the Adriatic into the lagoon. The channel used by boats to enter the lagoon through the half mile wide break in the Lido winds between treacherous sandbars and presents all entering vessels broadside to what at first glance is a rather picturesque building. It is a low and rather unimposing structure of brick and Istrian stone that seems nothing more than a warehouse with a number of open doorways that lead down a grassed bank to the water. These doorways are set up in tiers. One, exactly at water level, and one 10 meters above that. Behind each of these "doorways" however, was a cannon, and mounted on the top battlements another battery of them. A single volley from all of these would tear a vessel apart from the water line to its rigging and it's only when you ride a boat past this fortress that you realize how wonderfully lethal is its design.

Chapter 13

HORSES...

I have spent a great deal of time attempting to understand and mentally reconstruct the daily life of ancient Venetians, and in this pursuit, read all information about Venice that I can lay my eyes on. This information encourages my story into a living narrative and I look for verification in the streets and campos of modern Venice. The problem is that modern Venice is architecturally anything but modern, and I am often lulled into extrapolating ideas of 11th or 12th century Venice by looking at 16th and 17th century buildings. Reading that the northern area of Castello, where Zanipolo now stands was the site of the city's horse stables simply did not interface with the picture that I had created in my head, and so I pursued this information with zeal.

I find the fact that during this time horses were a major form of transportation around the city absolutely fascinating and realize that their presence has been totally absent for a long while. However, it is clear that the use of the horse once represented cutting edge technology especially in a military application. Any land battle was won or lost on the strength and capabilities of one's cavalry, and as Venice's ambition turned towards the Veneto and land conquest, the horse must have been a pivotal part of that expansion.

Among the great powers of Europe, Venice was outstanding in its participation in the religious crusades that were called by a variety of Popes. The papal call was to young Christian warriors, exalting them to drive the dreaded Muslims from the Holy Land. While the Islamic world was never in grave danger from the crusaders, it was forced to withdraw from much of the Levant and for almost 200 years Jerusalem was under the rule of Crusader Kings. Venice was a city of very pious people and their involvement was driven by this religious zeal. However, it would be denying the obvious to not see that the Pope wanted more than just Venice's citizenry. She possessed the most powerful navy in the Adriatic and possibly the Mediterranean and it was this presence that was required.

Venice played an extremely important role in all of the Crusades and their attempts to control the Holy Land. It was her navies that ferried most of the Christian zealots down the Adriatic to the Middle East. She played a major role in this religious zeal...But the fact that it was also a lucrative business should not escape our notice. A large part of the Crusader cargoes was the transportation of war horses, for those soldiers were of course, Knights. Of all the European powers, Venice alone was the most experienced in diplomatic encounters with the Middle Eastern powers, and in fact on many occasions entered into trading agreements with the non-Christians of the area. Venice was therefore the perfect choice to play a pivotal role in all of the Crusades and to the great credit of its citizenry it answered these calls when many others ignored them.

The first Crusaders literally walked to the Holy Land, an enormous trek through often hostile territory. One wonders how much war was left in a war horse by the time it had walked this incredibly long road. Richard the Lionheart of England radically changed this process. He taxed the English very heavily and his "war purse" was full. He could afford to be transported by boat to the Holy Land and established a tradition of levying a fee against his knights for the transportation of their livery. It was the great Venetian cargo vessels that were sought out for this task and the Venetians responded by redesigning their craft to accommodate this equine cargo.

The horses were stabled on the Lido before departure, but many arrived there from across the lagoon. The number of horses that were a part of this city is something that I cannot find out, and I am left with the fact that it's not just that their presence has long since disappeared, but also any memory of this presence. And so there are no horses in Venice... Such a statement is patently untrue, dear Reader, and the preceding page or so is just a way for me to introduce you to some of my favorite things in all of Venice...Perhaps all of the world.

After you enter the main front doors of the Basilica San Marco, you cross a small open space and its floor of exquisitely colored marble pieces and ascend a short flight of steps before entering the doors which will open onto the central nave of the church. At these doors, turn and look to your right and you will see a staircase of ancient worn stone ascending steeply into a tight and poorly lighted passageway. Years ago there used to be a small, simply lettered sign that said "Cavalli" and it occurred to me that only people who knew what they were looking for would venture into this gloom.

At the top of this quite steep ascent you will be confronted by a ticket booth and an attendant will ask you to pay an entry fee before you can proceed further. You are now in the Museum of San Marco which has been extended and improved over the past few years. Years ago, when I first came up these stairs there was really only one attraction, and you stepped out onto the balcony overlooking the open space of the Piazza San Marco to look at 4 glorious bronze horses standing guard over the front door of this ancient church. They are simply known as the horses of San Marco...I Cavalli.

The earliest history of Venice placed her firmly in the Byzantine world. It is often said that she was "born and brought up Greek" and her relationship with the Greek world is reflected in almost every element of her life.

The Basilica San Marco is considered by many to be the largest, most beautiful Byzantine church in all of the world. As Venice slowly gained control over the Adriatic and the Mediterranean seas, and her mercantile empire spread southwards, she maintained this Byzantine relationship and the ancient city of Constantinople, now Byzantium became a major marshaling place for her merchants. By 1167 it is estimated that there were as many as 60,000 Latins that were residents of Constantinople, and many of these were Venetians. They were riding a crest of success. They possessed the strongest navy, the most far flung trading organization. They had slowly taken over entire sections of the city and populated it with sumptuous palaces; they were proud and definitely not humble. In 1161, after an attack upon the Genoan enclave by the Pisans, both groups were expelled, leaving the Venetians once again to monopolize both the trade and maritime activity of the great city. In 1171 however, when the Latins once again were returned to their former trading presence, the Venetians attacked the Genoese sector and the Byzantine Emperor immediately arrested all of them and confiscated their property.

A period of negotiations and unstable treaties followed and by 1180 the tension between all parties had risen to a fever pitch. A public rally against the favoritism being shown the Latin traders spilled over into violence and one of Constantinople's worst massacres ensued. Any Latins, regardless of age or gender that did not escape the city were murdered and all of their properties looted. The clergy came in for particularly savage treatment and the Papal Legate, Cardinal John, was beheaded and his head dragged through the city tied to the tail of a dog.

Venetians were held captives of Constantinople for more than a decade and tension between the two powers remained at a fever pitch. Constantinople was such a linchpin in the Venetian trading empire that it was inconceivable that this situation would be allowed to continue, and the great prowess of Venetian diplomacy was put to one of its greatest tests. In this case, however, fate stepped in and presented a different resolution.

The fourth Crusade of 1201 was ill fated from its very conception. When Pope Innocent the III came to power in 1198 he made a commitment to mount a crusade to restore Jerusalem to papal power with an expedition that would enter the Holy Land through Egypt. By even the most optimistic evaluations, the preceding crusades had extracted a huge cost in human misery for what little was actually achieved, and his call to arms received a rather lukewarm reception among the European monarchies.

And so the Fourth Crusade was launched with no kings included in its membership, no fleet to sail them to the East...And worst of all, no money to purchase one.

However, through the meteoric preaching of a French cleric called Fulk of Neuilly, a level of interest was revived and the leadership of the crusade was given to a Frenchman, Count Thibaut who unfortunately died soon after. The leadership was then given to an Italian, Boniface I, who was Marquis of Montferrat whose brother and nephew had both been Kings of Jerusalem. Boniface was known to be an ally of the Genoans—and this did not put him in good stead with the Venetians.

The Doge at the time, Enrico Dandolo was 94 years old and blind, but was blessed with great health and vigor and an extremely nimble intellect. In 1201 he received a delegation of six French knights who had been sent to conscript the great naval skills of Venice into the gathering army that was to march on the Holy Land. To be sure, Dandolo was not surprised to be invited into the ranks of the Crusaders, but what the French knights asked of him was entirely another thing. The Crusade was expected to consist of 20,000 foot soldiers, 9,000 squires and 4,500 knights and their horses; and the Venetians were asked to supply the vessels that would transport this enormous army AND enough food to sustain it. In all probability the size of the fleet required could only be matched by some of the battles of the ancient Roman world. In other words an armada of this size was unknown in the contemporary times of the 1200's.

If Venice complied, she would need to build many new vessels, some designed specifically for the task, but more importantly would need to bring most of the vessels of its far flung merchant fleet back to Venice. The money lost in trade alone would be considerable, but these vessels would require about 30,000 sailors to man them which would leave a scant force at home in Venice should she need protecting. It was a wondrous mixture of piety, religious zeal, and mercantilism that eventually delivered the final deal to the French contingent and through them to Innocent III.

The Venetians agreed to transport 35,000 men, 4,500 horses and their food at an agreed price of 2 silver marks for each foot soldier and horse and 4 silver marks for each knight. The French would collect these monies and pay them in a lump sum to the Venetians. The Venetians also contributed, at no charge to the Crusade, an extra 50 fully armed war galleys, provided that all spoils were split between them and the French. They promised to assemble all of these vessels within an 18 month period of time to be ready to depart in June of 1202. The cost to both Venetian individuals and to the state was staggering and Dandolo somehow convinced them to do so, knowing that until the army arrived in Venice, none of this expenditure would be offset.

By June, the fleet was assembled and the knights and their horses began arriving. They were encamped in the sand hills of the Lido and the air was filled with the excitement of expected departure. However, by June 29th only 11,000 Crusaders had arrived and the atmosphere had soured considerably. A month later, only 1,000 more had arrived. Doge Dandolo was in serious trouble and his enthusiasm for the Crusades was now questioned by most Venetians. He granted an extension on the final payment, but by August, insisted that the Crusaders pay the 85,000 silver marks that had been agreed upon 18 months before. Knights were asked to pay much more than the 4 silver mark fare, but at the end of all of their efforts, the Crusaders could only come up with 51,000 marks—and they still owed the Venetians 34,000 more. With masterful diplomacy, Dandolo impressed upon his fellow Venetians how badly it would go for them if they just refused to join the Crusade. They would be seen in the poorest light by the religious community and far worse, stood to lose face with their trading partners in Europe.

It was clear that Venice needed to be rid of what was now an unhappy and potentially dangerous army that was camped literally on their doorstep, and equally clear that Venice would be financially ruined if some fiscal agreement was not concluded quickly. Once again Dandolo showed his great skills and he negotiated an agreement whereby Venice would loan the outstanding 34,000 marks to what was now a somewhat ragtag army. At last the armada made ready to depart. However, a stipulation of the loan was that the crusaders would winter in the port of Zara, on the east coast of the Adriatic in modern day Croatia because it was too close to winter and the weather and winds were not favorable to sail to the Holy Land. Zara had long been a problem to the Venetians for it was from here that the Zaran pirates routinely raided Venetian convoys as they made their way homeward up the Adriatic. To winter in Zara required that the fleet defeat the port city first. Not only was Zara a Christian city, but its king, Emeric of Hungary, had taken the crusader's cross the year before, and under canon law, was under papal protection. Three cities were attacked: Trieste, Moglia, and Zara and how these actions were finagled by the Venetians is not clear. What is clear is that after the fall of Zara, whose inhabitants hung huge canvases with painted crosses on them over their city walls to show that they were Christians (obviously to no avail), the Crusade stalled. Mired in guilt and discontent; with its major players unsure of how they had been so distracted from their goal, the Fourth Crusade looked as if it was over before it actually began.

What transpired then reads like fiction, but initiated a series of actions and reactions that would literally change the course of Western Civilization. A small German vessel arrived, carrying envoys from a powerful lord who was a pretender to the crown of Germany. He had aligned himself with all the powerful leaders that would listen to him and had thrown in his lot with the young prince Alexius II who was attempting to substantiate his claim to the Emperorship of Constantinople!

Alexius II was the son of Isaac II, the Emperor of Constantinople. Isaac ll was blinded and removed from office by his own brother (Aleius ll's uncle...also called Alexius.) This Alexius was dutifully crowned Alexius III and the young boy escaped to Europe where he toured the great courts attempting to rally support against his treacherous uncle. The envoys aboard the German vessel assured the Crusaders that the people of Constantinople hated Alexius III and would welcome the young prince with open arms.

The armada would have to pass right by Constantinople...Why, it was hardly more than a small side trip. But then the sugar was stirred into the mix. The young prince promised that once he was emperor he would resupply the armada so that it could continue on its way to the Holy Land...AND he would pay the Crusaders 200,000 silver marks. This was more than enough to garner the attention of most of the Crusaders. But wait...that's not all. He promised to add 10,000 Byzantine soldiers to the Crusader army!

...And that's not all. (And this is the part of the promises that clinched the deal)...He would place the Orthodox Church under the power of Rome. He promised to mend the great schism between the Eastern and Western churches that was more than a century old.

The Crusade was back on track!

Dandolo must have been a very worried man however. Constantinople was the most important city in the entire Venetian trading organization and the Venetians were only just beginning to return to their stature of favored trading partner after the conflict of the 1180s. The old Doge simply could not afford to jeopardize Venice's mercantile interests.

The armada of Crusaders and the young Alexius arrived in Constantinople... Declared to the people of Constantinople that he had returned to claim his rightful position as their King...and was showered with rocks and abuse. The people of Constantinople did not want this new emperor!

After suffering through several days of insults and showers of rocks, on July the 5th 1203, the Fourth Crusade attacked Constantinople.

The walls of this great city had never been broached in their long history and this situation seemed likely to persist. The attacking boats were consistently repelled by showers of stones from the top of the walls, and the day appeared to be lost. Then something almost miraculous happened. Dandolo, resplendent in his official robes aboard his official boat, a red trireme flashing with gold embellishments, ordered his rowers to bring all speed forward to beach the boat at the base of the walls. The red boat put on a huge spurt of speed and with Dandolo standing on the prow, drove itself onto the beach. It was apparently a galvanizing act of courage. (Of course it can be said that the old doge was blind and simply didn't know how bad the situation was) and it rallied all of the other boats which followed. The Crusaders managed to take control of only a small section of the great walls, but the Venetians set fire to a section of the city that housed many of the wealthy and it shook the great metropolis.

Alexius III continued in his treacherous ways, and gathering up a large horde of gold and jewels, fled. The young prince was quickly crowned Alexius IV in the hopes of restoring order and civility. He immediately delivered 100,000 silver marks to the Crusaders who in turn paid the Venetians the 34,000 owed to them. But Alexius could not raise the other 100,000 marks and he began to loot churches and treasuries, and in general behave in ways that did not endear him to the local Greeks, his new subjects. It made him and the visiting Crusaders immensely unpopular with the local population, and the Greeks began setting fires in the Venetian quarter along the harbor area.

On August 19th a group of armed Pisans and Venetians retaliated by setting fire to homes in the city center. A strong wind blew in and the fires quickly raced out of control. More than a hundred thousand Byzantines lost their homes. The city was now completely polarized and Alexius IV made it clear that he would pay nothing more to the Crusade. The winter was spent in stalemate; the emperor hid behind his walls, while the Venetians and French took over the north side of the harbor.

During this time the young emperor was assassinated and after the coup, a new emperor was crowned. Their champion dead, the Fourth Crusade declared war on Constantinople. There are many conflicting descriptions of the battle that ensued, and much should be said about the cowardice of this city's defenders, but when this great city fell it was largely due to the courage and skill of the Venetians sailors, and on April 13th of 1204, Constantinople capitulated.

What followed is almost impossible to comprehend; the attacking army fell upon the riches of Constantinople like slavering wolves. It is estimated that they looted 900,000 silver marks worth of riches in these 3 days of rapine. While the Venetians were as involved as any other of the Crusaders, it was said, however, that they were more circumspect with their looting, and that they had a more refined appreciation for the loot that Dandolo had crated and sent back to Venice.

There is simply no way to present what transpired in these three days in anything but the light of barbarism. Most historians believe that this heinous act so weakened the great city, that it was inevitable that it would eventually fall to the Islamic world. The great schism between the Eastern and Western Christians was now complete. On April the 14th of 2004, marking the 800th year of this desecration, Pope John Paul II officially apologized on behalf of the Western church. The great British historian Steven Runciman said "There was never a greater crime against humanity than the 4th Crusade"...

⊟⊟

A cold, wet wind swirls around the main doorway of the Basilica San Marco. It has blown across the Bacino from San Giorgio and rattled between the columns that surround the Piazza San Marco to push at me as I stand at the bottom of a long, dark stairway that ascends into the gloom above me. The steps look wet, and probably are, and the old metal railing is so cold that it nearly sticks to my hand. I'm going up. I've done it countless times, and every time I do what I'm doing now. I stand still and smile. I'm about to visit some old friends, some of my most prized moments have been had at the top of these stairs. Just for a moment, I hope that I will never become too enfeebled to climb them…and then I'm moving up.

Dear Reader,

It occurs to me that a little side note is necessary here, as I feel the need to explain what will follow. Rather than a dispassionate academic description; what follows are the words of someone who has become completely infatuated with four sculpted friends over a protracted period of time, and on many occasions. He has completely anthropomorphized them and the time that he spends in front of them can best be described as conversations.

John

Horses behave very differently in a stable than they do when they are out running free in a pasture.

The Horses of San Marco are now stabled. They live in a corner space of one of the most beautiful Byzantine churches in the world but without the artificial lights that surround them, cleverly aimed to accentuate their "best" features, these horses would live in perpetual twilight above the vastness of the central nave of San Marco.

My first reactions are always keyed by the turquoise, green and gold of them and there is a weariness about these four beautiful beasts that stand in front of me that is not easy to describe. The eyes have been worked in such a way that they are both alert and focused, but turned down towards the nose and accentuated by a slight raising of the eye brow…They are sad eyes. The turquoise gold patina is a result of long years of exposure and the inexplicable scarifying lines that seem to cover most of their bodies leave me with a feeling that they have been worked hard. They are certainly four individuals and it didn't take many visits before I could easily see the subtle differences each one displays.

They are the spoils of war, a part of the booty sent back to Venice from Constantinople by Enrico Dandolo all those years ago. Apparently they languished in the military center of Venice; the Arsenale, for 50 years before being mounted on the façade of San Marco, but since that time have insinuated themselves into the Venetian psyche in such a way that they have become an icon almost as powerful as St. Mark's lion.

They are a quadriga, a team of four horses, and they almost certainly at one time were connected to a chariot that would of course been equipped with a charioteer. Chariot racing was a profoundly important element within the social structure of the ancient world and the Hippodrome of Constantinople was as much the focus of this great city as any of its official buildings. We know that at least two different quadrige of horses decorated the great structure, and it is generally agreed that the four horses of San Marco are one of those. In those hellish days when the 4th Crusade raped and pillaged Constantinople, we can imagine them being lowered from their lofty perch and transported to Venetian vessels waiting at the docks.

The Horses of San Marco have had the reins and harness removed, their bridles taken from their head, and even the bit cut away from their mouths. They have been set free! The question of course is by whom, and the Venetian stories and myth that swirl through every calle and canal tell us that they were set free by their liberators…And then allowed to stand unfettered on their great Cathedral! They still wear their horse collars, but that presumably is because the collar actually serves to hide the joint where the head (cast separately) is attached to the body. Their mouths are slightly open to accommodate what is left of the bit which still exerts enough pressure on the lips to produce the small wrinkles at each side of their mouth; the sign of a correctly fitted bridle.

They each raise a leg...In salute we are told, but not by people who know horses. They are seeking attention and these legs would paw at the ground demanding a response were they not frozen in bronze. Perhaps the most perplexing question presented by these four most beautiful horses... How long have they been frozen in bronze? Most experts agree that Constantine decorated the Hippodrome of Constantinople with them. Did he bring them with him from his doomed Rome? Or did he collect them from the Grecian world that he had invaded?

Are they ancient Greek pieces or do they come from ancient Rome? They have been ascribed to the great sculptor/architect Phidias from 4th Century BC Athens and they have also been placed in 4th Century AD Rome! An enormous amount of scholarship has been brought to bear upon the conundrums presented by these horses. Style, structure, metallurgy, surface decoration and historic convention all present evidence to support a host of theories. Unfortunately, almost none of this information is in agreement and it cannot honestly be said that a conclusive decision has been achieved. In our 21st century, we are coming to a new understanding and definition of the term "bronze", and this reflects upon current and historic findings. It is now agreed that the term "bronze" is a rather loose definition and encompasses any metal made with a predominant body of copper and a host of other metals including tin and lead.

The four glorious beasts that I am looking at seem to be made from a very refined form of this alloy. They were moved inside...They were stabled...in 1982, and for the first time were examined using advanced technologies. A major discovery of this examination is that they are created from a bronze that is at least 98% copper, a fact that literally places them in a category all of their own. Not far from my home in Montana is a quite well renowned bronze foundry that casts large, monumental works for sculptors from all over

North America. When I asked if they could produce large sculptures with such a high content of copper, I was told that it was unlikely and that at any rate, they would not make such an attempt because the likelihood of a failed pour would be too great.. Research leads us to believe that the high copper content of the horses is because of the gilding process that has been used on their surface.

A layer of gold has been attached to the finished surface of the horses, and the way in which this has been done leads some experts to declare them of Roman birth. It seems that the Romans used a rather more sophisticated process than did the ancient Greeks, but this is far from conclusive data and new, revealing research of ancient Greek bronzes seems to be turning up evidence to refute these claims.

The arcane chemistry of mercury allows it to dissolve gold; creating a strange amalgam that will fuse to bronze surfaces. It can be achieved in two ways. The metal can be coated with mercury and then gold leaf laid over the top of it. The mercury dissolves the gold and then literally vaporizes leaving only the gold on the metal surface. The mercury can be mixed with gold to produce a bizarre paste which the bronze is coated with. Then the sculpture is heated and once again the mercury escapes as a gas. Gold leaf with no flux or mercury can simply be glued to a metal surface with a gum and then burnished into its surface. Gold is the most ductile of all metals and can be hammered into extremely thin sheets. An ounce of gold can produce enough gold leaf to cover 2 tennis courts and when it is burnished onto a metal surface it creates an almost molecular bond.

When mercury is used as a bonding fluxing agent it is most effective on bronze that has a very high copper content.

The lights trained on the horses is quite theatrical and outside of these focused spots the rest of the room is predominantly shadowed. Standing in the shadow, I am aware that it is possible that these 4 were once immaculately clad in a very substantial layer of gold and that if they still wore this golden skin, it would reflect the light so that most of these shadows would disappear. It is entirely feasible that they literally blazed their golden reflection over the ancient Hippodrome. At the "stabling" of these horses in 1982, many other discoveries were made. The scarifying lines that for so long were thought to be the destructive work of demented barbarians were measured and examined microscopically. They were found to be all exactly the same width and seem to be made with the same tool. There is clearly intention in these marks...But to what end? Offered up as an explanation by some historians, is the idea that these marks actually "tone down" the golden reflective quality of the surface. This explanation does not gain much traction with me, and I wonder if indeed we are not left looking at a layer of gold that is in fact an undercoat, that these scarifications are intended to help the final layer of gold leaf adhere.

I stand in front of the left hand side animal and have to control an urge to reach out and cup his mouth in my hand the way that I greet my own horse. The horse to his immediate left turns his head, making sure that my attention will come his way...and the same old dance begins. A dance where I walk up and down along the protective guard rail, smiling, visually patting and scratching. Those beautiful ears, so alert, the insides all ringed around with tufts of hair almost braided into a pattern...The sad eyes with a line deeply indenting the cornea. In the center of this the ancient sculptor shows his skill focusing the eye using a small crescent moon shaped incision...called a lunula. It is the final touch that establishes the intelligence of these animals.

It occurs to me that great poetic license has been taken by ancient sculptors and that even the proportions and breed characteristics exhibited by these horses are unique. They are swift and strong legged, without any of the almost effete finesse of an Arab horse; strong and powerful without any of the bulk and stolid qualities of the ancient European war horse; all of this overlaid with an air of intelligence, even prescience.

These four beautiful equine beings have been moved 6 times in their known history. It is said that on each occasion an empire has fallen. In 330 when

Constantine moved them to the new city that he named after himself, the western Roman Empire fell. They were "acquired" by the Venetians in 1204 in the sack of Byzantium. Napoleon stole them in 1797 and took them to Paris, only to have his own empire come crashing down around his ears. They were reinstalled on San Marco but were removed for safety during the First World War which saw the fall of the Austro Hungarian Empire. During the Second World War they were again moved to safety, and the Third Reich fell.

In the 1980's the horses were considered at risk and removed for restoration roughly coinciding with the fall of the USSR.

I never tire of looking at them and am always sad when I turn away to descend the stairs back down to the Piazza. I hear them nicker and call to me as I make my descent. I offer up a silent promise that I will return.

⚌

"Non rompermi i colleoni"

The large man sitting across the table from me is enunciating this sentence very clearly with exaggerated theatrical emphasis. He repeats this several more times and then I mimic his performance until I can say it with a rapid fluidity. He lifts the small glass of clear liquid in a salute and the six of us sitting around the table collapse in laughter. We have travelled over to the Lido to have dinner with one of Souheir's classmates and after a wonderful meal have moved on to the clear liquid—grappa.

The subject of profanity has arisen and Massimo who is the only Italian among the polyglot diners is leading us through the subtleties of cursing in Italian. Apart from him, each of us is a student at the Istituto Venezia and as superb as their language instruction is, it should come as no surprise that they have not spent time teaching us how to curse. Massimo's English is good… better than most of our Italian and he chokes back laughter and the last of his fierce drink and says,

"Don't break my balls!"

"Really? Colleoni means balls?"

"Si…testicles."

"The only Colleoni that I know of is Bartolomeo…"

"And his horse…campo Zanipolo. You must go back and look at the family crest."

"Why?"

"Just go look at it again…"

It is another Venetian horse and I have stood looking up at this great animal and its strikingly postured rider many, many times. I have certainly looked at the crest that is featured on the grand plinth of this sculpture, and am just a little piqued by the fact that I'm not sure what Massimo is alluding to. Clearly the first thing on tomorrow's agenda is a trip to Campo Zanipolo.

The water of Venice waits at your feet in every canal, splashes across the worn flagstones and cobbles during the rains that frequent every month of its year, and is often a part of the air that swirls down the calle and across the campi. The fogs and mists add mystery and wonder to the atmosphere of Venice, soft veils and tendrils of microscopic water particles that cling to eyelashes and eventually glaze all surfaces.

It was one of those mornings, and my muffled footsteps moved through the low fog down to the vaporetto stop at Sant' Elena. I stood in the rear of the vap for most of the journey around the "back" of Venezia as I rode past San Pietro and Bacino, past the rear entrance of the Arsenale to Fondamente Nuove. The black and white motoscafo travelled slowly through the silvery air, its sonar making slow revolutions on top of the wheelhouse. By the time I stepped up the gangplank, however, the silver was beginning to give way to gold and it was apparent that a warm morning sun was slowly making its way down into the layer of fog. Looking across the lagoon, I could just begin to make out the shapes of the trees on San Michele as the light began to warm them from a nameless dark tone into a recognizable green.

It's only a five minute walk down the side of Venice's major hospital to the campo of Zanipolo and I entered a space completely shrouded in muffled grey. A small café that takes its name from the famous sculptural monument of this campo is tucked into the row of buildings that line one side of it, and I move quickly inside and order a cappuccino while taking a warm brioche from the glass display case on the counter. The familiar thwack of the emptying coffee basket, hiss of steam, clank of porcelain, several swift flowing motions and the coffee arrives on the counter in front of me. By lunch time this café will assemble 20 or so tables in the space in front of its window. The platea...where its patrons will dine outside. Currently there are only two tables cuddled up to the front of the building, slowly dripping the moisture of the foggy morning. I take my cup and brioche and move toward the door. The barista raises a questioning eyebrow, but then he too sees, and smiling, comes around the bar and we exit together.

The golden light is slicing down through the fog which simply melts in its presence and the aedicula that sit atop the façade of the giant gothic church hiding in the fog across the campo are slowly being exposed. The effect, however, is reversed and instead of the light descending, the architecture seems to be rising.

"Bella, bella..."

I look over the rim of my coffee and smile my agreement.

The rest of the building is coming into view...and now its neighbor the hospital with its wonderfully complicated sculptural face. And then Bartolomeo

Colleoni rises up into the gold light. For a brief moment it is just him, and then the head of the magnificent horse he is astride. In another minute or two the entire campo has "arrived" and shines, sparkling in the newly arrived light. The barista and I smile at each other one more time and we return to the café where I pay and wish him good morning.

In the center of Campo Zanipolo across from the front doors of the hospital stands a tall cluster of 6 columns ringed round by an iron fence, and on the top of this stands a fearsome bronze horse and its equally fierce rider. The horse is straining impatiently forward, raising its left front leg...Almost pawing at the space in front of it. He is restrained by a barrel-chested bull of a man in magnificent armor who controls this quivering equine power simply with the posture of his body. The reins are not pulled tight, there is no tension from the bit into the horse's' mouth. Lightly holding the reins in his left hand, his right holds a symbol of authority and power... A short staff that is called a fasces.

You will need binoculars or an art history text to see the face above the huge chest plate; and it is here that I find myself emotionally disconnecting from the drama of this great sculpture. Colleoni's thick lips curl back slightly as he glares past all who would look up at him. He is contemptuous of we who are down here on the pavement and would have no compunction about riding this giant horse right over us. There is a cruelty in his face that poisons the posture and I can't seem to escape the disdainful arrogance that the figure exudes. Once you decide that there is a strong resemblance to Mussolini, you can never look back up there again without disquiet. And now dear Reader, I have sown that seed in you and in all probability, it will affect your viewing too.

Who is this man? What is this sculpture doing here in this place? Who produced it...And when was it completed?

I smile as I ask these questions because the mystery of Venice is immediately apparent...a story that is complex and arcane resides in every brick and flagstone of this campo...waiting to be told.

History is filled with moments in time when great changes occurred and historians spend their time looking for these moments. It brings order and sequence to their narratives; it's an attempt to make sense of events. Many historians see one of these fulcrum moments in the time when Venice turned its expansive energies away from the sea that it knew so well and began a series of conquests on terra firma. The land. It wasn't just that the technology and know-how of land battles were absent in the long history of Venice; it was in fact a good deal more complicated.

The territories that the Venetians initially moved on were typical of their time and geography. These city states were feudal and the organization of dukes, lords and serfs was completely foreign to the invading Venetians. The business of making war on land and the "business" of administering these territories once subdued was entirely new to Venice, and the prowess and power of its maritime experiences held little sway here.

The art of warfare was invested in a small group of highly trained generals who could be hired from all over Europe. They would, for a fee, organize the local citizenry and merchants into an army. They knew about fortification, the movement of troops and the rules of engagement. They were mercenaries...These generals were called condottieri. Bartolomeo Colleoni was one such condottiere. He was born in Bergamo and saw his first military service in Piacenza, and served under the famous Carmagnola who was eventually executed by the Venetians. Colleoni from then on, soldiered for the Serene Republic and although Gianfrancesco Gonzaga held the official office of Commander-in-Chief, Colleoni in fact controlled the army. His was a successful career and the Venetian Republic slowly manifested large holdings of land adding most of the cities of the Veneto to its territories. When peace was made with Milan, he went to work for the Milanese and then flip-flopped back to the Venetians but left again because they would not grant him the title of Captain-General. He briefly returned to the Milanese, but the Venetians induced him to return to them by granting him this title for life, and giving him a very large land grant. This maneuvering between powers left him with enemies within both empires and while no charges of treachery were ever brought against him, many of the Venetian patricians were wary of him. He seems to have left the scene quietly and withdrew to his estate where he was noted for his experiments in agriculture and his charitable works.

This civilized and somewhat benign character is nowhere present in the puffed up, pompous figure who sits astride the horse above me as I walk around to the stone plaque containing the Colleoni crest. In the lower portion of the crest are 3 fig shaped forms...Until now I always thought of them as such. Testicles? I feel like an adolescent milking double entendres out of every imaginable image. Is this where the myth that he had 3 testicles came from? Before I left the apartment this morning I checked the dictionary... testicles in Italian are coglioni. It's all a little silly, something of a fool's errand, but if I had not chased down this grappa lubricated rabbit hole, I would not be standing in this magnificent light, would have completely missed this amazing moment. I walk across the campo in the direction of the hospital and climb to the top step of the small bridge that spans the canal Rio degli Mendicanti. While the distance from the sculpture has increased, I am now closer to the level of the horse and rider and can now feel their motion in a different way.

At his death in 1475, Colleoni left 216,000 Ducats to the Venetian Republic to be used in the Turkish war with the one stipulation that an equestrian sculpture honoring himself was commissioned and erected in front of the Basilica San Marco. This was a huge amount of money and the Venetian state was unlikely to refuse it. However, there was a serious problem that had to be overcome; one that Colleoni himself must surely have been aware of. Before Napoleon's defeat of the city, no Venetian individual was permitted to be more important than the Republic. No statue to any doge was ever set up in a public place. No doge was ever interred in the Basilica San Marco. The Piazza San Marco is decorated with only three flag poles...It is the heart of the Republic and as such has always been sacrosanct. A competition was declared for Colleoni's sculpture and three finalists completed models. Andrea dell Verrocchio from Florence, Alessandro Leopardi from Venice, and Bartolomeo

Veltrano from Padua completed their models and in 1483 the contract was awarded to Verrocchio; one of the most talented sculptors and painters to be found in Europe at this time. History has not been kind to this remarkable artist and he is more often remembered for being the master of a famous apprentice, Leonardo da Vinci, than for the magnificent works he completed.

The final clay figure was finished and ready to be cast when he died in 1488, and Leopardi was commissioned to oversee the casting process. There is, of course, no way of knowing how faithfully Leopardi followed Verrocchio's preparations and there are many historians who offer up evidence of "meddling" on his part. No matter how collaborative his efforts, the end product was a tour de force of bronze casting and assemblage and probably the most outstanding piece of sculpture in the Western World at that time. Leopardi designed the 6 column base and the Venetians set it up in front of San Marco… But not the Basilica San Marco…The Scuola San Marco, which is the building that the hospital now inhabits! Subterfuge? Sleight of hand? Outright dishonesty? Maybe just more of the good old Venetian merchant skulduggery where you get the money no matter what…

None of this resonates as the truth with me, and I suspect the real story is buried in that place where anecdote becomes history. Looking across this space in this spectacular light, it occurs to me that there is no better setting in all of Venice for this sculpture.

Chapter 14

MORE LARCENY....

CA'D'ORO

I've had a rather aimless day and about half way through a morning walk, deep into the sestiere of Castello, I realize that I'm not far from a favorite little bakery tucked back into a cul-de-sac called Croce di Malta. The baker there produces a flat bread that has red grapes with rosemary and olive oil on it, and as soon as I think of it I can taste its sweet tanginess. It's not very far away, and it could have been on the way to somewhere...I move a little more briskly now that I have a purpose, and decide that I will make the bakery a stop on the way to the church of San Francesco della Vigna. Maybe the thought of grapes had something to do with it?

The Chiesa San Francesco della Vigna is a lost church. Tucked away in the northern edge of Castello one of its neighboring edifices is a disused gasometer which is a skeleton of rusted metal beams rising above weeds and rubble. It illustrates one of the great Venetian conundrums. The soaring real estate prices of Venice would lead you to believe that all of the city's land is being utilized. The effort to create this land--to literally put it where it is--was enormous, yet much of it sits vacant and ugly and in this case, toxic.

In some ways the Chiesa San Francesco is a no happier building than its dowdy neighbor. Tradition says that this church occupies the spot where a small chapel commemorated the very place where Saint Mark was shipwrecked and the angel came to him with the words "Pax tibi Marcus…"

What we know for sure is that the land surrounding this tiny chapel was a vineyard and was donated to the Franciscan order in 1253. They built a church which is largely gone, replaced by the current one in the early 1500's. One of the local grand palazzi belonged to the Gritti family, and when one of their sons: Andrea became doge he actively engaged in the restoration of what was his neighborhood church. The church was designed by the great Jacopo Sansovino, and Doge Gritti laid the foundation stone in 1534. Sansovino's design for the exterior was never realized and in 1562 Andrea Palladio submitted a plan that resulted in the current facade. It was Palladio's first church and while it is a little more three dimensional than his later works, it possesses all of the elements from classic Greco-Roman architecture that are the signature of so many of his designs. Consistent with the staging of ancient temples, Palladio was promised that the large buildings that hedge it in would be removed and his design would look out onto a large campo This proved to be an empty promise and to this day the beautiful edifice is constrained and restricted by the ugly blockiness of its looming neighbors. It was a great disappointment to Palladio and he carried a sense of betrayal about this building for his entire tenure in Venice.

The building's unhappiness is that it can never break free...Never stand alone where it can be viewed as an entity. Standing in front of it I always find myself feeling sorry for it. The white Istrian stone is never completely in full light and shadows hide parts of it for most of the day.

The bakery is only a short distance away and I have carried the white paper bag containing the flat bread to where I'm standing in front of San Francesco della Vigna. Consuming the bread is obviously the principal activity, but as I do, I find myself slowly counting off the classical elements carved in white stone that decorates this huge façade. The list comes from any art history survey class and it takes no imagination to decide that Palladio has simply stacked a series of temples into the single plane that is the front of this church.

Suddenly my morning has a new purpose...A new story....I know that I want to carry these images of white stone architectural elements to another place not far away to complete a narrative that is forming in my head.

I finish the bread and begin to retrace my steps, moving into one of Venice's most densely populated areas. The folk that lived here were the workers from the Arsenale and in a few minutes I'm standing in front of the grand entrance to this place.

You see, while I was standing eating my bread in front of San Francesco, I began to think about ancient Grecian temples and then about one of the most beautiful and famous of them all ...The Parthenon.

I am now standing in front of the gate to the Arsenale. In a previous chapter I described the group of stone lions that are arranged on each side of the grand entrance, and I walk over to the animal on the left. It is the Piraeus Lion and used to stand at the entrance to the Greek harbor city of the same name. It was such a famous landmark that the ancient Italians called Pireus Porto Leone.

Patience dear Reader, I realize that by now you are wondering where I am going with this tale...What on earth is the common thread here? The question can best be answered by asking another one...How did this Grecian lion get to be one of the guardians of a Venetian fort? This lion, carved sometime in the second century AD stood guard over Piraeus for 1500 years until he was carried off as plunder in what is yet another of the dark stories of Venetian history.

In 1687 during the 7th Ottoman-Venetian war, the Venetian military commander, Francesco Morosini had succeeded in backing up the Islamic forces until they took refuge in the ancient city of Athens. Morosini laid siege to the city and brought his advanced artillery to bear on the enemy within it. The Turks of course occupied the high ground and their forces were focused on the Acropolis. The ancient buildings on this hill top were world famous even in these times, and the jewel of the acropolis was the Parthenon. In 1687 this grand temple was largely undamaged. It had been preserved up there on its lofty perch as much as anything by the love and respect of all who visited it. The temple's measurements were astoundingly accurate and it is doubtful that modern day construction tools and technology could improve upon them. None of the beautiful columns are actually vertical. They all lean slightly inwards and are reaching for a common point. If you projected each one upward they would meet in a single point….About two and a half miles above the surface of the earth. The floor is not flat, but pillows in the center almost 1 ½ inches above the level of the perimeter. The roof was clad in tiles of pure Pentalic marble, cut so thin that they were translucent. When you stood inside the Parthenon the light literally shone through the roof! Some of the most prized sculptures in the world clung to its many surfaces, some in places that could not be seen from the ground below.

In this architectural statement of almost pure beauty, the Turks stored their munitions.

Enter Francesco Morosini…September 26th, 1687.

There are two reports telling what happened on that day. They are of course diametrically opposed stories. The official Venetian communique stated that a 'stray' cannon shell struck the Parthenon landing squarely in its center, detonating the munitions within, resulting in the almost complete destruction of the building. In a private letter Morosini wrote that it was a "lucky shot" and viewed the event as "a remarkable success." The beautiful temple lay in complete ruins…Well not quite. You see, the Venetian vandalism was not yet over. Each of the grand pediments of the Parthenon were still stand-ing and contained within them were some of the finest Periclean sculptures in the world. On the north end the entablature housed Athena, resplendent on a chariot drawn by a magnificent quadriga of horses. Morosini was clearly entertaining visions of repeating history, and like Doge Dandolo before him would return victorious with another set of horses to be displayed with the rest of Venice's booty. He set his men the task of removing these glorious beasts from the remnants of the building. What happened is not clear...Perhaps they underestimated the weight of the horses. As they were being lowered to the ground the ropes broke and the entire group of sculptures crashed to the ground and were broken into many pieces. Morosini abandoned them where they lay and a visiting Englishman brought the remnants that were then shipped to the British Museum in London where they still reside...The Elgin Marbles

Morosini was not to be thwarted however, and he took the Piraeus Lion as a consolation prize. Another lion for a city already filled with them...And at what cost? The destruction of one of the most beautiful pieces of architecture ever produced by man.

There is a cool wind making little waves in the canal as it blows in from the bacino, and staring up into the mouth of this giant white stone lion I find myself shivering. Antonio Palladio was obviously enraptured by the architec-ture of the Greeks. He must have loved the Parthenon...I wonder how he felt about this lion?

Chapter 15

"MAD DOGS AND ENGLISHMEN!"...

S ouheir and I had decided to take the train north to Trieste to spend a day in the port/city that sits at the farthest north point of the Adriatic. I had hoped to scope out the possibilities of a visit to Aquileia, the ancient Roman port that is to the west of Trieste and was surprised to find this ancient port now occupied a place quite a distance from the water.

This initiated a flurry of "map searching" that took up several of my days when we returned and is the reason that I'm riding a strangely modern glass and steel elevator to the top of a 16th Century campanile. It's not a pretty day outside. The wind is blowing across the Lido from the Adriatic. This is not a blustery and disorganized wind that snaps at Venice's flags and banners like an unruly dog. It is fierce and constant and everything seems to be pushed before it. As I walked along the Riva degli Schiavoni toward the #2 Vap stop, the public garbage baskets were laden with dead umbrellas, abandoned there after being turned inside out by this force.

Birds skid by overhead at speeds that they could not possibly generate by themselves and you have to wonder where they will eventually come to rest. Steel grey clouds move at about the same speed as the birds, but so far there has been no rain.

I'm in the elevator that will deposit me at the top of the Campanile of San Giorgio Maggiore. Alone. In fact I may well be the only visitor in this gigantic Palladian church.

"Only Mad dogs and Englishmen would venture out on a day like this..."

I'm talking to myself, enjoying my own private little joke; I fit both of those descriptions.

The light from above is getting brighter and the ascent slows and finally stops. The doors hiss open to an invisible chaos and the wind shrieks through the openings in the bell gallery, becoming mixed and confused. The pressure difference from inside to out is considerable and my overcoat lifts apparently of its own accord and billows towards the door opening. I snug my cap down onto my head, but think better of it, remove it and stuff it into a pocket.

There is no one else here, but if there were, I'm sure conversation would be impossible. I love it... Am transfixed by the sensations. I feel like I'm riding a kite high in the sky and the wind pulls and pushes at me. The wind has scrubbed the air clean of everything. No fog, no rain, no low cloud. In this polished state the air allows me to see forever.

I can see clearly from one end of the lagoon to the other. The cluster of buildings that is Chioggia at its southernmost point and the crooked Campanile of Burano in the north are not hiding in the mists that are so often present. Remarkably, from the east side of the tower I can look out across the Lido and see a line of large ocean going vessels making their way up the Adriatic.

It's perfect; and this is the reason that I have come here today. I've been struggling over the past few days to console some observations and facts into a new understanding. In a previous chapter I spent some time telling you, dear Reader, about the industry shown by the Venetians in the making of their city...the reclamation of land from the lagoon. I've come up here to look at that lagoon, because it has become very apparent that the Venetians have cultivated this 200 square miles of water, as carefully as any farmer tends his vineyards and fields. It is, in fact, the interventions of man that make this lagoon unique in the world.

Lagoons that form along coastal regions begin as a giant game of tug of war. Rivers that flow to the coast bring with them a constant sediment which is the byproduct of their eroding into the earth's surface. When the river is slowed by the barrier of the ocean, this sediment is deposited and collects as sand bars (interesting to note that in Venetian they are called a Lido). This sand bar grows and grows, pushed upon from both sides, eventually effectively "walling" in an expanse of water...The lagoon.

What happens to the lagoon is then decided by which force wins the tug of war. If the rivers dominate this contest they will eventually bring so much deposition to the lagoon, that it will fill in and go through a synthesis that will take it from low marshy swamp, to low wetlands, to dry flat arable earth. If the ocean tides dominate, the lagoon will remain open, its brackish waters captives of the tides which will wash over it every 12 hours or so.

The presence of the lagoon played such an important part in the military defense of Venice that it should come as no surprise that the preservation of it as a body of water was a major obsession of the Venetian Republic. It still is...At the beginning of the 14th century as many as 8 rivers emptied into the Venetian lagoon. Of them, 4 were considerable flows of water. The Bacchiglione, Sile, Piave, and Brenta were the largest of these rivers and legend holds that the Grand Canal is actually the remnant of the main passage that the Brenta used to push its way to the Adriatic. Like any good farmer, the keepers of the lagoon paid close attention to their "fields", and it became clear to them that the onslaught of the rivers had to be slowed and controlled. The Brenta and its massive flow received their first attention and a canal was cut to divert its outflow further south and away from the center of the lagoon where the city of Venice was flourishing. Throughout the entire 15th century, there were a series of projects which moved the Brenta further south until it now emptied into the lagoon opposite the point of Malamocco. In 1500, it was clear that even with all of these efforts the lagoon was silting up and the Venetian engineer Cristoforo Sabbadino presented a plan that would be followed almost into this century. He was a champion of the argument that all major rivers must be diverted. Some of the largest civil engineering projects in Europe were completed in the following years. The Brenta was moved yet again… All the way to Chioggia along a canal that was so large it was called the Nova Brenta. The Piave was diverted to the north. By the second half of the 16th century, attention was turned to the lagoon and the Santo Spirito Canal was dredged from Malamocco to Venice so that shipping could now enter the lagoon in the South. The Brenta and the Bacchiglione now both entered the Adriatic south of Chioggia and had long levees built along their banks to accommodate seasonal flooding. One has to believe that there was considerable trial and error in these efforts; in 1610 the largest canal yet built, the Taglio Novissimo (the Newest Cut) allowed water to flow back into parts of the old river bed of the Brenta to restore river traffic.

In 1791, the lagoon was finally defined and a series of boundary stones were placed to mark its extremities. A few years later, a new canal, the Taglio Sile emptied the Sile into the Piave which was diverted even farther north where it created a new outlet and a lake. At this time an extensive network of sea walls called "murazzi" were constructed along the coast in an attempt to control the Adriatic's aggression. In 1846 the Austrians defiled ancient Venice in an unimaginable act of vandalism and connected Venice to the mainland with a railway line on a bridge that was at that time the largest in Europe. The Venetians directed their attention to the building of jetties at the outlets to the Adriatic in attempts to control the flow of the sea water as it enters the lagoon. The Piave was moved again: this time away from the lake and back to Brandolo.

In 1932, the railway bridge was enlarged to accommodate automobile traffic. The new industrial center of Marghera was begun, and a channel directly from Lido to Marghera that would accommodate the new industrial shipping was created. Later in the 20th century, Marghera doubled in size and Chioggia was connected to the mainland by its own causeway.

The wind is shrieking and pulling at me and while it is not particularly cold, my time in this aerie is limited. I look carefully from each of the four sides, which are nominally lined up with the cardinal directions, and the most obvious thing apparent to me is that apart from the causeway and the giant cooling towers of Marghera, any visitor standing here could quite naturally decide that they were looking at a natural body of water.

Nothing could be further from the truth. If it were not for the considerable efforts of the Venetian Republic, this lagoon would have filled in just like the flatlands to the north and like Aquileia, Venice would have found itself surrounded by land and not water. Stepping back from the wind, I turn and sit on the step, blowing softly into my cold hands. I remove a small piece of paper from my coat pocket. It is a condensed map of the lagoon, showing most of the islands. Holding on tightly, I go back to the southern side and begin to mentally check islands from the map to the reality of the waters.

San Clemente is close by and the buildings of the old hospital are still clearly seen. Matteo tells me there are plans to house a large hotel there in the future. San Servolo, that served as a patrician mental asylum now houses the Venice International University and restoration school, but there is very little evidence of human activity here and the buildings seem to project a kind of lofty forlorn quality every time I passed them as I rode a #3 vap across to the next small Island.

San Lazzaro holds a special place in the ancient history of Venice, and it was here that the city's lepers were confined in the 12th century. It too became a haven for the patrician mentally infirmed, but in 1717 was given to a group of Armenian monks who were fleeing the Turkish invasion of their country. Under the leadership of a very charismatic Abbott by the name of Mekhitar (meaning the consoler), the monastery blossomed and became a hospital. The hospital was moved to the Scuola San Marco which is the site of Venice's existing hospital, but the church and library are still active here.

The small island of Santo Spirito where the channel turns toward Malamocco is barely visible and Povegia seems to be barely above the level of the lagoon. In a series of earthquakes in 1348, several small islands disappeared and were never seen again. It is recorded that the Grand Canal was almost dry for 15 days as well.

To the west, the tiny island of San Giorgio in Alga (literally in the seaweed) seems forgotten and inconsequential, but before the causeway, was a favorite halfway point for the gondoliers ferrying passengers from the mainland. Dignitaries coming from the mainland were often met here. In 1782, Doge Renier met Pope Pius IV here. It is said that more treaties were signed on this tiny island than anywhere else in Europe. I can clearly see the fish traps between Venice and Marghera and Mestre and the small islands of San Secondo and Campalto, their trees slowly being choked by creeping ivy. In the north, I have to look over the city of Venice and attempt to count off the islands that festoon away toward the decidedly leaning campanile of San Martino of Burano. The nearest of these islands were once the twin islands of San Michele and San Cristoforo but have been joined and are now the city's cemetery... The dark greens of their cypress trees are almost electric in this clear air. This was one of Napoleon's "gifts" to the Venetian people, a civilized gesture where the locals were taught to inter their dead in a necropolis. In the first days of surrender to Napoleon...days of ignominy, the Venetians were dispossessed of their wealth and their power, and over a longer period of time their culture and their art. Prior to Napoleon, the Venetians buried their dead in the floors of their churches and in the campi of their city. Each campo had a secular and a sacred end, and the spirits of the departed wandered freely among the living. In one clever act of "generosity", Napoleon also disconnected the Venetians from their dead.

Murano is a cluster of larger red roofs and the glass factories are seen as expanses of terra cotta tiles.

Vignole and Sant' Erasmo, the lagoon's market gardens are low and lush, and even at this distance present a quilt of varying greens. It is from here that the first green peas of spring were brought to be served as a special dish to the doges as a tribute and a way to mark the Day of Saint Mark.

The next tiny island I know is there, but it takes me several minutes of concentration before I can see it as separate from Sant' Erasmo; a small island between there and Burano that has carried about it a mystery and aloofness since the 13th century. It is San Francesco del Deserto. Legend has it that St. Francis decided to act as an intermediary between the Christian and Muslim religions and travelled to Cairo in Egypt where he met with the Caliph. On his way back from this venture, he rode a ship to Aquileia, disembarked and began his southward journey back to Assisi. For reasons that are not clear, he is said to have crossed the lagoon by boat and stopped on this island for some time. There has been a small but active monastery on this island ever since.

The cluster of Mazzorbo, Torcello, and Burano mark the end of the lagoon, the campanile of San Martino on Burano like a crooked finger rising up from the water. Burano is such a mixed bag of experiences. If you arrive on a sunny day in "high" season, you will fight your way through throngs of tourists and become part of 10,000 family picture albums spread all over the world, for you are in someone's viewfinder almost every minute you spend on the island. Off season, or better yet, in the cold winter months, Burano is populated largely by only its residents and you get a better feel for the fishing village that it actually is. At either time, the houses are resplendent in colors of such vibrancy and outrageous combinations that you too will be active with your camera.

While my vantage point enables me to see literally from one end of the lagoon to the other, it doesn't allow a view of what is man's most dramatic and controversial interventions in the ebb and flow of its waters. Hidden between the Islands of Vignole and Certosa is the largest of three channels which cut through the Lido, allowing the waters of the lagoon and the Adriatic to mix.

The Bocca del Lido (the mouth of the Lido) is a little over 900 meters wide, and has been the principle entryway into Venice since ancient times. It was often "gated" by a double row of floating logs chained together and if this did not stop unwanted "visitors", the Venetians cultivated the incoming channel so that all shipping passed very close to the ancient fort of San Andrea where a single fusillade from its many cannons would instantly destroy even the stoutest vessel.

Perhaps the greatest danger that menaces modern Venice is the very water that has protected her for so long. Uncontrolled flooding, the results of high tides. Offshore winds and rain swelled rivers bring aqua alta (high water) to Venice about a hundred days a year now. While fun-seeking tourists may enjoy sploshing about in rubber boots (and Venice must surely hold the world record for ownership per family), the damage done to both structures and services is very real, and is not appreciated by Venetians.

In the 1980s, the problem of flooding was finally given over to engineers and a series of fanciful and truly fantastic schemes were offered up as solutions. Finally one was selected with great optimism and no small amount of self-promotion, the project was presented to the world as the MOSE project (Yes…MOSES…They were going to part the waters). It is an acronym. Well, sort of an acronym. Desperately trying to maintain the Moses concept, the name comes from MOdulo Sperimentale Elettromeccanico. Vast amounts of money (the best number available is five and a half billion Euros!) have been spent on a highly experimental and entirely complicated program. Such an endeavor demands and deserves more than my few words, but here is a brief summary.

Both shores of the mouth have been massively fortified with mountains of concrete. The south shore becomes a sea wall which extends almost 2 miles into the Adriatic in an attempt to change wave action in the mouth.

A small island in the center of the mouth is now a complete concrete bastion which divides the mouth into a south and north flow. Even the seafloor has been reinforced and engineered and attached to this floor are a series of gates that are actually very large rectangular steel boxes hinged on one end. Normally, these boxes are filled with water, the weight of which sinks then to the sea bed. Connected to these boxes, however, is a massive compressed air system and when air is pumped into them, the water is displaced. The free end of the box then floats up to the surface while the hinged part remains fixed to the sea bottom. It is a floating gate...And a complete wall of them will stretch from one side of the Lido mouth to the other. When the elements of aqua alta threaten, the gates will be raised, keeping the Adriatic on one side and the lagoon on the other. When the aqua alta subsides, and the gates are no longer needed, the compressed air is released, water re-enters the box, and it sinks back to the sea floor. The other Lido mouths at Malamocco and Chioggia are being fitted with these gates as well.

It has been an extremely controversial project from its conception, and the arguments that rage around it continue. Aside from the spiraling price tag, the major criticism comes from a group of marine biologists who believe the whole project will end in disaster. The natural state that currently prevails in the lagoon allows a delicate balance of fresh and salt water to be maintained. The bio system of the lagoon tolerates spikes in both directions of salinity, but could not tolerate prolonged periods of either. The scenario that the biologists fear is one where the flood is extreme, requiring the MOSE to remain in place for a prolonged time. The salinity of the lagoon will change dramatically, beyond the tolerance of its waterborne inhabitants. Some biologists believe this will result in the death of the entire biomass of the lagoon....An ecological disaster that probably couldn't be reversed.

I am now definitely cold and shivering, and take one long last pan from Torcello down the coast to Marco Polo Airport where a toy airplane seems to fly away from a white stack of Lego blocks. Then I look back all the way to San Marco just across the Bacino; and move into the sanctuary of the elevator. Fifteen minutes later, I disembark at San Zaccaria and head to my favorite lunch spot for a Tramezzino and Spritz.

Chapter 16

"WHEN YOU HAVE TO GO"...

The love/hate relationship between Venice and the tourists that visit it is a long, long story, and the tourists (and you need to read "us", dear Reader) have been accommodated into the fabric of this city for many generations.

Just inserting the word "Venice" into any search engine on the web will result in pages and pages of responses. One of the official websites of the city is called "HelloVenezia" and it offers reduced rates for tourists that cover transportation, museum and church entrances, and a host of other important activities. They come as a "package deal" and if you click on the "City Pass" it will explain the benefits of purchasing such a package.

Prominent among these benefits is a two word description...

"Toilet Facilities"

Yes dear Reader, we have reached the chapter that I promised at the beginning of this writing adventure.

My observations lead me to believe that many of the "tourist hours"... (That is, hours spent in Venice by tourists)... are spent in the search for public bathrooms.

Public bathrooms have long been a part of this cityscape and many descriptions of paintings of the Piazza San Marco from the past point out the poetic license of the painter that has resulted in the omission of certain elements that were not considered beautiful. The public latrines that occupied the Piazza are seldom seen in any paintings, but they were an extremely important part of its function.

I am asked to give directions to a toilet facility…and if the person asking is desperate enough, any toilet facility, about as often as I'm asked to help people who are completely lost.

A major complication to this dilemma is created by the WC stickers that can be found adhered to the pavement all over Venice. The letters WC are cleverly worked into an arrow design that clearly points the way…But to where? I would not tell you that I have made an extensive study of these ubiquitous little signs, but I have attempted to follow enough of them to know that they must surely be the end product of a deviant sense of humor. My best advice to those of you who are desperately attempting to find a public restroom is to completely ignore them!

There are public toilets in Venice. They are not hidden away. They are, however, not clearly marked…And you must pay to use them.

In truth, I can't imagine that any day tripper tourist would be able to easily find any of them except for those in the railway station…So let's start there.

There is a large public toilet in the railway station. The station has been undergoing improvements for a protracted period of time, and it is possible that these facilities might be moved, so some effort may be needed to track them down in the building.

Most tourists will find themselves on or in the vicinity of the Ponte Rialto. On the San Marco side in the little Campo Bartolomeo that has a bronze sculpture of Carlo Goldoni smiling above the crowd, there is a public toilet hidden away just along the calle which exits the campo into the Corte del Tentor at its northern end.

Another important landmark for the tourist is the Ponte Accademia or the wooden bridge. On the Dorsoduro end of the bridge, cleverly concealed under the entry stairs is a public toilet.

If you exit the Piazza San Marco on the western end and pass in front of the entrance to the Museo Correr, you will find a small alleyway that leads to a large public toilet.

All of these facilities cost at least one euro, unless of course you purchased a 'City Pass' and you can cash in your 'toilet tickets'.

Perhaps it is too much to ask someone who desperately needs to use a toilet to understand some of the complexities of this problem, but I am constantly amazed at how outraged some of Venice's visitors become when confronted with it. The first thing visitors need to remember is that everything is transported into and out of Venice. It is simply a logistical problem that most other places don't have to deal with. It is entirely reasonable to expect you to help pay for this. Therefore the primary thing the visitor needs to come to grips with is that this service is going to cost...Which brings us to the next technique used for finding a toilet.

Almost all bars, and certainly all restaurants have a toilet and bathroom. They are almost always exclusively for the use of patrons, and the only way that you will get to use them is to become one of these patrons. You buy a coffee, sandwich, a drink...Whatever it takes! And then you too can use the facility...Of course emptying your body of fluids while at the same time topping them up with more is probably counterproductive.

As I have pointed out previously, riding the large vessels called auto nave will allow you to use the onboard toilet, and you will find toilets in all of the large museums.

Remember... When they say good luck to you. The Italians say,

"In bocca al lupo"

In English it means... "In the mouth of the wolf"!

If you are frantically looking for a toilet in Venice, it might serve you well to remember that you are in the mouth of the wolf.

Chapter 17

BRIDGES...

Many years ago, when I was a student in Australia, academia was filled with a refined cadre of teachers who (and I never knew if this was conscious or unconscious on their part) were quite Anglophile. Their speech and accent were more refined and they did not use the colloquialisms or profanity that decorated Australian "common talk". One such of these wonderful, old gentleman when completely frustrated and exasperated, would break down and exclaim,

"Shit...oh dear!"

...Whereupon those of us in his class who were usually the source of his frustration and exasperation would dissolve in laughter. It has always seemed to be a rather benign way to show frustration and is the most memorable part of an art history class that was as dry as the searing Australian summer that was beating against the windows of the lecture hall.

"Well, shit...oh dear!"
    Tarik looks across at me and says,
    "What? The John Rawlings infallible compass has broken down?!"

He and I are standing at the end of a long and narrow alleyway and are look-ing down at the surface of a canal that is a couple of feet below us.

"I've never said that I don't get lost…That's just a story your mother made up."

There is no fondamente here. The walls of the buildings on both sides of the alley go directly down into the canal. Leaning out and turning our heads to the left we can see the place that we were heading for, but our passage forward has been stopped by one inescapable problem. There is no bridge to cross this canal. We will have to retrace our steps to find the bridge that we can see to our left. We are deep in Castello and I promised Tarik to walk him along the tall wall topped with castellations that encloses the Arsenale. My plan was to end in San Francesco di Vigna, but it has clearly gone wrong. It is won-derfully quiet in this small place and we sit and allow our legs to dangle just above the water. This young man is not a waster of words, and we sit without speaking for quite a while before he looks at me and says,

"If you had a boat, you could get to any part of this city…couldn't you?"

I simply smile and nod and watch this realization working its way into his understanding.

Depending on your source of information (and even the "official" sites can't seem to agree) there are between 378 and 408 bridges in Venice. Most of them are relative newcomers. Sources for information on the building and rebuilding of Venice's bridges are not easily accessible to me. The state archives are only available by invitation and the limits of my Italian language make it extremely difficult reading for me anyway. The major changes to the bridges of Venice occurred during the French and Austrian occupations and so we are disconnected from human memory of these events. However, by piecing together some ancient texts and looking at paintings and drawings from Venice's wonderful collections, I think we can draw some conclusions that are really quite interesting. In what was probably a rather romanticized depiction of Venetian life, the Roman Historian Cassiodorus in 537 AD describes a vehemently independent populace that lived half in and half out of the water… "Whose dwellings cling to the banks of the rivers and marshes, reflecting the character of the rushes and reeds that also grow there." Their shallow draught boats were light and nimble and they used them with complete freedom, moving about like the wind and the tides that swept across the lagoon. Some rather crude and unsophisticated drawings that date from the 11th century can be found in the Biblioteca Marciana. They show houses of wood with thatched roofs clustered in rather disorganized groups, with little apparent concern for any kind of grid street system or organization. Many of these houses show gondola-like boats tethered to their front entrance. No bridges are depicted.

I conclude that the earliest Venetians moved around as often in their boats as on foot. That boat ownership was ubiquitous and very high. That a major way that Venetians exercised the qualities that they held so dear…that made them Veneziani…was to be found in their relationships with boats. They didn't need bridges. They could access any part of their city in their boats. The first major bridges were designed in a typical Venetian manner, with commerce in mind. Bridges that crossed the Grand Canal and the Canal Cannaregio certainly allowed foot traffic but were designed with the specific idea of effectively precluding incoming trading vessels from entering the city. Goods carried by these vessels had to be off-loaded onto the blunt ended Venetian boats called "toppi" and then taken to storehouses. The Venetians charged for these services and this was a major source of employment for the boatmen.

While it is not clear how many bridges existed in ancient Venice, we do know something of their character. Paintings and drawings from these times show bridges with no parapets. No railings… Nothing to stop the pedestrian from falling sideways into the canal below. Nothing much is said about why they were designed this way until we read the complaints from the local populace about how the Austrians had defiled their bridges by adding railings.

In the Museo Correr there is a marvelous painting depicting a rather peculiar Venetian activity. Sometimes the result of nothing more than high spirits, but often driven by a fierce sense of pride in parochial neighborhoods or sestiere that quickly manifested raw violence, groups of young men "faced off" in the center of a bridge (often the bridge that connected one sestiere to another) and then began to "push" on each other. The painting shows the Ponte Pugni and the Campo San Barnaba can be seen clearly in the background. Two large groups of men clash in a crush that is obviously open conflict…An enormous fight with the intention of pushing the opposing force off the bridge.

Such activities were not looked upon kindly by the local constabulary but the narrative of the painting tells its story clearly, and the hysteria and mayhem of a crowd that is obviously unmanageable would have been a serious deterrent to any police intervention..

There are only a few of Venice's bridges that still exist in their original state… that is, without railings. A small one spans the Rio Felice canal, just around the corner from the giant barn-like building of the Scuola Nuova di Misericordia. It is one of those bridges that spans a canal only to reach a doorway of what is now a rather dowdy old building. Without the brick or metal railings there is a lightness about this bridge that immediately declares it feminine and the smoothness of its arc possesses the verve of a line in a sumi-E painting.

I often get students to stand on this little bridge for group photographs, and the way that they walk out onto it always surprises me. They are tentative; some actually hold their arms out as if they are balancing on a narrow beam, and there is always a sense of relief about them when they return to the fondamente. I fantasize about ancient Venetians skipping across these slivers of stone, flung like arced ropes across canals, just another way to show their relaxed expertise when crossing water. It is an easy piece of mental gymnastics for me to look at the current bridges of Venice and see the stolid, sensible and heavy Austrian characteristics weighing down the lightness of the original Venetian span.

The proliferation of bridges under the French and Austrians was the act of an occupying military force and facilitated rapid movement of military personnel from one part of the city to another. They were not boat people and the bridges served to equalize a profound Venetian advantage. It is quite clear, however, that once in place, these bridges were utilized also by the local population and Venetian life was irrevocably changed.

In 1834, the residents of Dorsoduro petitioned the city council to build a bridge that would connect their sestiere with that of San Marco, so that they could "enjoy the life and prosperity which others enjoy". A site spanning the Grand Canal at San Salute was examined and then abandoned because it would bespoil the vista of the entrance to the Bacino, and another site opposite the Scuola Accademia was decided upon. A bridge and a tunnel were envisaged, but it was not until 1854 that a final plan was conceived and by that time the idea of the tunnel had been abandoned.

An English engineer/architect by the name of A. E. Neville won the final contract and a single straight span constructed entirely from cast iron that had been prefabricated in England was built. This structure was controversial from the beginning and the stiff, straight, vaguely Art Nouveau bridge inserted a discordant note into the flowing music of the Grand Canal. This style of bridge, called the "Austrian bridges" by the Venetian populace slowly proliferated around the city. Neville established his own foundry in the San Rocco area and in 1865, constructed bridges at the Scalzi, close to the railway station and the Ghetto Nuovo.

A ground swell of negative responses to those structures gathered momentum and in 1931, a new competition was announced for a bridge to replace the Ponte Accademia. Both metal versions of the Scalzi and Accademia bridges were

demolished in 1932 and Eugenio Miozzi, native son and vehement Venetian produced winning designs for their replacement. Miozzi produced a wooden "temporary" version of the Accademia bridge first, and I suspect that he was making
sure that his design would integrate itself into his beloved city before constructing
it from stone. He boasted that it was a bridge "in the Venetian manner" and it
was instantly and almost universally accepted and loved. Once again, the strange,
uniquely Venetian ethos exerted its influence and the local population decided
that they loved the bridge as it was, and voted to leave the temporary structure. It
is now simply called "the wooden bridge" but has been reinforced with steel in an
attempt to ensure its longevity.

Miozzi's design for the Scalzi was a sister to that of the Ponte Accademia and
was completed in stone, giving us a clear idea of what the wooden bridge was
designed to look like, but, to date, there are no plans to change this giant
wooden structure.

The northernmost end of the Canale Cannaregio is spanned by one of my favorite bridges in all of Venice and true to its name, Tre Arche uses two short and
one long span to cross this water thoroughfare. It is the last of these tri-arched
structures, but there is evidence to support a theory that perhaps many of the
larger canals were spanned using this technique. When you enter room 20 of
the Accademia Museum, you are instantly surrounded by a collection of large
canvases that depict a series of civic and religious ceremonies. These paintings
have great historic and artistic value, but I find them most engaging because of the
many small details that they contain. The artists have taken great pains to show
life as it was. They were recording an event at a specific time in a specific place,
and we are treated to careful depictions of clothing and shoes, architecture and
boats, and above all, the contemporary landscape of ancient Venice.

In Gentile Bellini's painting called "Miracolo della Croce", he tells the story of an annual procession of one of Venice's major religious confraternities
where their most treasured possession, a piece of the true cross which had
been brought from Jerusalem through Cyprus in 1369, is paraded through the

streets. It somehow falls into the canal and the painting depicts that moment of horror and then miraculous discovery as people plunge into the water to look for it as Andrea Vendramin rises to the surface with the relic in his hands.

This event unfolds among the houses and palazzi of a Venice that, while ancient, can still be recognized. The oars and forcole of the gondola, the clothing drying on the roofs, the clerical dress of the clergy...All can be seen with a clarity that allows us to know a great deal about these ancient Venetians. The entire tableaux presents itself below, in front of and on top of the Ponte San Lorenzo, shown in the painting to be exactly where it is today. However, instead of the graceful single span that you and I would cross, the bridge is depicted as a sister of Tre Arche and is supported by three spans.

No matter what their number actually is, there is only one bridge that steals the attention and imagination of visitor and resident alike...Ponte Rialto. The bridge that connects Venice across the Grand Canal at the Riva Alta, or high banks, remains the focal crossing point from San Marco to San Polo and literally millions of people cross its span every year.

In Act 3-Scene 1 in Shakespeare's "Merchant of Venice", we find the line "What's new on the Rialto?"

... And as silly and trite as it sounds, I seldom cross this bridge without whispering them to myself. Because this is the Riva Alta and it is reasonable to extrapolate that the first building in Venice was done on its highest ground, the Rialto Bridge spans the Canale Grande at one of the oldest parts of the city. Its western ramp of stairs leads directly into the marketplace which unfolds through narrow passageways choked with small stalls, to the sounds and smells of the fish market and the stalls of the fruit and vegetable vendors.

In 1181 it was built as a pontoon bridge that was called the Ponte Moneta (presumably because of the proximity of the mint). It allowed foot traffic from San Marco to San Polo, but it restricted the passage of boats along the Canal. In 1265, this was solved by building another wooden bridge that consisted of ramped stairs on both sides with a moveable central section between them. This section could be raised to allow the passage of boats.

In an ill planned and astoundingly unsuccessful attempt to seize the ducal power for himself, Bajamonte Tiepolo led a band of followers through the streets into San Marco. Legend has it that as this band burst into the Piazza, a leader of the group was felled by a cast iron pot that had been flung out of an upper storey window by an irate housewife. Coming from above, perhaps this was seen as something divine? They immediately turned tail and were pursued down the mercerie and across the bridge at Rialto. Tiepolo stopped long enough to set fire to the wooden structure and in this way avoided capture. It was rebuilt, and in the early 1400s two rows of shops were added to the structure. In 1444, a large crowd gathered on the bridge to observe a parade along the Grand Canal and the entire central structure collapsed. It was rebuilt again, and in 1503 discussions began to explore the possibility of replacing it with a more secure stone structure.

The second collapse of the wooden structure in 1524 was the galvanizing moment however, and in 1551 a formal competition was held to receive architectural proposals for Ponte Rialto. It was the grand time of the Italian Renaissance and the contestant list reads like a "who's who" of classic architects; Sansovino, Vignola, and the great Andrea Palladio all offered up drawings and models. It is said that even Michelangelo was invited to compete. However, all of the proposals reflected the classical vocabulary of the time and to the Venetians credit, they realized that any of these proposed works would strike a discordant note among their existing architecture. In the Palladio Museum of Vicenza, there are detailed plans and renderings of what Palladio proposed and it is difficult for me to believe that many people would have been comfortable with this grand anomaly sitting astride the Grand Canal.

In 1588, the commission was awarded to Antonio da Ponte (obviously bridges played a large part in his family!) and it was completed in 1591. It was his aesthetic that flung this long (about 94') gorgeous arc across the Grand Canal. You need to pass beneath the span to feel how breathtaking this leap really is, and the stretch of the span is never more real than when you are on the water beneath it. Scamozzi was sure that Antonio had in fact overstepped structural possibilities, and predicted its collapse.

It is still with us.

"What's new on the Rialto?"

Unfortunately I have to report that the newest arrival on the bridge is graffiti. Spray painted words and "tags" adorn the rear walls of the northern side shops and as much as I want to conjure up a marauding horde of pirates or barbarians to lay the blame upon, I suspect we are seeing disgruntled Venetian youth at work.

The Ponte Rialto was not the only bridge used for commerce, and in the heyday of Venice's lascivious years, many of the city's 15,000 registered prostitutes stood on bridges to attract customers who passed below on the canals. An ingenious underwired, support system allowed these ladies to wear gowns that completely covered them, but allowed their breasts to be open...A way of displaying the merchandise. A bridge in San Polo in the Carampane area (that housed the bordellos and brothels) is called Ponte di Tette...Literally the bridge of tits, and it was over these parapets that the ladies "let it all hang out." Interestingly, there is another Ponte di Tette over in Castello near Zanipolo. I presume they were quite popular. Perhaps each sestiere had one!?

It is virtually impossible to walk any distance in Venice without crossing a bridge. Very few are alike and each has a character, even a personality. Almost every time you find yourself stopping to look around at the wonder of this city, you will be at the top of a bridge.

Chapter 18

TIME...

An intellectual "game" played with friends who have spent time in Venice and come under her spell, is to describe something that is truly unique about her. The list is long and varied, but contains a group of interesting common denominators, and among these one seems to stand out. All of us have decided that the passage of time in Venice is somehow not the same as in the rest of the world.

In an earlier chapter I told of the bells of Venice and how most of them marked liturgical time. They are tolled to mark the end or the beginning of a fixed time...And this time is itself measured by a device or mechanism. There are many clocks in Venice. In fact among all of the city's clocks, she boasts one of the world's most famous. The Basilica San Marco and the Palazzo Ducale (the next chapter, dear Reader) have always been the focus of the considerable propaganda of the Venetian Republic. The grandeur of this architectural cluster is inescapable and visiting dignitaries were exposed to as much of the wealth, power, and technology of the Republic as could be crammed into these buildings which are still the "front door" of the city.

A visiting monarch would be met at the small island of San Giorgio by the Doge in his private vessel called the Bucintoro. There were 4 major incarnations of this splendid barge dating back to the 13th century. They were grand vehicles of pro-paganda and were highly decorated and gilded with only one intention, they were built to impress the visitor. They were an extension of the Doge's Palace...a two decked, floating Palace, and were never intended to perform any tasks beyond the ceremonial. The last great Bucintoro built in 1729, at the cost of 70,000 ducats, was 115 ft long and about 26 ft high. It had 168 oarsmen that propelled the vessel with 42 oars that were 36 ft long and weighed more than 200 lbs each.

This grand vessel would, of course, have an accompaniment of military boats and with oars dipping in flawless unison, the entire flotilla would cross the lagoon, come down the Canal Giudecca, and across the Bacino di San Marco to a mooring right in front of the two giant columns with Theodore on the left and Mark's lion on the right.

Stepping ashore, the monarch is immediately presented with a view down the Piazzetta San Marco to the city's most beloved timepiece; the Torre dell' Orologio.

Why would this Republic give such prominence to a clock? And why such a complex and clearly expensive structure? The monarch is moved in proces-sion down the Piazzetta and taking a right hand turn, enters the governmental inner sanctum of Venice through a gate that actually connects two buildings, the Basilica on the left and the Palace on the right. The sacred meeting the secular; a sculpture over the lintel shows Doge Francesco Foscari kneeling before the lion of St. Mark.

Ascending a series of grandiose staircases, our Monarch is moved into some of the most ornamented rooms in all of Italy; each successive room progressively competing for attention with more...More of everything: Scale, gold, paintings, furnishings and in the first few of these rooms, enormous clocks.

All of these timepieces are patiently measuring the most abstract of ele-ments. The Venetians are showing how ordered and precise they are...How aware they are of their part in time's passage; their history. The clocks are huge and opulent and beautifully complicated...and they are owned by the Republic. The message is clear...Venice controls and owns everything here... Including time.

Without a means to measure time, mariners cannot navigate, cartographers cannot make maps. The great Venetian skill of rowing without cadence, timing, is impossible. The rise and fall of the lagoon in tides that peak every 12 hours also keeps time, and the water level in the canals is a time signature that these mariner people read like a wrist watch.

It's a grey morning and I'm walking down the small calle called the Frezzeria (in some very distant past this was the area of the city where the arrow makers had their workshops. They were the fletchers.) It's a narrow way that always seems to have too many people on it. A man in front of me stops and opens a map that takes up at least a half of the calle and I control an urge to burst through it to continue on my way. He shuffles to one side and is almost pinned to the wall by a porter pushing a barrow loaded with boxes.

"Attenzione"

I slide to one side of the barrow, and map-man sort of squawks as he is confined to a much smaller space than the one he had been occupying. I love this place…the proximity of people demands that we share. The porter shakes his head slightly and raises an eyebrow towards map-man. I smile at him. A little knowing smile is returned.

And then with one quick step I am out of the crush of the street. I have stepped into Claudio's tiny office.

"Ciao Claudio!"

"Ciao John!"

His eyes peer over the top of his computer screen.

"I'm very busy here…"

"You have time for coffee?"

"Of course…but I must stay in the office until Agnese comes."

"Where is she?"

"At the clock"

"What clock?"

"THE clock!"

And once again, Claudio plays a part in my exploration of this city. "THE clock", is of course, the Torre dell' Orologio, and it turns out that Agnese is also a guide who conducts tours inside this wonderful mechanism. Over the course of a couple of days, I meet with her and she organizes my inclusion into one of her tours. She is bright, vivacious, wonderfully engaging, and her English is flawless. She quickly engages the small group (limited to 12 people) and we are captivated as she walks us up a series of very narrow staircases, stopping at each level to narrate history and explain mechanisms. Finally we exit onto the very roof of the tower to watch the two giant bronze statues strike the bell and take in one of Venice's most breathtaking views.

It is simply too much information for me to take in at one viewing and I attach myself to two more tours over the course of a couple of weeks in the pursuit of understanding.

In the 1400s, there was a clock in Piazza San Marco. It was the clock of St. Alipio and occupied a place somewhere in the northwest corner. However, by the 1490s, this mechanism had stopped functioning reliably and consistent with the beautification taking place throughout the city, it was decided that a new, far grander clock should keep time in San Marco. To this end the Senate voted in 1493 to allocate funds for this purpose. Two major commissions were granted: One for the clock mechanism itself and another for the building which would house it. Master clockmaker Gianpolo Ranieri and his son Giancarlo from the city of Reggio Emilia were awarded the commission for the clock and the architectural element was to be the responsibility of Mauro Codussi although no copy of a formal contract survives to confirm this. It was decided that the tower should straddle the street of shops, the Mercerie, and that it should be tall enough to have a presence that rivalled its neighbor, the giant Basilica of St. Mark. Codussi produced a plan that called for a centralized tower, but revised this idea to incorporate two side wing buildings that were added after his death.

In 1496, buildings were demolished and the tower was started. On the 1st of February 1499, the clock was formally inaugurated and its long relationship with La Serenissima began.

In 1500, the elder Ranieri died and his son Carlo was induced to stay in Venice and become the formal keeper of the clock. By the time he died in 1531, the clock was not functioning well and in 1581, the great architect, Sansovino was instructed to remedy its problems. It was cleaned and re-gilded in 1663, but by 1750 it was clear that the great clock was in need of a complete restoration. In 1751, Giorgio Massari received the commission to do this and he entered into a program that would last for the next six years. He added to the wing buildings, raising them two more floors, so that the clock took on a more commanding architectural presence. Eight columns were added to the facade of the grand floor in what may have been an attempt to stabilize a building that was now much larger. However, as radical as these external modifications were, it was the interior workings of the clock that received the most dramatic transformation.

Bartolomeo Ferracina set about restoring the mechanism that was largely unchanged since the Ranieri built it. He changed the movement of the clock from a foliate escapement to a pendulum system which was much more accurate and removed the mechanism in the main face that showed the stars revolving around the earth.

The striking mechanism of the clock was changed to a 12 hour cycle and in 1759, the procession of the Magi was repaired. 1855 found the clock in need of repairs again and during this process something remarkable was added. On either side of the giant Madonna on the 4th level, the world's first digital clock was installed!

The most recent chapter in the story of "the Clock" was written from 1998-2006 when the world famous Swiss company Piaget entered into a contract to undertake a complete refurbishment of the entire mechanism. They celebrated its 500th birthday in 2006 by removing scaffolding to reveal the Torre dell' Orologio restored to its external glory while its interior workings contained the most precise mechanisms available in the world of timepieces.

If you enter the Piazza San Marco a few minutes before the hour at almost any time of the day or night you will find a cluster of people standing in front of the three flag poles that face the Basilica. They are all looking upward at the clock and are waiting to see the two giant figures on the very top of this structure strike the bell that stands centrally between them.

It is not a tower in the classic sense of a singular tall structure; rather it is a building with five frontal sections, where the center one rises two levels above the sides. These wings contain none of the clock's mechanisms and are in fact now apartments and stores (on the ground level). The Torre dell' Orologio is clearly divided vertically into four sections. These separations rise from the street level of the piazza, each divided from the other by horizontal architectural elements.

The lowest element is an archway which rises two stories to span Venice's oldest "shopping street", the Mercerie. It is one of the main entrances to the grand Piazza, and most visitors are not aware that they have passed through the clock tower until they are in San Marco and turn to look back. Above the archway the next squared section contains the giant clock face that is a remarkable combination of metal surfaces covered in an enamel of lapis lazuli and gold leaf.

Most people simply look at the giant golden single "hand" which is in the shape of a blazing sun, and tells the time. On closer perusal, however, this face is measuring far more than just the hours of the day. At the center of the large blue face, the hemispherical form represents the earth, and all things revolve around it. This was consistent with scientific and religious theories of 1493. (It would be 90 more years before Galileo postulated the theory of the planets revolving around the sun.) If you look closely you will see a series of concentric divisions that did revolve about this center sphere, and the relative positions of Saturn, Jupiter, Mars, Venus and Mercury could be read. However, in 1751 as testament to the acceptance of Galileo's theories, this mechanism was disconnected.

On this center face the moon is also represented, with a clever sphere inside a sphere mechanism that documents the phase that the moon is currently in from new moon to full moon. The next band is divided into twelve and contains the zodiac symbols. This band is married to the giant sweep hand with the blazing sun at its "pointer" end, and makes only twelve moves in a calendar year, thereby measuring the months of the year.

The metal circles are contained within the white Istrian marble façade, and the next band of the clock is carved into this marble. This final band contains the twenty four numbers of the hours in the day in Roman numerals and was covered up in 1755 to reflect the new and more universally accepted twelve hour clock. The twenty four hour numbers were "rediscovered" in the renovation of 1896 and restored to their present state. The next band above the clock face provides the clock with some of its most unique elements. Seated on a throne that is centrally situated on the tower, a large Madonna and child created from beaten copper and gilded in gold, looks out over the Piazza.

To her left and right, two rectangular openings display the digital clocks. To her right and the left of us, looking up to the clock, the numerals are Roman and count the twelve hour clock. To her left and our right, the numerals are Arabic and count every 5 minutes of the hour. Lamps were once placed behind these revolving numbers so that the time could be read in the evening hours. However, these digital mechanisms were only added in 1858 and prior to this, these doors served a very different purpose.

A circular track passes from behind the Madonna in the interior of the tower, out through one of these doors, passes in front of the Madonna and then back through the other door to the interior. Four carved wooden figures with moveable mechanical parts can be fitted to this track and when activated will exit from the left hand door, pass in front of the Madonna and re-enter the tower through the right hand door. As they pass in front of the Madonna another mechanism trips the moving parts of each figure. The first figure is an Angel and he raises his trumpet. History records that this trumpet actually made a sound, achieved by a bellows system much like a pipe organ, but there is no evidence of these features left.

The next three figures are the wise men and they raise their crowns in respect. This display is only activated twice a year: on the day of the Epiphany on January 6th, and on Ascension Thursday, which is 40 days after Easter. On these days the digital drums are moved to one side to allow the figures to pass.

The next band above this now contains a winged lion carved in white marble standing in front of a large blue panel encrusted with a regular pattern of gold stars. In 1499 when Doge Agostino Barbarigo inaugurated this clock, he left behind a statue of himself in white marble kneeling before this great lion, but this was removed and destroyed in 1797 by Napoleon.

The very top of the tower (the roof) is called the "Moor's Terrace" and contains a large, centrally placed bell which is supported from beneath and flanked by two giant mechanical men holding hammers. These two male figures cast in bronze at the Arsenale are wearing the sheepskin attire of shepherds. One is young and strikes the bell two minutes before the hour, the other is old and strikes the bell on the hour. They are fashioned so that the top part of their bodies, from the waist up, pivot on a mechanism that brings the hammers into contact with the bell. They are called "I Mori" (or the Moors), and you would expect therefore to find negroid characteristics in the faces of these sculptures. But they are obviously European and it is believed that the name simply reflects the fact that the surface of the bronze has blackened with oxidation over the years.

The bell is struck by each Moor once for each hour of the twelve hour clock: but at midday another set of hammers strikes six groups of twenty two blows for a total of one hundred and thirty two. These blows represent all of the hammer blows delivered over the preceding twelve hour period. There is a very interesting reassertion of the power of the Republic in the overall organization of the Torre. The Lion (and until 1797, the Doge) occupy the top, higher most level. They are above everything. The Madonna and Child are a level below. Is the message, "You are Venetian first and Christian second"?....

...Looks like it to me.

This beautiful timepiece is positioned so that our visiting monarch was aware of it the moment that he disembarked. It commands the view down the Piazzetta in a most theatrical way. The two great pillars of stone on the Molo where the Piazzetta empties into the Bacino were the place of execution in ancient Venice, and these executions were often carried out at noon. The condemned person would be set to kneel so that he or she could look down the Piazzetta to the clock. The crowd gathered and awaited the moment of execution, which occurred when the clock struck twelve. On the twelfth strike the executioner beheaded the prisoner and it is said the crowd would call out,

"He knows what time it is now!"

Chapter 19

"IT IS NOT WHAT IT APPEARS TO BE"...

A considerable amount of the energy that I use walking around Venice is consumed by my conscious efforts to stay away from the dreaded tourists, and such a statement should bring a smile to your face, dear Reader, because what could be more obvious than the fact that I am of course one of these tourists. My pretense at being otherwise often results in situations where I resist doing certain things based entirely on how "touristy" I think they are. It transpires that this is a rather unjustifiable criteria which often precludes me from pleasurable, and sometimes enlightening experiences. I resisted riding in a gondola for almost ten years; not solely because I thought that it was too expensive, but because I did not wish to be counted among the droves of people who make this a focal point of their six hour attack on La Serenissima.

One afternoon when walking through the quiet of Campo Santa Maria Formosa we were approached by a gondolier and his quiet,

"Gondola?...Gondola?"

It became one of those "Why not" moments and we climbed down stone steps, green with moss into his waiting craft.

I was transfixed…

It became one of my most moving Venetian experiences and I saw this city in some ways, for the first time. It was also a great lesson, and since that time I have curbed my rather haughty anti tourism attitude.

I'm sitting at the dining table in the Sant' Elena apartment…Afternoon light shafting through the open window passes through the delicate fabric of the lace curtains and is broken into soft dapples that dance across the table's patterns that are inlayed veneers of woods from who knows where. I am not alone, for across the table from me, sitting in this moving light display is a Venetian mask. It's a bauta, which is the most authentic and ubiquitous of all the Venetian masks. The bauta is quite a simple design... A wrap of material over the eyes, a nose piece, and then a sort of shovel shape that extends over the mouth area. It allows the wearer to drink, eat, smoke, and converse. Most other masks preclude these activities. This mask is black and the eye holes allow light to shine through them. He is definitely looking at me.

I've had a very interesting morning and have returned to the apartment for some quiet time. I'm trying to digest information that I've been chewing on for several weeks and this morning's outing has definitely moved these thoughts closer to a conclusion.

I look across the table again at my companion, and resist the urge to speak to him. Perhaps I'll ask him what he thinks...But of course he is designed so that you don't know what he thinks. You hide behind him. That's the function of this device. You see IT...Not what's behind it.

And that is what I'm looking for!

The key...

Thoughts tumble into new configurations. Not exactly a "Eureka" moment...but close.

This morning, after coffee and brioche at the corner bar, I walked slowly all of the way along the waterfront to the Palazzo Ducale where I lined up with a gaggle of tourists and bought a ticket for "The secret tour of the Doge's Palace". That's correct, dear Reader, one of those dreadful touristy excursions that I have been resisting for a long time.

For the past couple of weeks I have been spending a piece of each day in the Basilica San Marco and the Palazzo Ducale. Standing in dark and out of the way corners. I've been haunting these places...Stalking something.

In the previous chapter we walked through a scenario that had a visiting monarch arriving in Venice, explaining the grand entrance that is the cluster of architecture arranged around the Piazza and Piazzetta San Marco.

The Basilica and the Palazzo take the principle roles within this cluster of magnificence.

They are presented to us by Venetians saying...

"Look at our magnificence...This is Venice...This is who we are."

As my search for understanding continued I became obsessed with these two building complexes. It became clear that there was quite a lot of both of these structures that could not be studied unless permission was given to do so. In other words you may only look at what "they" want you to look at. (And no, I don't know who 'THEY' are) And so I lined up with my fellow Anglophones, a little adhesive badge on my coat lapel, and waited for the young lady who would conduct the "Secret Tour".

True to form, it was wonderful...Something I obviously should have done years ago.

She greeted us in excellent English and explained the parameters and restrictions of the tour, where we were permitted to take photographs and where we weren't, and then we followed her like ducklings after their mother on the most amazing journey.

Standing in the main courtyard next to one of the beautiful bronze well heads, she directed our attention to the façade of the building that rose up before us. She counted the clear architectural separations of each floor and then told us that this number would not correspond to the number of floors within the building: because...

"It is not what it appears to be..."

She unlocked a small metal door, and after we had all passed through, closed it with a theatrical clang behind us. We had entered the building at the ground floor level and immediately found ourselves in a windowless maze of prison cells that even in the their twenty-first century cleanliness and sanitized state, elicited a visceral, wrenching sensation that would have turned to blind fear if someone had extinguished the lights. We ascended a long winding staircase and entered a room that immediately set me searching for reasons. The floors, walls and ceilings were made from rough cut lumber. The ceiling was low (a couple of the taller folk in our group were close to touching it with their heads), and the windows were small, with almost the feel of a porthole.

Maritime!

It felt as if we were below decks in a wooden ship! But where were we?

Let's return to our monarch who has disembarked, walked up the Piazzetta, turned into the giant doorway that connects the Basilica to the Palazzo, proceeded slowly up the grand staircase, passing between the great stone sculptures of Mars and Neptune (an interesting combination), into an enormous building of four floors. He ascends a golden staircase to either the living quarters of the Doge or one floor above, the varied chambers of officialdom; each performing a specific task in the governance of this great Republic.

We (and I presume we represent the behind the scenes Venetians, the worker bee Venetians), had passed through one of the nastiest dungeons on the planet, ascended a tight, dark wooden staircase, and entered a labyrinth; a warren of rooms that are actually hidden between the four great floors.

Our tour guide led us on through these rooms, stopping in each one to explain its function, and sometimes its proximity to the grand chambers literally on the other side of the wall. Simple doors on this side of the wall opened into opulent spaces decorated with gold and exotic woods. However, on the Palace side the door showed as nothing more than a panel. No hinges or door handle were to be seen. It was a secret panel.

Our monarch on his procession through the grand rooms and chambers may have at times felt himself all alone. It is clear, however, that Venetian eyes were on him at all times.

We continued on through the office of the Chancellor, a Venetian public servant with enormous powers of oversight. He was elected for life by his peers: and his job was to oversee all of the peregrinations of the state. He was the principle filter through which everything passed. He worked in tandem with the Doge...And the Doge did nothing that he didn't know about, or approve. He was paid a huge salary, presumably to ensure that he could not be corrupted. His office was about fifteen feet square; walls and low ceiling still showing the saw blade marks of rough cut lumber. The desk at one end of this small room was about five feet by three feet, behind it an ordinary wooden chair. A small painting hung on the wall behind the desk, illuminated by the wan light coming through a small window.

The tour guide led the group into the next room, but I was completely captivated and stood there, finally alone, mesmerized by this small desk. I could somehow feel the power of this Republic. Such determination and commitment to an ideal. Behind all of the clamor and color of the "official" state, this austere, practical, faceless and therefore somehow dispassionate force ensured that the ideals of state trumped all personal ambitions. A polite cough from the door reminded me that I was part of a group and we moved on, passing into a hidden courtroom where enemies of the state were tried by a triumvirate of judges. Connected to this chamber was a larger room left theatrically dim, but surely not easy to illuminate in distant times. Most of us have used the term "torture chamber", but how many have actually entered one? Once again, wooden all around, the space reached up two floors to a ceiling probably twenty five feet above our heads. Hanging from the center of it a single hempen rope, the free end dangling just above a small set of wooden steps, looking somehow alone in the center of the floor.. A desk with three chairs occupied one end of the room. (Always three…No even numbers…Always a decision never made by an individual). At the other end on each side wall a single prison cell somehow suspended out over the floor, with a small window in each that enabled a clear view of the small set of steps at the end of the rope that had now taken on a certain sense of menace.

Prisoners were brought to stand in front of these prosecutors and if they did not confess in ways that satisfied, were taken to the set of steps. They were made to ascend and then had their hands tied behind their backs to the rope hanging from the ceiling. A simple push from the top step left them dangling, usually resulting in dislocation of arms, always in considerable pain. The prisoners in the cells above who were the next "customers" could view this physical horror, could not escape the screams of pain. The torture was therefore both physical and psychological. I'm sure that I would sing like a canary long before they connected me to the rope. Of considerable interest to me is the fact that the Republic abandoned the use of the torture chamber in the 1400's because they realized that the information gained this way was highly unreliable. Apparently this is a lesson that some of the world's contemporary super powers have yet to learn.

There was a sort of involuntary shudder from the group as we moved out of this place and an almost audible sigh as we entered a large open space which was the room where all official documents were recorded, copied and stored. Even here a triumvirate of overseers sat at a desk at one end of this long room, and the copiers (who could only work here for one month and could never copy an entire document) worked at desks arranged down its length. We moved on, upwards along dark narrow passages, eventually arriving at a level directly below the roof of this great building. The roof is sheeted in lead and the rooms and cells on this level are referred to as the "piombi". These cells reserved for political prisoners of patrician status bear no similarities to the horrors of those on the ground floor, but are still decidedly uninviting. The young woman stopped here to tell the story of Giacomo Casanova and his miraculous escape and we were encouraged to enter his cell and that of his co-escapee. We were then led back down the main flight of stairs to a chamber where she thanked us and told us that we could continue through the 'rest' of the Palazzo Ducale without her. She opened a door that deposited our little group on the landing of the staircase leading to the first of the Institutional Chambers, bid us farewell, and walked back down the stairs. I was left with the strangest feeling. I fantasized walking behind an old dowager in a richly brocaded and decorated gown which swept down to the floor. She stumbled and as I moved to help her she exposed her underwear; I was struck by guilt that I had actually looked up her dress. After she regained her feet and straightened her dress, I found myself wishing that I hadn't looked. Our journey through the "secret" part of the Palazzo had exposed something that clearly was never meant to be seen publicly.

It was the fourth time in less than a week that I had visited the Palazzo, so instead of wandering back through its vastness on the way to the exit, I too descended the stairs into the bright sunshine of Riva Schifanoia, and went looking for white wine and tramezzini.

Duplicitous…No matter how I say it (in my head or out loud), it is always a pejorative.

The mask is still looking at me across the table, and as the sunlight dapples across it, one of his eyes is thrown into bright sunshine while the other remains dark. Did he just wink at me? I find myself smiling and winking back. Almost nothing in this city is as it seems at face value. There is always a front and a back…An up and a down…Positive…Negative…Yin and Yang.

However, there is nothing capricious about this subterfuge, and the facades are extremely protective. The State, the Republic of Venice, reigned supreme throughout its long history. Very few individuals attempted to wrest that power from her. None succeeded.

Her…La Serenissima. She was the entity that received love and obedience from all levels of society. It was in her that this polyglot society became one…

"Sono Veneziano"

The riches of the state belonged to and were the pride of every one of its citizens, regardless of personal position or wealth; her perpetuation was undertaken by all.

If you enter the institutional chambers of the Palazzo Ducale you are immediately in the presence of HER.

Although this building complex was initiated in 810, it has suffered through several disastrous fires and reconstructions, and perhaps the final indignity of a modern restoration, and yet it still possesses a magnificence that is inescapable.

There is an inter connectedness to each of the chambers; each serving the State by performing specific tasks that ranged from fiscal, to military, to social activities. SHE is present in most of them. Portraits depicting her receiving patronage and gifts cover the ceilings and walls. She is always beautiful, blonde, and wholesome. She regally sits among Doges and Saints, the Madonna and Jesus, as their equal. Some images are purposefully ambiguous and she plays a part that has multiple attributes. Is that a statue of Justice that stands high over the main façade of the Palazzo Ducale?...Or is it Venice standing blindfolded, the scales of justice held aloft?

My favorite depiction of her is Tiepolo's painting of Neptune emptying his horn of plenty onto the hem of her golden gown which is obviously the robe of an empress. Should the gown not be significant enough, you need to focus on the scepter in her left hand and the crown upon her head. It is the relationship between the god of the sea and the empress that I find so compelling. Naked from the waist up, Neptune leans toward her; there is a longing; even lust in his eyes that are locked with hers. She seems to diagonally withdraw, but reaches forward with her right hand....For the riches?...Or for him?

Throughout the Palazzo, giant clocks measure her time, and maps and globes her domain. She is everywhere, and in everything.

The chambers lead onward to the front of the Palazzo which presents its major façade to the sweep of the Bacino di San Marco and its sparkling waters. Room after room of furnishings and fittings made from the world's exotic woods and fabrics lead the visitor forward. No surface is left undecorated, or empty. The visitor has to be reaching a state of visual and tactile overload for that is the intention of such opulence; but then, just as this state of overstimulation approaches, he enters one of the largest rooms in Europe. The Chamber of the Great Council is one hundred and seventy four feet long, eighty two feet wide, and the ceiling hangs incongruously without obvious support forty feet above.

This was the most important chamber of all, and housed the most important political body of the Republic. Every male member of patrician families (those whose names were registered in the Golden Book) was eligible to sit on this council. Republican equality indeed... But only for the patricians. The ceiling is resplendent in enormous paintings, with equally enormous frames, the walls covered with paintings by a list of painters that any museum in the world would covet.

Just below the ceiling cornice runs a frieze of portraits by Domenico Robusti, son of the great Tintoretto. It contains portraits of the first seventy-six Doges, each holding a scroll on which is written his greatest achievement.

In the left rear section of the room the space allocated to Doge Marin Faliero is hidden by a painted black curtain. He attempted a coup d'etat in 1335 but Venice's loyal subjects came to her rescue and he was tried as a traitor and beheaded at the top of the Grand Staircase...His head rolled to the courtyard below. The black curtain records his infamy, but is also testament to the fealty that she commanded. No Venetian ever rose above her. She reigned all powerful and supreme until the end.

The sun is sinking and the patterns of light on the table have been extinguished. It occurs to me that I have been sitting here for too long, and I stretch and stand up. I reach across the table for the mask to return it to the wall where it was hanging, but without thinking, place it on my face and tie the strings behind my head.

Chapter 20

SAN MARCO...

I have no story to tell about the Basilica San Marco. No interesting, unexpected series of events. No hook to catch you with, dear Reader.

In fact, every time I enter this amazing church I end up castigating myself for not paying enough attention. Each time this building envelopes me... Wraps around me with images, smells and sounds that result in such theater that I am never allowed to be the dispassionate observer, and instead allow myself to be transported to a place where the rational collection of information has no part. There is a feeling of lift--not lightness, but lift--to almost all other Venetian structures, but the Basilica San Marco has a weight and gravity powerful enough to anchor the entire space of the Piazza in front of it. The lightness of the Palazzo Ducale is the product of the beautiful pink stone from Verona and its curious upside down architectural elements. Even the grand scale of its squared blockiness gives way to the Basilica and its cluster of domes and spires.

Almost every visitor to La Serenissima will enter the Basilica; in fact it is often the focal point of many tours, and tourists are clustered in front of its doors in pods that often stretch back down the Piazzetta for most of the hours of the day that this great church receives visitors.

It is therefore virtually impossible to have a private moment within its gloom, and because visitors are trafficked along the same route, you cannot sneak off into a corner to be alone. I have visited at almost every hour of the day, even attended worship, but have yet to find the lone, still voice that I know this place must have.

There is no grand architectural sweep into San Marco. You step up from the level of the Piazza, but then down into an entry vestibule or narthex that is considerably lower. You then climb an almost uncomfortable series of steps (look to your right into the dark maw of the staircase that leads up to the horses), and enter through a set of double doors to find yourself standing at the western end of a central nave. Unless there is a service being conducted, and it is any time of the day other than the hour between 11:30am and 12:30pm there will be no artificial lights illuminating the interior and most people will stop just inside the double doors... Not just because of the grandeur of this wonderful space, but because they are waiting for their eyes to become accustomed to the gloom that drapes its mystery over everything.

Arching above, the upper stories consisting of domes and ceilings are covered in some of the most impressive mosaics in the world. Most of the eight thousand square meters of surface consists of tiny golden tesserae that await any light source to excite them into spangling brilliance. Biblical characters and narratives are woven into all of these surfaces and it would take many visits before you became conversant with all of them. Purists among art historians lament the fact that these mosaics have been almost continually restored, and that little of the existing surface reflects the original Byzantine workmanship; but for most of us with less refined expectations, the effect is breathtaking.

In truth this church has a long history of building and rebuilding, and this ongoing restoration is still reflected today. I can't remember seeing San Marco without some form of scaffolding attached to some part of its structure.

There is no caprice to the fact that the church and the palace are in such close proximity. Until the interference of Napoleon in 1807, San Marco was the private church of the Doge and had served that function since 832. When Venetian merchants returned from Alexandria with the stolen body of Saint Mark in 829 a building program was initiated, and San Marco's history began. That building was burned in the political rebellion of 976 and was restored in 978, but the current structure probably needs to be dated to around 1093, which is the consecration date most agreed upon. The building possesses asymmetrical elements, and this leads historians to believe that certain preexisting parts were absorbed into the "new structure": but there is no clear indication of "which is which".

In 1106 the church was again damaged by a fire that gutted a large section of the city, and many historians believe that all of the mosaic interior dates from this time. The mosaics record this long series of refurbishments and you can clearly see the older sections use the Greek of the Byzantine Church to label saints and individuals, while the newer sections change to Latin for their titles.

The old saying "all that glitters is not gold" probably doesn't hold up in this church, and I tell my students that a good "rule of thumb" to remember is that if it looks like gold...It probably is gold.

However, staring up at this heaven of gold the viewer often overlooks, and of course misunderstands, some of the most precious elements of the interior. The lower levels of the basilica; all the walls and pillars, are sheathed in exquisite, figured marble slabs. Our current technologies allow us to cut any stone into wafer thin slabs, but the slabs in San Marco represent an effort of stone cutting that would have been absolutely extraordinary. These beautiful, book matched pieces of exotic stone were so difficult to achieve that their inclusion in such quantities would have rivalled the opulence of the gold mosaics above them. While Venetians and visitors of the twelfth century were certainly aware of this fact, most modern day viewers, like magpies, are fascinated by the glitter of the gold above, and the stones below get little attention.

One of my favorite elements of the interior of San Marco is its floor. Tessellated in tiny tiles, the floor is a marvel of geometric and narrative panels, many of them using animal and plant motifs. Concomitant with the rest of the building, the floor too has undergone continuous restoration and reflects these changes in differing styles and levels of craftsmanship.

I feel that the floor tells a very different story than the lofty mosaics that steal so much of the visitors' attention. The floor tells the story of the age of the building in ways that are unintentional... Somehow organic.

The Piazza and Basilica occupy some of Venice's lowest lying areas and when the waters of the Lagoon rise in the floods of "aqua alta" they are at their deepest here.

When the Piazza San Marco has a meter of water covering it, that water is also very deep inside this grand old church, and of course, the floor is affected. It is no longer flat and seems to have abandoned any pretense that it might be. There is a sort of a relaxed quality to the way that the floor sinuously undulates as it moves on its rather fluid foundation. I again fantasize about that same old attractive dowager, fashionably dressed, even resplendent in a glorious gown and shoes. She bends down, removes the shoes...And reveals feet that are old, bunioned and calloused, reflecting the long years that she has walked on them.

These wonderful floors are the feet of this grand basilica.

Uncountable feet have worn the floor smooth and shiny and this means that it becomes quite slippery when wet. Coarse, textured matting is used to ameliorate this problem, but it also means that much of the floor is often covered, and its marvels are not always available to visitors.

The interior form of this church is absolutely Greek and its overall shape is that of a Greek cross. Each arm is divided into three naves with its own dome, and there is a large central dome above the crossing. The central focus of the church is held by an altar screen constructed of eight columns of a deep red porphyry stone that have a centralized crucifix and statues placed on the beam that they support. Behind this screen, Saint Mark's sarcophagus is the base for the high altar. It is a rather simple stone box that still bears the chisel marks of the stone mason, and it creates a discordant, but clear note among the surrounding sumptuous opulence of highly polished exotic stones.

For an added fee, you can walk through a turnstile on the southern side of the altar and pass behind it to the Pala d' Oro and the incredible array of jewels that encrust it. When Napoleon plundered Venice, San Marco was not spared, and most of the church plate was seized and melted down for coin. The pieces that are extant today, and mostly displayed in the treasury, were hidden away by the clergy before Napoleon could steal them. Looking at the breathtaking treasures, reading the indignantly righteous tone of the description of Napoleon's plundering, it is not difficult to sympathize with the Venetians. Unfortunately, it is only a part of the story and it would be wrong of me to not remind you, dear Reader, of Doge Dandolo and his exploits of 1202. When he and his troops sacked the city of Byzantium, they brought back a good deal more than just the four horses that are stabled upstairs on the first floor of San Marco. Most of these beautiful jewels, metalwork, and vessels arrived as loot in the returning warships, and as such were stolen objects… The very situation that the Venetians found so odious. Because of this history, the treasury contains some of the finest examples of Byzantine metalwork in the world.

There is no way of knowing about many of the building's design elements. It is my opinion that the ancients possessed extremely sophisticated understanding and expectation of the architecture they created, and it is no stretch for me to believe that they, with great purpose, created San Marco's acoustic interior. In its most simplistic explanation, it is the combination of the shape, scale, and surfaces of San Marco that allow sound to do such wonderful things. At each end of the North and South arms that act as transepts, there is a choir loft and an organ. They are about two hundred feet apart, with the top of the central dome ninety two feet above them. Different parts of a musical piece can originate in each transept and then "meet" in the central area of the church where they become a single entity. Music was written specially to explore this phenomena. Stereophonic music was discovered in this church.

The vast interior simply became another instrument and over the centuries many composers rose to its challenge and created marvelous works especially for San Marco. Andrea Gabrieli and his nephew Giovanni wrote antiphonal compositions for brass instruments especially for this building and I can't even imagine what they might sound like.

As I exit the grand Basilica, I often play a little mental game with myself which is really quite simple. I estimate how long I have been inside, and then look up at the Torre dell' Orologio to check the time. I always underestimate my stay; sometimes I'm in there three or four times longer than I think. Earlier I spoke of the theatre of San Marco…It is very real, and continues after all these years to spin its magic around visitors. Time seems to stop for me when I enter its doors.

The exterior of the Basilica San Marco is an entirely different story. Firstly, you have to be a fairly determined viewer to take in all of its vistas, and very often the most revealing views come when you are off exploring something entirely different.

If you have never stood on the Moors Terrace of the Torre dell' Orologio then one of the most compelling views of this church still awaits you. Coffee in the café of the Museo Correr is not particularly memorable...But the view of the Basilica out of the window is.

From the top of San Marco's Campanile the view of its roof, looking for all the world like the display window of Borsalino's famous millinery shop, shows multiple domes stacked like hats on top of the building, revealing a structure strangely eastern, the lead sheathed onion domes an incongruous element among the terracotta rooftops of Venezia.

Seen from another Campanile, that of San Giorgio Maggiore across the Bacino, it is obvious that the Basilica and the Palazzo Ducale are cuddled together. Most visitors simply view it from the Piazza, where it anchors the Eastern end with its stunning façade.

Churches often present something of a conundrum for art history students, not only because of the complexity of their architectural elements, but because a church is a living entity. It is inseparable from its congregation that will venerate it, love it, repair it, make additions, change it...All so that it continues to function within some sense of contemporary time. Earlier I talked of Byzantine mosaics, but standing in front of this building it is obvious that some of the cycles of mosaics on the façade have an almost modern look to them, and are indeed 19th century restorations.

The narthex and façade only date from the thirteenth century and at that time the present domes were also added, presumably so that they could be seen over the new façade. Like the interior, you would spend a great deal of time and do some serious research if you were to attempt to examine all of the narratives and motifs that cling to the Basilica's exterior.

The west façade is divided into three sections: lower, upper, and domes.

The lower division consists of five round arched portals, two smaller at each side of a large central portal. This section contains a vast array of columns of an almost endless variety of different colored stones and decorative elements. They are sometimes in clusters, and at others singular, creating an asymmetry so complex it doesn't register with most visitors. They are as foreign as the horses and the contents of the treasury, and while I'm sure many are the result of trade, most of them, just like the horses, are objects looted from far distant places. Many are ancient enough to be pre Christian and therefore pagan, and you might ask how they can be used to decorate a Christian church. Ancient theologians quoted the Book of Kings where the Queen of Sheba gave Solomon gold and materials to build his temple, and reasoned that it was permissible to use riches from pagan sources (Egyptian gold) to glorify God.

The upper division is encrusted with statuary and flamboyant elements, and another cycle of mosaics fills the lateral arches on each side of a giant central window. In the center above this window Saint Mark and his winged lion look out over the Piazza.

Few people would argue with the declaration that this is a beautiful church. It is considered one of the finest Byzantine churches, but as much as I love it, I am constantly disturbed by it. In daylight hours, when the Piazza San Marco is dense with tourists and pigeons, where at every turn and in every moment you become a part of some family's photo album, with the sound of camera shutters whirring like crickets in a field, this beautiful building is lost in the din. Wait for the coffee bars to close and for the "battle of the bands" to finally wind down...For the street vendors selling flowers and silly laser lights to go home for the evening. Then you can have a very different San Marco experience.

I walked there at 2:00am on a cool moonlit night and of course had the place to myself. I walked slowly down the Piazza and turned to look back at San Marco as I retraced my steps. I walked until I was standing in the shadow of the West façade with Mark and his lion high above. The horses kept their patient vigil, all pigeons' heads were under their wings.

I was finally alone with it.

The mosaics were nothing more than dark shadows, but not quite shadows, because every so often a small sparkle of light from some active tesserae escaped like a miniature flash camera. The gold showed a metallic sheen, but strangely its luster was almost blue... Statues only silhouettes against the starry sky.

There was great mystery to this place, and as I walked quietly away I knew that it would take someone far brighter than me to unravel it.

Chapter 21

ANCIENT MARINERS AND DOGES

E xit the Piazzetta San Marco, turn left onto the Molo, and continue along the Riva degli Schiavoni… Past the vaporetto stop at Zaccaria Jolanda… Past Vivaldi's church with its giant plain white façade, which looks in envy across the Bacino at San Giorgio and its magnificence. Continue over a small bridge past the Arsenale Vaporetto stop to the next bridge which spans the Rio Arsenale.

Something almost miraculous happens here. The tourists, especially the day tourists who are deposited in groups along this waterfront (these groups are often incongruously large) thin out…The bridge seems to be a natural barrier that they are unprepared to cross. In truth most of them are headed in the other direction, map and guide book in hand, as they rush to count coup on San Marco.

Each time I reach the top of the Ponte Arsenale I release an involuntary breath…A sigh…And I swear I can hear the Venetians do the same. As you descend the bridge you enter a strange irregularly shaped campo that runs off to the left along the Rio, and on the corner stands a large architecturally bland, almost blank building with giant ship's anchors on each side of its front doors.

It is Venice's Museo Navale, an enormous repository of all things maritime. Some artifacts seem to have been collected with little concern for a historical narrative, and are almost memorabilia, but it is a vast collection. I have visited this place many times and have never shared it with more than a half a dozen people at a time. Perhaps its disastrous visitor rating is simply because it is on the other side of the tourist "border line"? Perhaps if you only have the six hours that we are told is the average length of time that the typical tourist spends in Venice, that you simply can't include this in your frenetic schedule?

Of course I would like to tell you I went looking for a specific piece of information, and by clever sleuthing arrived at the front doors of this building. What actually happened was that I was returning from a morning walk on a blustery day that had threatened rain since I set out. I had no rain coat and no umbrella, and just as I began to cross the Ponte Arsenale a dark squall came scudding across from San Servolo and began to pelt me with rain. The customary sigh that I have spoken of was replaced by a squawk and several expletives, and then doing what seemed entirely sensible, I bolted into the open doors of the Museo Navale. I arrived a little out of breath but not too wet, and was instantly intrigued. The entry is filled with military naval paraphernalia that ranges from flags and pennants, a cannon, to the giant two-man submarine that takes up most of the entryway.

In the first room on the right there is a monument to Admiral Angelo Emo that was carved by Canova!   I was hooked at this stage and walked through to the ticket office. The attendant almost apologetically told me that the entry fee was one Euro, fifty and presented me with something that looked like a train ticket and bore no resemblance to the full color varieties used by the city's other museums.

I exited the building three hours later to a world that was dry and even a little sunny, walked around the building to the canal side, and sat down on a public bench to think about what I had just been treated to.

I admit to being a little obsessed with my profession, and it is the excitement that I feel as a teacher in moments when it all comes together for students that has sustained me over the years. Much of pedagogy is a slow synthesis involved in the building of an architecture of knowledge and information. There comes time in this process, however, when the architecture becomes an entity, has a singular voice; is more than the sum of all of its parts. Those are the moments that we teachers live for.

Sitting looking at the water in the canal as it smoothly answered the call of the tide and flowed beneath the bridge, I was having one of my own moments.

Among the rest of the Italians, Venice is often called "Un altro paese"…Literally "another country". Everything about this amazing city is different. Different from where?…From anywhere. She is undoubtedly unique in the world, and aside from all of the physical elements that constitute much of this unique character, it is the way that the Venetians organized themselves that sustained this Republic and enabled it to become so wealthy and powerful.

Because there was literally no land, the feudal system could find no political traction, and with no agriculture the ancient Venetians literally remained hunters and gatherers. They were fishermen and they harvested the salt from the shallows of the lagoon. As they became more numerous and their population centers grew, mercantilism was the element that drove their organization. They became the "middlemen" in the exchange from producer to consumer and it was their skill in boats, their maritime prowess, that enabled them to travel far afield collecting all manner of exotic goods and bringing them back to Venice where people from all over Europe would come to buy them.

Because of the nature of the ocean there was always an element of risk inherent in every transaction; and risk taking, gambling, was an inescapable element in everything they did.

On a boat the crew knows that their safety is invested in the safety of the ship. There can only be one captain and they are betting on his experience, skill and knowledge to keep them safe. On a "free boat" the crew can register their dissatisfaction with the performance of the captain by meeting and discussing the situation. It was the right of a crew to be able to meet whenever they desired and in some situations even vote for another captain. (This is also called mutiny.) These meetings were the "aregnos" of ancient Venice. An ad hoc group of citizens could come together at any time to register their discontent with any situation. It is my contention that the original republican ideals of ancient Venice were no more than the normal expectations of any crew member of any boat. Captains quickly realized that they had to be competent and skillful, and above all had to ensure that their crew was happy and safe. The crew had to put all of their confidence in the captain if they were to respond to his commands. And it was the resultant symbiosis that enabled complex and often arcane maritime activities to be melded into a smoothly operating entity...The 'running' of the ship.

On the 2nd floor of the Museo Navale there is large scale model of one of the famed vessels of the Venetian Navy, the trireme. It is a long, low slung, sleek vessel bristling with 90 oars. These oars are operated in gangs of three. Three sailors sit abreast on a bench and these three oars will sweep as one. On a slightly elevated rear deck stand the captain and his immediate officers, one who calls cadence to the crew. They stroke on his command. One of the most compelling feelings that you have as you walk around the glass case that holds the model, is just how easy it would be for everything to go wrong. One small falter, one small slip in timing and the tangle of oars would be catastrophic. Making this vessel simply function would have been an amazing undertaking. Turning it into a high speed, lethal weapon that could turn extremely quickly (because one side of oars could backstroke), and literally cut the enemy boat in half with its rostra or beak, would require skills that are almost inconceivable.

Looking at the model, I felt as if I had been given a brief glimpse into how Venetians interacted with each other. After minutes of literally standing there shaking my head in disbelief, I wandered over to another display, and there on the floor was a full sized reme or oar. It was almost 25 feet long and weighed 170 pounds! I walked back to the model and was impressed all over again.

The Museum's collection of models continued to illuminate and instruct. The variety of vessels that have originated in this Republic are amazingly organic and simple, and yet so lively and sleek that it is clear that a highly developed set of skills was necessary to pilot them.

For me, Venice was the boat and her citizenry the crew. The captain was the doge and the crew were the citizens, often divided into groups according to their skills. "Doge" ....Venetian for Duke. The supreme ruler of the republic...But was he? There were 120 men, who over a 900 year period of time held this, the highest position in the Republic. What were the responsibilities of this office? ...And how did one get to be a Doge?

Over 900 years and through 120 incarnations, the position changed enormously. In its earliest forms there was little formality and not much organization to this process but this could also be said about the Republic itself. As Venice grew in stature and influence and her power extended its will over larger and larger areas, the complex organization of this burgeoning mercantile state demanded more and more of its highest office. In their newly formed mercantile world the compelling element was trade and its successful by-product, profit. More than any other nation in the then known world, the Venetians entered into treaties and agreements with other states, always to ensure that the exchange of goods would continue profitably. They became masterful negotiators and many of these agreements were quasi secret. It was not uncommon for Venice to have agreements with both sides of combatant states in wars and skirmishes. Were they being disingenuous to one or the other of these combatants? They presented themselves as being neutral, often negotiating for a peaceful outcome, but in truth the stable world of peace ensured the flow of goods and money into state coffers. This was often a difficult course to navigate and diplomacy became one of the most important requirements of Venetian officers. This diplomacy was focused internally as well, and the Republic went to great lengths to ensure that no mercantile preference was seen to be given to any individual or family.

A major obstacle among the early Dogeships was the concept of succession. If this office simply passed from father to son it would quickly become a dynasty that would exert a system of nepotism allowing one group or family unfair access to the market. While it is true that some families produced more Doges than others, a process of election was initiated and refined until it became impossible to allow direct succession to occur. However, the paranoid concern for secrecy and impartiality produced the following entirely arcane process.

At a meeting of the Grand Council, the youngest sitting member was identified (He had to be at least 30 years old before he could take his place on the Council). He then went down to pray at afternoon mass in San Marco. As he exited San Marco he was instructed to return to the Grand Council with the first boy that he encountered as he left the basilica.

This boy was then called the "Ballatino", a title that he would hold for the entire tenure of the new Doge. It was his responsibilities to count, record, and destroy all of the vote slips.

Everyone's name was in a basket, and the Ballatino withdrew 30 names. Then...

These 30 then elected 9

Who elected 40

Who elected 12

Who elected 25

Who elected 9

Who elected 45

Who elected 11

Who elected 41

Who elected the Doge!

Preference was given to older candidates, in fact, the average age of the doges was 72 and the process has jokingly been called a gerontocracy. Young men are filled with passion and hormones, and can be led much more easily into conflict than their older counterparts. Older men have lived a life where they have established wealth and influence and can now focus on public life without the distractions of family. In fact, many had outlived spouses and there were very few Dogeresses in the long history of this office. Once elected, the Doge was expected to do a number of things. He was to make a gesture of munificence. This usually entailed a procession around the Piazza San Marco where he threw coins into the crowd. He had to furnish the Doge's apartments in the Palazzo Ducale, and commission a number of paintings showing himself in interaction with saints and the Republic of Venice, usually depicted as a beautiful, matronly woman. He was then literally imprisoned in the Palazzo Ducale. He could never leave the building without at least two chaperones. He could not meet any other head of state unless he was accompanied by two chaperones. He could never receive a letter addressed directly to him. It was always opened and inspected first. He could not own land in a foreign country, although he was expected to stay abreast of current trading activities from these countries. He was elected Doge for life. Although several were forcibly removed, most simply served until they became too infirm, and then chose to abdicate and spend the last of their days in a monastery. At the end of his Dogeship a committee was formed to pass judgment on his tenure. Should he be found to have committed any acts that cost the Republic, his estate and those of his family would be charged with recompense.

Just to add a little more misery to his life... the Doge's salary was considerably less than the Chancellor's. Looking at all of these facts one would wonder who on earth would want such a job?

What is clear, is that this system of organization never allowed any individual to act entirely on his own volition, never allowed anyone to be the "King of Venice". He was always the figurehead who was the representative of the Republic. But the Doge enjoyed considerable power, often pursuing personal agendas. To achieve this, however, he needed to be constantly marshalling supporters and allies in an ongoing internal diplomacy. The arcane organization of state simply served to slow everything down, and it was almost impossible for Venice to act in haste.

Chapter 22

GHETTO...

G hetto...It's a Venetian word... A simple word... A word that has found its way into the English language. It can be quite innocuous, and even a little humorous. Before Ipods, we had ghetto blasters.

But we all know that the word "ghetto" has insidious connotations that speak of horrors. The almost incomprehensible acts of barbarism by Adolf Hitler's Germany in the 1940's has so poisoned this word that there is no chance of presenting it in any other way. I discuss it here as a short chapter that is almost a postscript, solely because it is obvious to me that so few people who write about Venice and its history are prepared to be completely honest.

The earliest documents of Venetian history talk of a Jewish population. In fact, anywhere nascent mercantilism slowly exerted its influence, a Jewish population sprang up. Usury was one of the seven deadly sins, and mercantilism in its earliest stages was continually thwarted by this religious tenet.

Christians enthusiastically entered into a situation of deflection. If they borrowed money from Jewish folk who were non-Christian, then the transaction--the sin--would not cause any Christian to fall, and apparently God would "look the other way".

In the 5th century, the Venetian Jewish population was relocated to Mestre on the mainland and remained there for the next 850 years. In 1516 a decree was passed that required this population to leave the mainland and be

moved to a place that was being prepared for them in Cannaregio. As you
may imagine this place was not the most desirable real estate in Venice; in
fact it was on a site that had been heavily industrialized and had housed the
city's foundries before they were moved to the Arsenale. The Venetian word
'gette' describes the slag metal by-products of a foundry, but came to be the
word used for 'foundry'. Many of the first Jewish residents were Ashkenazim,
originally from Eastern Europe and their guttural pronunciation of the word
changed it into 'ghetto'.

In 1541 the New Ghetto (so called because it was the site of the newer
of the disused foundries) was completed and its Jewish population installed. The Venetians had taken this industrial area and turned it into
a campo which was enclosed on four sides by buildings that were quite
different from any in Venice. They are still some of the tallest residential
buildings in the city, and because they were designed with low ceilings,
contain more floors of living space than can be found elsewhere in Venice.
The Ghetto was designed to be a place of intense population density. The
canals which flowed around its perimeter were made wider and deeper and
the two bridges that spanned them were complete with gates that remained
locked from dusk to dawn. The Jewish folk were allowed to enter the city
during daylight hours, but had to wear a red cap. They were restricted to
a list of rather menial occupations, including pawnbrokers and rag sell-
ers, but Jewish medical doctors were highly prized, especially in times of
plague. (The doctors were the only people permitted to leave the Ghetto
at night, so that they could respond to the calls of their Venetian neighbors.) There seems to be no formal justification for the decree of 1516, but
clearly this was not a capricious undertaking. I think that over the centuries, the Jewish population took an everincreasing role in the security of
Venice's finances, perhaps even a pivotal and essential one. If the Jewish
population continued to live in Mestre there was always the possibility
of them coming under the influence of some of the Veneto's other cities.
Venice needed to keep this population where they could be controlled.
At this point, dear Reader, you must surely be wondering what would
compel a group of people to voluntarily allow themselves to be confined

in such a way? The answer reveals either a real beneficence, or the genius of the Venetian business acumen, depending how cynical you are. The Jewish folk confined in Venice's Ghetto were allowed to practice their own faith, with no restrictions or fear of reprisals, or external violence. In the mid 1500's there were very few places in Europe that granted their Jewish populations such latitude, and what began to happen was remarkable. Jewish people from all over Europe came to Venice to voluntarily become a part of the Ghetto. Here they could be the one thing that they were often forbidden to be…Jewish. They built their own synagogues and schools and controlled life within the Ghetto according to the strictures and calendar of the Jewish religion. Five of these synagogues still exist and can be visited at different times of the year, and of course I attached myself to one of these tours. They are fascinating pieces of architecture and give a very different insight to the quality of life within the Ghetto. Many of its Jewish inhabitants were wealthy (perhaps you had to be to be in order to afford migrating there from other parts of Europe), and that wealth is no more apparent than in some of the synagogues. The Sephardic Synagogue of the Spanish/Jewish population is an opulent building of fine stone and woodwork with an altar designed by Baldassare Longhena, the architect of Salute. However, one amazing fact is reinforced by the time that you complete your tour. None of these synagogues are on the ground floor. No synagogue was allowed to be built on Venetian soil. Nor were any of the Jewish dead buried in its soil. As early as 1386 the Republic granted an area for the Jewish cemetery at Saint Nicholas on the Lido and on this outer island all Jewish inhumation took place. It was abandoned in 1938 and has only just undergone an attempt at restoring what is basically a collection of ruins. By 1633 there were in excess of 5000 Jewish people living in the New Ghetto and it was expanded west toward the Canal Cannaregio in what was called the Old Ghetto (because it occupied the area of the previous old foundry). The Ghetto continued in this configuration until 1797 when Napoleon occupied the city and destroyed the gates to the Ghetto in a symbolic act that showed himself to be the great liberator of all.. What ensued then was something of a tennis match with

Venice being the ball. La Serenissima went from French control in 1797 to Austrian in 1798...Back to French control in 1814...to Austrian in 1815.

It is interesting to note that each time the city fell back into the hands of the Austrians, the gates were repaired and restored and the Jewish population returned to the Ghetto.

We need to insert some information here that will help take a little of the vitriol out of my writing, and even show a degree of justification for what I'm describing. It was not uncommon for the Venetians to restrict the movements and activities of certain groups of foreigners (foresti) who lived in their city. Most of Venice's trading partners had a physical presence within the city. They were given certain areas, and sometimes buildings within which they could carry on their mercantile activities. However, they were strongly discouraged, or even prohibited, from going outside of these areas and lived literally confined lives. None of these groups were saddled with anything near the restrictions and demands made of the Jewish community, even the contingents that came from the Islamic world. In 1866 Victor Emmanuel scored some victories in his campaign to unify all of Italy under Italian rule. One of these victories forced Austria to finally and irrevocably leave Venice. On that day the gates were removed for all time and the Jewish community was formally given citizen status.

This, dear Reader is where the story could have ended; in fact, it seems to in most history books. This is where we could look at a great wrong and see that it had played itself out over centuries of prejudice and hate. Where we could decide to let ancient history be just that, and embrace a common future.

This is not where it ended.

Under Benito Mussolini's National Fascist Party racial laws once more deprived the Jewish populace of Venice of its civil rights. In September of 1943 as the allied invasion of Italy gathered momentum, Italy shifted from a position of being an ally of Nazi Germany to being an occupied state, and the Germans rapidly took control of the country. They came to Venice to rid it of its Jewish population and pressured the leader of the Jewish community, Professor Giuseppe Jona to give them a list of Jewish residents. He committed suicide rather than do this, but it was clear that the hunt for Venice's Jews was about to begin.

In November of 1943 Italian Jewish people were declared "enemy aliens" and were ordered arrested, their properties seized, and the search took on heinous qualities. Between December 5th, 1943 and August 17th, 1944 more than 200 Venetian Jewish folk were arrested and deported to German death camps. Only 8 of these people lived to return to Venice.

Just around the corner from the Levantine Synagogue in the Old Ghetto, you will find a wonderful bakery. Among the many kosher delicacies that it produces for a small Jewish community is a bread called "Pane Veneziano". It is an extremely moist bread that comes in tiny loaves that seem to be at least 50 percent dried fruit. It reminds me of the bread pudding that my mother sent to school with us in our lunch boxes; and is one of the things that I look forward to each time I visit La Serenissima.

I stood patiently behind two young boys who ordered an assortment of cakes and cookies in a language that I presumed was Hebrew or Yiddish (which is a little silly, due to the fact that I have no idea what either of these languages sound like...but they were not speaking either English or Italian.)

My presumptions were based entirely on the way that these two young-sters were dressed. They both wore tight fitting skull caps of a black satin material, white shirts and a dark waistcoat, and were girdled about their waists with a belt of white strings which hung down almost like an apron. On either side of their head they had allowed the hair at their temples to grow long, and it hung down in two wispy curls on either side of their faces.

They laughed with the little woman who was serving them, the three of them sharing a joke in this language that I could only guess at. Then, with their white paper bag of goodies in their hands, they turned to me and said, "excuse me" in perfect Italian as they passed through the door. Sometimes when you are close to children, you can feel their youth...that eager energy that overflows out of them. These two--so alike to surely be brothers--had a great sweetness about them, and my smile followed them out of the bakery. I paid for two "pane Veneziano", watched as the woman slid them into a white paper bag, and bid her good morning as I left.

I stepped into a street so narrow that I suspect the sun seldom shines on the paving stones, and I walked in shadows over a small bridge and into the open area of the Campo Ghetto.

The glory of the sun was everywhere here, and I sat on a bench and began to pull pieces of the sweet bread out of the bag to eat it. Aside from the building on the north side of the New Ghetto everything is much the same as it was. The building that now replaces the apartment building which used to occupy this northern site is only three stories tall and has a vaguely "official" look to it. At its western-most end it connects to a tall brick wall which is topped with strands of barbed wire. The Gestapo used this building as an office in 1943. It is a kosher restaurant now, but even such an innocuous façade can't cover up its history. On the tall brick wall and at the low end of this building a series of bas relief sculptures have been erected as memorials to those deported souls. I seldom come here without seeing flowers of tribute on both of these memorials. It is the saddest place in Venice.

Putting the bread back into the bag, I walk over to the memorial that shows two scenes of people being herded onto trains. Behind the sculptures a simple wooden wall bears the names and ages of the people who were taken by these trains.

I begin to slowly read; names and ages...This sad list, incomprehensible in warm sunshine with the taste of sugar in my mouth.

Alberto Leone Todesco 14

Bruno Todesco 7

Emilio Todesco 16

A family of brothers...And of course I'm thinking of the two boys in the bakery. I reach out to touch the names.

No matter how small the part Venice played in this horror. No matter how active or passive...or indifferent...

Nothing will eradicate this stain from her history.

Chapter 23

"THAT DAMN NAPOLEON!"...

"So, what about the Republic?"

"What Republic?"

"The Republic of Venice"

Tamir and I are walking towards Sant' Elena along the fondamente which skirts the outside of the Giardini, trees and the rather incongruous architecture of the Biennale pavilions on our left and a waist high wall of pink bricks on our right. I have no idea why he has asked the question

"What do you mean? ...What about it?"

"Well, does it still exist?"

"No"

"Where did it go?"

"The canned answer would be that Napoleon Bonaparte defeated and looted it"

We have stopped and I'm leaning on the warm brick wall. A dark green lizard blinks at me and disappears into a crack. Tamir hikes himself up onto the wall and turns and dangles his legs over the lagoon side in one smooth action. My response to this is 4 or 5 rather ungainly actions accompanied by a fair amount of scratching and scraping, and then I'm sitting up there with him too; dangling my legs and looking at San Servolo.

"That damn Napoleon!"

He turns his head and pretends to spit, and we both laugh.

Months before we had been talking to a young friend of Tarik and Tamir who was a student at Ca' Foscari; she was recounting a list of the loot removed from Venice by Napoleon and the Austrians. Each time she said the name Napoleon she theatrically spat to one side. We thought it was very funny and were so impressed that we had affected her little "spit" every time we used the name too..

"Napoleon… (spit)…Would certainly tell the tale of great conquest. He… (spit), the great liberator entering the city, knocking down the gates of the Ghetto, and erecting a tree of liberty in Piazza San Marco. You know he … (spit)… Ordered the destruction of every lion in Venice?"

"Really?"

"Well it's a good story…I don't know!"

And it occurs to me that I don't know many of the details of Venice's demise, and I begin to think about where I might go to discover them. The sun is wonderful, the wall warm and somehow comforting, and the view is world class. The Lido on our left and then a long pan to the Bacino San Marco "all set about with" astounding architecture. We stare down into the waters lapping below and it is clear that those details are going to have to wait. It's one of those magical moments where words are superfluous

When we do move; we say,

"That damn Napoleon"… (spit)…

And swing our legs back to the Giardini side of the wall.

I spent the next couple of days wandering the streets of my favorite parts of Venice, looking for answers. My questions were simple enough; perhaps too simple. I could stand in front of buildings, churches, monuments, and know that they had been placed there many hundreds of years ago…And they were still there. But the "stuff" that was Venice, that ineffable organization of people. Was that still here? None of the people of history are still here, but those who are here now consider themselves vehemently Venetian. In 1797 the last Doge, Ludovico Manin removed the "corno" of office (that strangely shaped hat that commanded more respect than many of the gilt crowns of Europe) and turning to his manservant said,

"I won't be needing this anymore".

Well, at least that is one of the stories. No matter what actually transpired; he abdicated quietly. The Republic ended with a whimper, and not with a bang.

The Doge and the Grand Council decided that they would capitulate without any physical resistance. They made this decision for the entire city just as they had made all of the decisions in the past. The tradesmen, craftsmen, street vendors, merchants weren't consulted. They were not asked if they would like to fight. I think it proved to be a huge mistake, but perhaps by this time it was too late for anyone to fight.

History is mostly written by the victors, and in this case the Venetians would not be doing the recording. What were the details of the demise of the Venetian Republic? Even with the perfect vision of hindsight it is difficult to know when the apogee of the Republic occurred. The theory of 'tipping points' tells us that irrevocable change has already transpired long before we are cognizant of it. Few geopolitical organizations can boast a longevity of more than a millennia, mostly because it is incredibly difficult to sustain order and obedience for such a period of time. The Venetians sustained their Republic for 1300 years.

Over a span of 1300 years the world had undergone dramatic changes at every conceivable level. Nations had fallen, disappeared entirely; and new ones had risen in their places. Mercantilism had flourished and the industry of banking had been birthed. Technologies had changed and sophisticated all manner of enterprise, and the maritime industry was among the first to be revolutionized. It was probably impossible for Venice to stay current and competitive with all of these changes and it simply makes sense that she was increasingly less capable of holding her old place in the pecking order of the European powers. As convenient as it may be to demonize the final players in the demise of La Serenissima, it is clear this process involved a long, protracted 'running down" that was more about fatigue than intrigue.

The story of the rise and fall of Venice is the stuff of great tomes and towering intellects and I would not consider even a condensed version in this little book. I'm hoping that a short list of dates, numbers and statistics will give some idea that this was a steady downhill trend and not a precipitous drop.

Before 1400, Venice possessed an indisputable dominance in the trade between Europe and the Levant. The exotic goods of the Middle East, and through the Black Sea--Asia as well--passed through La Serenissima in a most profitable way. All of this came about because of her outstanding maritime presence. In 1410 the Venetian navy numbered 7,300 ships and 36,000 sailors. On May 29th,1453 the great city of Constantinople fell to the Ottoman Empire and Venice's dominance began to wane. What became quite clear then, still in some ways persists. In the preceding millennia an enormous amount of money had flowed into this city. It was reflected in the grand churches and civic architecture, and it had become the personal fortune of a number of its grander families. In this, the 21st century, much of that wealth still resides among these families. By the end of the 1400's Venice had 180,000 residents and was the second largest city in Europe after Paris; she was certainly the wealthiest city in Europe.

1545 marked a year when a seemingly small change in maritime organization occurred. Up until then all of the sailors who rowed the ships of Venice were "free men". They "owned" their oar. They signed on as a part of the crew, but also to share in the profit of each voyage; this speculation as much as anything fuelled Venice's engine of mercantilism. In 1545 the Republic assumed control of all maritime activity and many sailors were chained to their seat. In 1563 the population had slipped to 168,000 residents and it went on to take some precipitous drops, due to plague which repeatedly visited this city more often than it did its neighbors. In 1581 it boasted a stable population of 124,000.

The Turkish Empire continued with its dominance of the Eastern Mediterranean and a long, slow withdrawal was forced upon the Venetians. In 1669, Crete, the island they had so cunningly acquired, was lost, and in 1714, the Turks formally declared war on the Republic of Venice. Only Corfu managed to withstand these advances and the trade of the Levant was slowly lost. In the 1700's Venice was being pushed to compete with other maritime powers, and her wars with Genoa forced her trading vessels into military use. The trade monopoly was broken and Venice found herself competing with many "newcomers" to the Adriatic trade routes. The dukes of Tuscany created a large port at Livorno and the British chose it as the staging platform for their entire Mediterranean fleet. Closer to home, the papacy invested in Ancona, turning it into a flourishing port, and the Austrians did the same with the great natural port of Trieste.

In 1779 Carlo Contarini addressed the Great Council in an attempt to change the political stagnation of Venice, and said,

"All is in disorder…Everything is out of control"

These remarks were seen as traitorous and he was locked up.

However, in 1784 an even more powerful Venetian, Andrea Tron, addressed the Council and said,

"Trade is falling into collapse. The ancient and long held maxims and laws which created and could still create a state's greatness have been forgotten. We are supplanted by foreigners who penetrate right into the bowels of our city. We are despoiled of our substance, and not a shadow of our ancient merchants is to be found among our citizens or our subjects. Capital is lacking, not in the nation, but in commerce. It is used to support effeminacy, excessive extravagance, idle spectacles, pretentious amusements and vice, instead of supporting and increasing industry which is the mother of good morals, virtue, and of essential national pride".

Venice's fleet had dwindled to 309 merchant vessels by 1792, and by 1796 only 11 of these remained; 4 galleys, 7 galliottes, and a few brigades of mostly Croatian mercenaries were all that was left to protect Venice. Obviously incapable of defending herself, Venice fell back on her last and final resource; Diplomacy.

In 1796, the great combatants of Europe were the French and the Austrians and a major area of this conflict just happened to be south of the Alps in territory that was Venetian.

Napoleon offered an alliance against the Austrians, and the Venetian story is that they chose neutrality. What really happened is that they thought Austria would prevail, and were secretly seeking an alliance with them.

In 1796, Napoleon out maneuvered the Austrians and pursued them across Venetian neutral territory. He of course left a French "presence" in the lands he crossed. At the resolution of this action, both Austria and France were ostensibly occupying Venetian territory and there was nothing that La Serenissima could do about it. In 1797 in the small Austrian town of Leoben, a treaty was signed by the two warring nations. Venice had no presence in this process, but secret and undisclosed elements of this treaty divided Venetian territory between France and Austria. Even though it should have been clear that Venice could not offer any military threat, Napoleon was unprepared to leave a potential enemy force on his flank while he pursued the Austrians, so he began a process of demonizing Venice. She was presented as a republic of oligarchs, where the wealthy few controlled everything and forced a large working class population into servitude and penury. His coming would therefore be an act of liberation, and he moved from town to town and city to city across the Veneto erecting his "trees of liberty" and setting the poor free from their shackles. When these towns and cities began to resist this "liberation", the French blamed this on the political machinations of the Venetians, and tensions were raised another notch.

On April 25th, in the old city of Graz, a frustrated Napoleon replied bitterly to the Venetian contingent that came looking for leniency,

"I want no more Inquisition, no more Senate. I shall be an Attila to the state of Venice!"

On April 30th he gave orders for a small group of ships to enter the mouth of the Lido. The lead vessel, called the "Liberator d' Italia" was captained by Jean Baptiste Laugier, and of course had to pass in front of San Andrea and its guns. What transpired then is reported in many ways and perhaps the clearest statement would be one that says it is not clear what happened.

Cannons were fired…How many?

Given the military advantage of such a fortification, if all the cannon of San Andrea discharged a salvo it is inconceivable that any vessels would have survived. One cannon was certainly fired, apparently by Domenico

Pizzamano, and this shell struck the "Liberator d' Italia", killing Laugier and 4 of his crew.

In reaction to this singular act, Napoleon issued a declaration of war on Venice on May 1st.

The drama of the next 11 days is beyond my imagination. Ludovico Manin, the last Doge of the Venetian Republic desperately explored every avenue of diplomacy and acquiescence, however Napoleon would accept nothing but total surrender.

"…And as he had clipped the wings of the imperial eagle of Austria, he would compel the lion of Venice to lift his paws from the earth and leave them but little on the ocean"

Manin turned to the possibility of defense, but it was here that I think the old system failed him. He could only consult with the Patricians that remained in Venice. (Many had fled to their summer homes along the Veneto rivers and beyond). These were largely merchants and bankers who perceived any military exercise as damaging to enterprise and profit, and who by their very nature were unlikely to be physically involved in any activity that would endanger them.

The lower classes and the Arsenalotti, who would have fiercely defended their beloved Venice were never consulted, and perhaps even worse, never considered.

On May 12th the Grand Council met for the last time. It was not so Grand (in fact not enough patricians turned up to create a quorum), and they voted to give their power to a "Provisional, Representative Government".

The vote was 512 for…And 10 against.

Ludovico Manin quietly abdicated and the entire Palazzo Ducale was abandoned.

On May 17th General Baraguay D' Hilliers arrived at San Marco with 7,000 French troops and the surrender contract was officially signed.

Napoleon then began to "liberate" Venice. It has been described as a "civilized looting".

In the initial few months of the first brief French occupation of Venice, Napoleon emptied the coffers of every Scuola in the city. These confraternities effectively performed the duties of the Republic's social services. They were charged with administering schools and hospitals, looking after the poor, the indigent, the widows and orphans. Many, especially the six Scuola Grande had amassed huge amounts of money which would now fund the great war machine of Napoleon instead of serving the citizenry of Venice. This single act of larceny had a sociological impact that would be felt for decades to come. The gates to the Ghetto were torn down and burned, and the population inside granted citizenship; but it also effectively brought them into the greater population where their numbers swelled the tax rolls, which brought more money into Napoleon's war machine. On December 13th the four horses which had occupied the façade of the basilica San Marco since Dandolo had brought them from Constantinople, were removed and taken to Paris, along with the winged lion that had stood on its column in the Piazzetta since the 1200's

The Bucintoro, the wonderfully decorated barge of the doge, was broken up and taken to the Island of San Giorgio where it was burned to recover the gold that decorated it. On December 25th the entire work force of the Arsenale was dismissed with one week's pay. The Arsenale was completely sacked. Boats were scuttled at their moorings thereby rendering most of the wharves inoperable; buildings were ransacked and burned.

However, Napoleon's enormous war machine was being stretched in too many directions at this time and he needed to focus his aggressions. On October 18th 1797, he signed the Treaty of Campoformio which gave Venice and all of her possessions to Austria in return for guarantees of non-aggression.

On the 18th of January 1798, the Austrians entered the city under the leadership of General Olviero Van Wallis, by all accounts a rather conservative being, who began to exert a series of rather oppressive controls over the fallen city. To shout the words "Viva San Marco" was punishable by death. The next few years were not going to be happy ones for La Serenissima. However, they were the 'glory days' of Napoleon's conquests, and he moved from victory to victory, slowly acquiring more personal power than his ego could control. In 1804 in the Grand Cathedral of Milan he crowned himself King of Italy.

By 1805, he had the upper hand of his Austrian nemesis and snatched Venice back for a final time. In December of 1805, the Austrian Emperor formally returned Venice to the French at the Treaty of Pressburg.

Napoleon's stepson (who was now a Prince) was in Padua when this treaty was signed and four days later he attended the theater to celebrate the arrival of French rule. He chose to do so by ordering a sixty cannon salute before he entered the building! In March of 1807 the Palazzo Ducale was decreed crown property, and in one piece of legislation it was made clear that the French intended to make profound architectural changes to Venice. The most controversial of all the building programs; the redesigning of the Piazza San Marco and the Procuratie Nuove, and the building of the Palazzo Reale, were initiated.

Napoleon himself visited Venice on December 2nd of 1807 and ensured that La Serenissima greeted him with all the pomp and splendor that she had shown previous visiting monarchs. There was a floating triumphal arch in the Grand Canal near Santa Lucia and the Grand Canal was crowded with decorated boats. Napoleon traversed the entire Grand Canal and disembarked at the Piazzetta San Marco. However, instead of turning right into the Palazzo Ducale, he turned left, walked up the main Piazza and went to the new Palazzo Reale in the New Procuratie. Before he attended the opera, La Fenice was refurbished so that it incorporated a royal box, changing forever the acoustics of this wonderful building.

Then on December 7th he announced the grand new plan for Venice.

San Cristoforo would become the formal cemetery of the city. Riva degli Schiavoni would be widened and extended east toward the area that would now become Venice's first public gardens. One of the most ambitious parts of this plan was to build another huge Piazza (larger than San Marco) on the eastern end of the Giudecca just across from San Giorgio. This was projected to be a parade ground for the military and a place for the passeggiata of the people. Funds for these projects were thankfully scarce and many of the more grandiose were trimmed. The Giudecca Piazza was scrapped entirely. However, it was necessary to "prepare ground" for the projects that were accepted and the only way to do that was to "find ground". The only way to do that was to demolish existing buildings and fill in canals. The Rio di Castello was filled in and it became Via Eugenia, and later took on its modern name: Via Garibaldi. It was at the northern end of this Via that the real destruction was being done, and the space for the Giardini was found among some of Venice's most densely populated areas. This was the part of Venice where many of the Arsenalotti lived...The workers that Napoleon had come to liberate. Untold numbers of their houses were levelled, along with three of their beloved churches. San Antonio, San Nicolo and San Domenico were demolished, although the Lando Chapel within San Antonio was thought too beautiful and its Doric arch entry was somehow preserved among the rubble. It now stands, incongruous and disconnected among trees and hedges, a silent memory of a beautiful church, and testament to French vandalism.

The seminary of the Cappuccine order was toppled. But the worst cut of all came when they destroyed the Hospice for Retired Sailors. Back in San Marco the new Procurate marched around the square to meet the Old Procurate, and swallowed up Sansovino's beautiful little church of San Gimignano. There had been a religious architectural entity on this spot since 552, and Sansovino's final incarnation was considered one of Venice's gems. The grand staircase which currently climbs up to the Correr Museum is the same one that Napoleon used to climb up to the Palazzo Reale. The next time that you stand in front of the metal gates on your way up to the museum, look back over your shoulder. There on the floor, in the center of the arcade is a plaque with a linear drawing of a church façade and a Latin inscription. Go over and have a look at it. It's all that is left to mark the place of San Gimignano.

By 1814, Venetians who returned to their city after only a ten year absence were incredulous of the changes that had occurred. Napoleon's military aspirations eventually depleted all resources, and on the 29th of April, 1814 he abdicated, allowing Austria to simply step back into Venice to continue the control it had given up nine years before. They intended to keep it this time and in the Congress of Vienna, Venice was formally declared an Austrian possession.

She was a strict, conservative, imperial power, and Venice and the Veneto became a source of considerable income. It was not uncommon for the profits from these territories to be as high as 50,000,000 Austrian lire a year.

At the end of Napoleon's control of Venice, the Austrians had taken a leading role in assisting with Venetian requests that their stolen art works and treasures be returned. It was Austrian troops that in December 1813 forcibly removed many of these works from the Louvre in Paris.

The great Venetian sculptor Canova had championed this cause for years and had consistently placed these demands before the monarchs and governments of Europe; but it was the action of the Austrians that finally initiated the repatriation of Venetian treasures. On December 7th of 1815, the four horses arrived back in Venice where they were welcomed by a contingent that included a descendant of Doge Dandolo himself. On December 13th they were ceremonially restored to their place on the Basilica San Marco. The winged lion was not quite so fortunate and was smashed into 84 fragments when it was removed from its Parisian perch. It went directly to the Arsenale foundry where it was repaired and then returned to its column on the 17th of April in 1816. Even though Austria played such an important part in these repatriations, she too coveted many of Venice's beautiful things. Over the years of Austrian occupation there was a constant and continuous drain of art, artifacts, and intellectual materials from La Serenissima.

Even though "that damn Napoleon" (spit) was no longer on the scene, the Venetian relationship with their Germanic overlords was not a happy one. The Austrians kept the Palazzo Reale which became the closest thing to a royal court that Venice had ever experienced, and many Venetian patricians found this to be personally elevating (which of course caused dissention within the Venetian population).

The factors that moved Venice inexorably toward open conflict with their captors were also at work all over Europe, and it was the emergence of a politically active middle class that fueled fires of dissatisfaction all over the continent. The world too was changing, and the industrial revolution was making demands of populations that had never been made before. In 1882 the first mention of connecting Venice to the mainland with a railway was presented, and it was clear that this modern invention would change her forever. Some early plans had tracks that would violate the city all the way to Salute, and the final span from Mestre to Piazzale Roma was actually quite a compromise. Upon its completion In 1846, it was one of the longest bridged spans in the world, and as such, a marvel of engineering. As industry and commerce grew so did the gap between those who embraced the future and all of its changes, and those that counselled preservation of the past; but it was the overarching and almost universal disdain for the Austrians that melded the population. Daniele Manin was a young lawyer who was actively involved in the Venice/ Milan railway venture, and was committed to improving Venice's ability to be competitive in the greater theater of European economics. He had personally initiated a petition to the Austrian Governor asking that the shipping trade that was currently being sent to Trieste, be directed to Venice instead. He has been described as a "local middle class patriot", and was clearly a charismatic man with excellent oratory skills. He saw the power in the working classes of Venice, and they embraced him as 'one of theirs'.

Niccolo Tommaseo was an intellectual from Dalmatia, but was such a committed "Venetian" that he wrote about her in impassioned eloquent prose. His was a clear voice of reason and was held in high esteem by many. Both of these men voiced their criticisms of the Austrian government and on 18th of January, 1848 were arrested and imprisoned. This act further united the Venetians and they rose as one to confront their oppressors. Family feuds that had stretched over a century were ended so that a unified front could be presented. The Venetians of their own volition banned smoking and Carnevale just so that they would defy the Austrian taxes on tobacco and feathers!

The people wore scarves and sashes of red, green and white. Opera houses presented powerfully patriotic and even pro-revolutionary operas. On the 6th of February, 1848 La Fenice was closed when a performance of "La Siciliana" was received too enthusiastically. When the Austrian military band struck the first note of their evening concerts in Piazza San Marco, this was the signal for every Venetian in earshot to stand up and leave.

Things were not going well for the Austrians even in their own homeland, and on the 17th of March 1848, a revolution was declared in their beloved Vienna.

Taking this as their cue to do the same, the Venetians stormed the Palazzo Reale and demanded the release of Manin and Tommaseo. The Austrian governor received their demands and, discretion being the better part of valor, allowed the revolutionaries to go free. They were carried through the streets to San Marco, and the Venetian revolution against the Austrians had begun. Unlike the 1797 capitulation which was largely decided by the upper class citizens, this revolution was fuelled by the zeal and patriotism of the workers, and Manin made his first move at the Arsenale where he was welcomed by both the Arsenalotti and the soldiers charged with guarding it. They marched down Riva degli Schiavoni and captured the Austrian cannons in front of San Marco. In Naples, Bologna, Milan, and Vienna the revolutionary cry was,

"Viva la Liberta"

Manin and his followers cried,

"Viva la Repubblica…Viva San Marco…Viva la Liberta!"

While the Austrians may have been dislodged from the Venetian islands, it was clear that they had no intention of going very far. They quickly gained an upper hand in Mestre and in the waters off the Lido. Venice was blockaded, and for the first time the lagoon could not offer the defense it had historically done. In Mestre the first 5 spans of the railway bridge were dynamited and the island of San Giuliano was made ready to receive Austrian cannon.

And then the beautiful Serenissima, who, for so long had remained aloof from external military invasion forces, was defiled for the first time in her long history. The Austrians launched balloons from which they dropped incendiary bombs. Between May 4th and May 24th of 1849, the Austrians launched 60,000 projectiles into the lagoon. The sestiere closest to San Giuliano's canon was Cannaregio and the population was evacuated to Piazza San Marco on the evening of June 29th in 1849.

The Venetians could do little more than hunker down and endure what was happening. Resources simply could not handle the population density that now existed in Venice's eastern most places, and concomitant with the degradation of drinking water, cholera broke out. Food was rationed, and many of the dead were left lying above the ground around the grand church of San Pietro in Castello.

The Austrians, who had spoken with such affection for 'their' city when they liberated her from the French, now indiscriminately raped her with cannon and bombs.

Tommaseo wrote,

"...The former Queen of the Seas...became a slave girl, and the winged lion no more than a water rat"

On April 2nd of 1849 in the giant room of the Grand Council in the Palazzo Ducale, the assembly under Manin passed a decree that simply said,

"Venice will resist the Austrians at any cost"

...And the Venetians fought on until conditions had deteriorated to such an extent that they could literally go no further. On the 19th of August 1849 the Venetians surrendered. In his book "The Narrative of Scenes and Events" Pepe wrote,

"Thus fell Venice, not vanquished by a great empire, but because she had neither bread nor powder. She fell after sustaining a thousand misfortunes and after sacrifices on the part of the population which were almost incredible".

The Austrian General Radetzky entered Venice on the 30th of August. Assurances were given that the revolutionaries could leave safely and all lesser officials and military personnel were pardoned. However, even the great Austrian Empire could not hold back the sociological changes that rode the industrial revolution into Europe, and calls for liberty, equality and representation echoed around the world.

The Risorgimento raged up and down the Italian peninsula for the next 15 years and its history mostly points out just how regional and disconnected the people who would become Italians were. Venice was offered as a bargaining chip once more and in an almost incongruous process was given to the French, who gave her to the Italian States, and on November 4th 1866, she became Italian under Victor Emmanuel.

I think the most telling part of this rather amazing story is that in the brief moments that Venice rose up to confront her oppressors, those two years where the populace endured unimaginable hardships, they gathered behind Daniele Manin, and as they marched virtually weaponless to the Austrian palace they called out,

"Viva la Repubblica!...Viva San Marco!...

It is this quality that I find in my Venetian friends. They possess a profound sense of being different, and take fierce pride in this difference. They are Venetian above all other things. What does it mean to be Venetian?

Cento percento Veneziano...100% Venetian?

One of the most sensible things to do would be to ask one. Matteo and I are sharing lunch at one of his favorite places. We have cemented a friendship that I value highly and he has become one of my most valued sources of information. Beyond the fact that he is "cento percento" and can answer with such personal depth, I am drawn to his quiet ways and gentle intellect. We are clearly quite dissimilar souls, but in the parts where our sensitivities overlap and meld, we have created a strong kindred spirit. It's a simple repast of salad greens and tuna over which we have liberally drizzled excellent olive oil and balsamic vinegar, and the magic to its simplicity is that everything is absolutely fresh. Over coffee he looks across at me and answers my question with an elegant simplicity that is perfect.

"We have been Venetians for more than 1500 years...And Italians for less than 150... Of course we are Venetians first."

Chapter 24

IT'S A LOVE STORY....

I t was during my fifth visit that something quite strange transpired. I woke early on the first morning and walked down to my favorite local bar for coffee and a brioche, but was only about half way there when I was literally consumed by how happy I was to be back in this city. I stopped on a small bridge in the early morning quiet and literally said out loud,

"I love this place…"

And then came the realization that I was truly in love with Venice, all the while thoroughly aware that she was loved and adored by countless others.

Many of you who read these words know exactly what I am describing and must surely have asked how this comes about. Venice obviously has a great number of people under her spell and many of us are moved by her to do things that we would not normally do,

…Like write a book.

POST SCRIPT

I was never quite sure how to begin this little book and still visit the first page in hopes that the words that eluded me so long ago are hiding in the margins waiting for me to find them. If you remember, dear Reader, I began this book with a confession and as I write these words I realize that I'm about to conclude it with a confession as well.

It has been seven years since I wrote the first page and a great deal has happened in that space of time.

Armed with the store of information collected during my sabbatical leave, I returned to my school in Montana and spent an intense semester planning and seeking endorsement for a study abroad program in Venice. All of this was accomplished, and a pilot program left for Venezia in January of 2009. It proved to be very successful and for the next 6 years earned accolades and praise from the Venetian educators with whom we were collaborating. However, after almost 50 years as an educator, it came my time to retire and I passed the program onto others.

Souheir and I immediately created our own small company, called Art & Soul… I'm Art and she's Soul… (www.artandsoulinternational.com), and we direct annual Artist Residencies in Venice for the month of April…Our commitment to La Serenissima continues.

...And so the person writing these words is decidedly not the person who wrote those on page one. My relationship with Venice has deepened and mellowed, and in many ways is now much more honest. I am still deeply in love with this place, and can't imagine that feeling ever going away. Every day she reveals herself in yet another breathtaking moment. Standing on a vap from Arsenale to San Zaccaria I always have to remind myself to breathe as the Palladian vista of San Giorgio, Zitelle, and Redentore aligns itself along the horizontal line of the Giudecca.

But we are practiced lovers now and she has worn a groove in me and I in her. I move around her entirely intuitively...she is part of my unconscious—Sometimes I step off a vap and onto another with only a couple of minutes ashore--and I expect to move like that. Every day is still an act of discovery...myriad textures, colors, sounds and smells...all with an advanced familiarity.

In the six years of directing the program I was also seriously tested by Venezia. Seeking permits and authorizations, I had to confront the ponderously gnashing teeth of its bureaucracy, had to learn to smile and reserve my comments as I watched graft and corruption nibble at the edges of almost every financial transaction I made. When I introduce new students to Venezia we spend time exploring and discussing the Lagoon. It is the major defensive barrier of the city and one of its most beneficial qualities is that it is largely opaque—you can't look down into this water...and it conceals the muddy sand bars that will ensnare the unwary.

I am now experienced enough to be able to penetrate that barrier...I can look beneath the sparkling surface of Venice and she keeps far fewer secrets from me than she used to. I hope, dear Reader, that you won't see these words as cynical—because there is none of that in me. My intention in them is to let you know that my relationship with this city, tempered over time, is now more real...more honest.

So, I'm sitting looking out of the windows of my apartment on Via Garibaldi in Castello, watching my Venetian neighbors as they go about their daily lives. The little bakery across the via wakes me every morning, first with the delicious smells of its products cooking and then with the rattling of the metal shutters as they are raised from the windows of the storefront.

As I close the shutters on my windows in the evenings, I often nod to the man across the via who is closing his bar, softly whistling as he takes the chairs and tables in for the night. If you live in this city for more than a brief tourist visit, you find yourself adjusting to her restraints and requirements in subtle ways that affect almost everything you do. Beyond the ache of legs unused to walking all day; often climbing stairs and bridges; beyond the obvious demand to function in another language, I am aware of changes in me that literally adjust core behavior. In Montana, if I am driving to town in the morning and half way there realize that I have forgotten something and have to turn around to go back for it...I am truly frustrated...even angry.

In Venice, if I'm half way down Garibaldi and realize that I have left something in the apartment, it is nothing more than an inconvenience; something easily dismissed. The effort required to walk back, climb two flights of stairs and unlock the apartment is considerably more than turning my vehicle around and driving back, so what is different? Part of it is because in Venice I get the chance to walk back along this street where I have to react to all around me. I am not encased in a steel and glass container; isolated, even insulated, from the reality outside.

Sitting to think about this though, I realize that the compelling difference is that in Venezia I feel like I have the time to go back...that things will wait for me. The time that I talked about earlier in this book has taken on proportions that I would never have understood without an extended residency.

The more time I spend in my Venetian life, the more information I have to compare it with my Montanan life and I have long ago given up on the idea that I am the constant in these situations. For me, the greatest shift is from my rural Montanan schedule to my urban Venetian one. The constraints and requirements of being a city dweller differ enormously from what is required of me to live in my mountain home.

I sometimes wonder how many words I use to function in both places. While it is not infinite, or perhaps even very large, the vocabulary of my native tongue doesn't feel constrained. Any time I want, I can reach beyond the several hundred words that I probably use for my daily functions. There are literally no constraints that I am conscious of. However, I function with a much smaller Italian vocabulary, consciously acquiring words almost daily; but for all practical purposes repeating and recycling a stock series of phrases.

Another confession…My Italian is still atrocious, and continues to be a source of embarrassment for me; which of course, changes how I function. While I do not feel schizophrenic or a Jeckyl and Hyde, it is clear that I have a Montana persona and a Venetian one and I have no problem moving from one to the other. While I don't think of myself as being brash or overconfident in my Montana life, it is clear that as a Venetian I am a much more humble person. Most of the things that I need or do, require the assistance or intercession of another person. If I am asking even a complete stranger for something, he or she needs to make a concession to my inexpert use of their language and if that fails; has to agree to my request to speak English. I am not at the 'mercy' of anyone, but am poignantly aware that my life functions only with the assistance of others. I enjoy the man that I become, who quietly makes his way among a population not renowned for its acceptance of strangers and who seem committed to the philosophy that there is very little worth hurrying for.

The question that I find myself asking is, "If I have changed in this time… has Venice also changed?"

I want this place to be immutable, implacable, unaffected…but of course that is not possible and as my residences have allowed me to see the different perspectives of Venetian life, they have also allowed me to be aware of the subtle physical changes that are occurring around me. I watch the cancer of graffiti inch slowly from the dark, uncared for places where few people go, into and onto thoroughfares and campos. No one seems concerned enough to stop it—It is seldom removed and therefore begins to become acceptable… even the new face.

Because this is the city of some of the world's greatest merchants it is constantly involved; embroiled, in the many processes of mercantilism. The goal and end product of all these activities is money…and if money was a driving force behind ancient Venetian merchants, it is no less today. In the complex fabric of Venetian life, this scramble for wealth seems to be moving from peripheral, decorative threads into the very warp and weft of the weave.

A few weeks ago, Souheir and I were waiting for a vap at the Arsenale stop. It was a cool afternoon and the light was being absorbed by the moisture of a misty sky. I looked across past San Giorgio to the Canal Giudecca and almost choked on my own intake of breath. An enormous white mass was coming out of the mist, its bulk dwarfing Palladio's San Giorgio, and two tugs pulled a huge cruise ship slowly into the Bacino San Marco. We watched, speechless as its great bulk bore down on us. Vibrations from its huge engines, still several hundred meters away, sent the entire fermata rattling and humming and eventually our bodies also hummed along as well.

Then, incongruously as it passed, the entire fermata rose about two feet on the water that this vessel displaced. It passed; the vibrations diminished, and then it was gone; and the fermata settled back down as water flowed back into the Bacino. Venice has accommodated the rise and fall of the tide for 1500 years. Each cycle wearing slowly at its bricks and stone. It was diurnal...every 12 hours...something to set your clocks by...it now occurs every time one of these giant ships passes by.

It is difficult for me to believe that the danger of allowing such a huge vessel into this narrow channel is not apparent to everyone...That the crass, invasive, incongruity of its presence is not offensive to all, not just Venetians. There has been a concerted effort to ban these large vessels from entering the harbor; promises have been made...but still they come. Why? Because it is estimated that each visit by these giant vessels, and their sometimes 5,000 passengers, will leave behind a million euros.

And the money flows in.

The tourist trade is of course about selling 'stuff', and I have discussed this in a previous chapter, but the drive to sell more 'stuff' has simply created more tourists, and Venice is now the destination place for many more millions of people than it was when I started this book.

In a world where some of the most visited tourist cities like Paris and Rome report statistics that document 18 visitors for each resident, Venice stands alone. It is calculated that in Venice, the ratio of tourist to resident is now at about 600 to 1.

And the money flows in.

This year when we turned up at our favorite trattoria on the Giudecca we were received by the brother of one of the owners. He gave us the news that the trattoria had just been sold to a Chinese family. He delivered this information in much the same way that you would expect someone to report a death in the family, but said that he had been retained for one month so that he could show the new owners how the establishment functioned. He assured us that all of the cooks would be retained and that the recipes and menu of the past 30 years would remain. Dinner was chaotic, but it was obvious that everyone was working hard trying to accommodate this interface, and the food was excellent.

We revisited two weeks later and our friend was clearly unhappy and frustrated. One half of the kitchen staff had been replaced and it was the pizza cook's last evening. The food was a little disappointing and the menu had been reduced by about a third.

A week later when we decided to give it 'one more try' the waiter stood at our table with tears in his eyes,

"My family kept this alive for 35 years and in less than a month it has almost gone."

"Why?", I ask

"Before, people came to Venice to share in our foods and wines, to eat our fish…to love our Art…to share in our culture. These people only come here to make money!"

I am too polite to ask him the obvious question,

"Why did you sell it to them?"

One look around the trattoria filled with people, many now Asian, all enthusiastically involved in the eating and drinking ritual. The answer is clear.

And the money flows in…

One of the most glaring examples of Venice's headlong plunge into mercantilism is to be found in the giant engineering project called the MOSE that I have described in chapter 15. This enormous experiment in marine biology and tidal control is now many years past its projected completion date, and as would be expected in such a situation, many Euros beyond its projected budget.

How many Euros?

Five billion Euros! However, ongoing investigations reveal an even more alarming statistic. Three of these five billion Euros that have been overspent cannot be accounted for. Most of the principle Officers from the project's contractors are under indictment or in jail. The Mayor of Venice was under house arrest, but has since been released. It is clear that a great deal of money has been used to discredit and silence the research from marine biologists from around the world who believe that the implementation of this system will result in the biologic death of the lagoon. A common sign seen on flags and posters around the city is "VENEZIA E' LAGUNA"...Venice is the Lagoon.

Why would anyone take such risks with the very life source of this city?

Because the money flows in.

The paradox of each of these examples is that failure and success chase each other around in an apparently endless spiral. The success of modern day Venice's mercantile efforts (its pursuit of money) is matched and often outmatched by the negative effects that are by products or results of this mercantilism. Venetians have lost control of their city to a horde of visitors that dramatically outnumber them, and as the cost of real estate spirals, the Venetian population of the city is constantly dwindling. The very ownership of their city is in contention.

Voices of caution, reason and intelligence raised in defense of Venice's ecosystem and the quality of life of its inhabitants are effectively silenced by a blanket of Euros that settles over everything.

And the money flows in...

This spiral that is apparently endless, is of course not, and there is surely an end game that must be reached. What will that look like? Entropy or collapse? Some will say that I am only talking about a fugitive, ethereal thing...a way of life...which is of course an aesthetic value and therefore something that we seem to be incapable of measuring or quantifying. As long as it is seen in this light there will never be consensus...never a point of general agreement. And it will be unlikely that any substantive changes will ever occur.

What of my beloved Venezia?...Our beloved Venezia, dear Reader?

Can she survive the onslaught of the 21st century with its hordes of visitors, spiraling mercantilism and rising waters?

I'm afraid the answer is…probably not…Certainly not without the intervention of man…People like you and me.

When I began this book I could never have imagined that I would conclude it on such a dour note. Venice is unique…she is unlike any other place on the planet, with a history that literally links this current Western civilization to its roots. It contains some of this civilization's finest, most important works of art and architecture. It is the birthplace of so much of its music and theatre, and it refined the Republican ideals that so many political organizations have embraced.

She is no longer safely protected by her placid lagoon and is suffering under an attack, whose ferocity and magnitude are beyond anything that she has ever experienced.

La Serenissima is no longer serene…and she is calling out to us dear Reader… she is calling to us.

GRAZIE

Sitting to write this page, I am surprised at the compulsion driving me to thank everyone in my entire life! However, it is clear to me that I do have a great deal to be thankful for and that this is perhaps a perfect vehicle to accomplish this... So, I will begin by thanking dear, dear Lilian my Mother, who at 93 is still a major source of inspiration in my life.

I resonate with the influences of great teachers, with the energies of my past students, and with the understanding that I am just a small part of a much larger collection of skills and knowledge. I'm a little embarrassed that the writing of this book has taken so long and would like to thank the following people who were so influential in pushing me toward its completion:

Without the encouragement and skills of Mikie di Muro the book would have stalled in its infancy. She was the brave soul who first pulled and pushed it toward its current state, and she will always occupy a special place in it.

Dan Yuhas was an early reader, when that entailed wrestling with reams of loose pages and obvious determination. His demands for "more" helped enormously.

Barb Myers not only read it, but actually told me what kind of a book I had written... and removed the last block to my conviction.

Deena Dietrich was an enthusiastic early reader and her encouragement and suggestions carried me through the entire process. Matteo Savini--who has played such a pivotal role in all of this--was my mine of information, my confidante, and the venturi through which all things 'Venetian' passed. He is a wordsmith in his own right and was extremely patient when my capabilities could not quite meet his demands. However, beyond all of his contributions to this book, I value his friendship most of all. He is simply one of the nicest people I know. Claudio Vianello is one of Venice's "characters" and I thank him for all that I learned while chasing after him as we strode around the city... and the many cups of coffee we drank along the way. I need to thank Aga "Agnese" Agnieszka Sudnicovicz for all the technical information about "The Clock", and for being such a wonderful support person in our many visits.

My sons Tarik and Tamir, who were such a part of this story, receive my love and gratitude for being such easy and rewarding fellow travelers. Over the years we have slowly learned some of the things that they were involved in on those afternoons when they "ran away" to the streets of Venezia... and it is clear that they 'know' a Venice quite different from the one described in these pages!

Finally, of course there is my beautiful Souheir, whose sharing, comfort, advice and love I cherish above all. Beyond that, however, she is an amazing and demanding editor, and the final draft would simply have been impossible without her. Grazie mio amore... John

ABOUT THE AUTHOR

John Rawlings is an artist and educator who has explored the world extensively. He was born in London and raised in Australia. He earned his MFA from the University of Guanajuato in San Miguel de Allende, Mexico.

Rawlings fell in love with Italy after living in Florence and Venice for extended periods. He has introduced the beauty of Italy to hundreds of students over the past twenty years while leading arts programs.

A teacher of art and history for over thirty-five years, Rawlings was named the 2014 Association of Community College Trustees Faculty Member of the Year for the North American Western Region.

Rawlings is a sculptor and painter who finds inspiration in found objects and natural materials. His work was displayed at the International Biennale in Egypt in 2006, and is in collections around the world

Rawlings lives with his wife, Souheir, in northwest Montana.

Made in the USA
Lexington, KY
01 June 2017